Short Escapes
Near
New York City

Fodor's Travel Publications, Inc.
New York * Toronto * London * Sydney * Auckland

▼

SHORT ESCAPES NEAR NEW YORK CITY

Contributors: Nicola Coddington, Janet Serra, Glenn Scherer
Text Design: Nancy Koch
Map Design: John Grimwade
Map Coordinator: John Tomanio
Maps by: Alex Reardon, Andy Christie, Joyce Pendola, John Grimwade, John Tomanio
Editors: Nicola Coddington, Martin Everett
Research Associates: Paul Rogers, Betty Villaume
Cover Design: Guido Caroti
Cover Illustration: Edward Parker

Special thanks to Diane Abell, Robert Jonas, and Ronald Dupont.

Copyright © 1995
by Beachscape Publishing, Inc.

Also available:
Short Escapes : Country Getaways in France
Short Escapes : Country Getaways in Britain
Coming in 1996: *Short Escapes in New England*

While every care has been taken to ensure the accuracy of the information in this guide, time brings change, and consequently, the publisher cannot accept responsibility for errors that may occur. Call ahead to verify prices and other information.

Please address all comments and corrections to Beachscape Publishing, Inc., 145 Palisade St., Dobbs Ferry NY 10522; tel. 914-674-9283; fax 914-674-9285.

ISBN 0-679-03092-1
First Edition
MANUFACTURED IN THE UNITED STATES OF AMERICA
10 9 8 7 6 5 4 3 2

To my wife, Shawn Bolger, and children, Kate, Chris, and Elizabeth, whose loving support helped make this book possible. And to all the volunteers who have worked so hard to build and maintain the area's beautiful trails.

♦♦♦

To Kristin and Ben, for bringing laughter to each day. And to Terry, for showing them the way.

ABOUT THE AUTHORS

Bruce Bolger, an avid traveler and experienced walker, has explored the countryside in more than a dozen countries spanning four continents. Currently head of a book packaging and electronic publishing company, he has extensive experience in the travel and publishing fields. He is a graduate of the University of California at Santa Barbara and attended the University of Paris in France. He lives outside of New York City with his wife, Shawn, and children, Kate, Chris, and Elizabeth.

Gary Stoller has been an editor at *Condé Nast Traveler* magazine since its startup in 1987. Considered a pioneer of the concept of "investigative travel reporting," he wrote articles that were cited by judges when the magazine twice received National Magazine Awards. His articles have also won awards from the National Press Club and the Aviation/Space Writers Association. He has a journalism degree from the University of Colorado and now lives outside of New York City with his wife, Terry, and children, Kristin and Ben.

Contents

▼

▼

Introduction

When you travel outside New York City in search of nature and history, you can find beauty alongside country roads and monuments to the past in small villages and towns. But not until you get out of the car and stroll through villages and countryside can you really escape the pace of modern life that forever disturbs our effort to experience the past.

This guide is for everyone who would like to escape to the peace of the countryside and soak up a more complete sense of the way life once was and is today. It will take you away from the tourist spots to unique places with spectacular vistas and remarkable histories. You can stroll alone on a path once used by George Washington's troops, follow a trail that Walt Whitman loved, or picnic without neighbors on a hilltop overlooking a ghost town. You can continue the mood at a recommended restaurant in a picturesque setting and then complete the experience at a charming country inn or bed-and-breakfast.

Short Escapes Near New York City brings you to special places, often little known to local residents. According to your tastes, you can tramp around hidden historic landmarks, plunge deep into farmland and forest, or just sit undisturbed for hours looking at a view that will take your breath away. Through the quiet, you will be able to feel what it might have been like when the Native Americans roamed the land, when the Revolutionary War soldiers fought, or when the great Hudson River painters set up their easels to record the region's staggering vistas. Many of the book's suggested walking tours cover country roads and footpaths in use for hundreds, perhaps thousands, of years.

▼

The 25 experiences in this guide are scattered around different regions—each with its own distinctive character, flavor, and points of historical, cultural, or natural interest. Each experience is centered around a walking tour, which can be anything from a short stroll to a five-hour hike. Nearly all the walks can be shortened to suit your schedule, and several are accessible by train or bus. All are an easy daytrip from the New York metropolitan area but can be extended into weekend trips or longer. Also included is information about the history or nature you will encounter on your walk, as well as listings of recommended inns and bed-and-breakfasts, restaurants, other attractions nearby, and information for serious walkers.

These experiences cost less than other forms of travel. Nobody charges admission to villages or the countryside, and rural hotels and restaurants often match their urban counterparts in comfort and luxury at somewhat lower prices.

Short Escapes Near New York City is more than a travel guide. It's designed to awaken the traveler's senses to the moods and flavors of a place and its people and to help evoke a real sense of the past. We hope that the 25 experiences in this book will have the same uplifting effect on you as they had on us. You will thrust yourself into the soul of the countryside and learn about the land and its people in a way that can't be done simply by reading a book or observing artifacts in a museum.

WHERE TO FIND EACH EXPERIENCE

NEW YORK

North/South Lakes **9**

Woodstock **8**

Kingston

Lake Minnewaska **7**

PENNSYLVANIA

Schunemunk Mtn. **6**

High Point **22**

Wawayanda **21**

Norvin Green **20**

Delaware **25**
Water Gap

Jockey Hollow **19**

Delaware Canals **23**

Bowman's Hill **24**

Philadelphia

40 MILES

NEW JERSEY

Stissing Mtn. **11**

Mills Estate **10**

Poughkeepsie

Cold Spring **5**

Dunderberg Mtn. **4**

Rockefeller State Park **3**

Piermont **1**

Irvington **2**

Whitman House **13**

New York City

Newark

Fire Island **12**

Peoples Forest **16**

Hartford

CONNECTICUT

Mine Hill **17**

Guilford **18**

Shelter Island **14**

Hither Hills **15**

How to Use Short Escapes

We selected the 25 experiences in *Short Escapes Near New York City* for their historic, cultural, or natural interest and for their general proximity to areas popular with travelers. At each location, walking tours permit visitors to get out of their cars or the train and experience special places up close. All include private, easily accessible spots to picnic or enjoy memorable views. When possible, itineraries provide optional walks for strollers or serious walkers.

Itineraries are organized by region and are chosen so that travelers visiting in one of the selected areas can easily enjoy multiple experiences during their stay. We followed every itinerary mentioned in this book personally and purposely omitted others that gave us difficulty.

To bring your visit to life, each experience comes with a narrative on historical, cultural, literary, or natural points of interest. Other unique places to explore nearby are also suggested, so you don't have to be a walker to enjoy this book.

FINDING YOUR WAY

We designed the book to make it as easy as possible to follow the directions. For your convenience, each walking tour begins with basic information on duration, length, and level of difficulty. Walks marked "easy" have few ups and downs, no areas of tricky footing, and no navigational challenges and are appropriate for anyone capable of walking. Tours labeled

▼

"moderate" require a little more physical commitment and might have an area of tricky footing, but they require no particular navigational abilities or physical endurance. The few itineraries marked "difficult" are appropriate to regular walkers who feel comfortable walking in a few tricky areas and finding their way in forests or hills. The text fully details whatever difficulties the traveler might encounter along the way. Serious walkers will probably find even "difficult" trails relatively easy. And even the least experienced walkers can safely follow almost all "difficult" and "moderate" itineraries just a short way to a nice view or historic site, and then retrace their steps.

Unless otherwise indicated, all itineraries are loops; and walking time is based on a very leisurely 2 mph, except in itineraries with exceptional ups and downs. The numbered text directions enable you to complete a walking tour without using the map, but some may find it easier to simply follow the map and refer to the text when necessary. We strongly recommend that you use both the text and the maps, which provide navigational aids. At each numbered point on the map, the same number in the text gives the information you'll need to find your way from that location on the map, as well as additional observations about the terrain.

For the few difficult itineraries, experienced walkers might enjoy having a compass and a more detailed topographical map, which can be purchased at various stores throughout the region or by mail. (*See* For Serious Walkers section below).

Most of the itineraries follow footpaths marked with colored trail blazes that indicate the way for at least a portion of the route. A word of caution: Trailblazes can mysteriously disappear and footpath conditions change. While we have made every effort to select well-established itineraries and have walked every single one, we cannot guarantee that the character of an itinerary has not been altered or deformed. If you encounter a dramatic change, we'd like to hear from you. Contact us at the address provided on page II.

▼

THE REGIONAL FOOTPATH SYSTEM

Before you head off on a walking tour, familiarize yourself with the trail system. Trails are blazed with different colors and shapes depending on the area. For information about the blazes, check each chapter's Walk Directions introduction. Generally, three of the blazes placed together in a triangle indicates the beginning or end of a trail. One blaze placed atop another indicates a curve in the trail: If the top blaze is to the right of the lower blaze, the trail goes right, and vice-versa.

If the instructions tell you to follow the blazes during a certain portion of a walking tour, don't change trails unless directed to do so by the blazes. If you're not sure you're on the right trail, retrace your steps until you pick up a blaze, then turn around and resume your walking tour, keeping an eye out for the next blaze.

PRECAUTIONS

Although most of the itineraries require no special athletic abilities, all travelers should dress appropriately for the weather and wear shoes or sneakers designed for walking. Always carry the clothing you'll need for a worst-case change in the weather. A daypack generally can handle whatever clothing two people might need, plus drinks and a picnic; these small packs, when empty, fit easily into your suitcase. Please remember to carry out whatever you bring in.

You might want to bring insect repellent and take precautions against deer ticks: Wear light-colored clothing; pull your socks over your pants legs, and shower thoroughly after your walk. No one involved with researching this book was bitten by a tick.

The usual countryside obstacles—such as muddy and rocky trails, fallen trees, and poorly cut footpaths—pose the greatest risks. Since you can accomplish the longest of these itineraries in about a half day, there's no need to race through your walking tour. Take the time to enjoy the beauty, and watch your step. Be sure to pay attention to any warnings or advisories in the Walk Directions.

Although we have never seen a copperhead or a rattlesnake in the wild, people walking in the countryside should know that these poisonous snakes inhabit parts of the region. You will have no problem if you take the same precautions you would in just about any forest: Watch where you sit down or place your feet and hands.

Finally, the deer hunting season varies but generally lasts for several weeks in late autumn. In each chapter, you'll find the number of a local tourist office or a park ranger who can provide specific dates for hunting in the area you're visiting. You should wear bright-colored clothing if you're walking through forests during hunting season.

WEATHER

Generally speaking, spring and autumn are the region's best seasons for walking. Temperatures on summer days often exceed 90 degrees with high humidity, although you are just as likely to encounter a beautiful day. Even on hot days, you can usually beat the heat by setting out early or late in the day. The region's mild weather during recent years has made winter walking feasible for many, but snow still accumulates in the mountainous or inland regions and may even last until May in the highest elevations.

GETTING THERE

Although those who travel by car have the greatest and most flexible access to the area's hidden treasures, even train travelers can enjoy some of these short escapes. Wherever there is rail access, it is noted in the Getting There section.

If you are driving to a short escape, use the directions in the Getting There section and the small regional map alongside the walking tour map. A more detailed, commercially available road map will also help.

Almost all itineraries have been selected in regions already

▼

popular with travelers. So if you plan on going to a popular tourist attraction as well, you won't have to travel far out of your way to enjoy a short escape.

OTHER PLACES NEARBY

For those who prefer to tour by car, we've provided suggestions on how to visit the high points of our experiences and have pointed out other places of interest in the region that are often overlooked by tourists. This way, you can enjoy the highlights of our itineraries and uncover other special places without driving more than a short distance.

DINING & LODGING

For those who want to continue the mood created by the day's experience, we've selected a few restaurants, inns, and bed-and-breakfasts in the countryside near our itineraries.

To be included in *Short Escapes Near New York City,* a restaurant must either have an excellent view, be rustic or historic, or serve good food that's popular with the locals. Restaurants fall into four categories based on the average cost of dinner for one person (including appetizer, main course, and dessert, without drinks, taxes, and tip):

Very expensive .... **More than $50**
Expensive .... **$31-$50**
Moderate .... **$16-$30**
Inexpensive .... **$15 or less**

Keep in mind that you may be able to spend less, depending on your order. If possible, make a reservation, especially on weekends and holidays.

All country inns, bed-and-breakfasts, and other lodging establishments we've chosen either are rustic or historic, have character or an excellent view, or are a great value. Most have less than 20 rooms and are located in quiet areas. Almost all

▼

have private bathrooms with shower and/or bath. We have checked each one for cleanliness and up-to-date maintenance. Most bed-and-breakfasts include a Continental breakfast in the price, and a few offer complete American breakfasts and/or an afternoon tea. Be sure to inquire when you book.

In general, you should request a reservation well before you go, since many of these small inns and B&Bs fill up fast on popular weekends in spring, summer, and fall.

Lodging prices are double-occupancy for a single night and are designated as:

Very expensive .... **More than $180**
Expensive .... **$111-$180**
Moderate .... **$76-$110**
Inexpensive .... **$75 or less**

Prices are based on weekends and peak periods; you can often save money by staying during the week or off-season, or by getting a smaller or otherwise less desirable room. Keep in mind that many of the places listed have two-day minimum-stay requirements on weekends during peak periods.

You'll find that some hotels and restaurants well suited for one itinerary may also be within easy access of another recommended itinerary. Some areas do not have a wide selection of restaurants and hotels in keeping with the standards of this book. In such cases we recommend establishments that come as close as possible to our standards.

All hotels and restaurants in this book accept a major credit card unless otherwise noted; the most inexpensive restaurants and bed-and-breakfasts usually require cash.

TOURIST OFFICES

Most of the areas featured in this book have tourism offices that can provide you with the latest information on restaurants, hotels, and other attractions.

▼

FOR SERIOUS WALKERS

The New York City region has nearly 1,000 miles of blazed trails within a day trip of the city. Many are maintained by volunteers for the New York-New Jersey Trail Conference, and new trails are always on the drawing boards. The trail conference publishes an extensive collection of superb walking maps, which you can find in many book and outdoor sports stores. To order maps by phone, call the New York-New Jersey Trail Conference at (212) 685-9699, or visit their office at 232 Madison Ave., Room 401, New York, NY 10016. It's open Monday through Friday, 11-5. Serious hikers who expect to extensively explore the region should pick up the trail conference's classic *New York Walk Book,* now in its fifth edition and available at the address above or in area book and outdoor sports stores.

The Footpath
From Gotham

EXPERIENCE 1:
PIERMONT-ON-HUDSON

To escape New York City, you don't need a car or mass transit. You can walk out of the city across the George Washington Bridge onto a 240-mile footpath that plunges immediately into the forest and leads all the way to the northern Catskills. On this

The Highlights: Sweeping river views, ancient forest roads, an abandoned industrial site, a picturesque village.

Other Places Nearby: A Revolutionary War village, the boyhood home of painter Edward Hopper, a great town for antiques.

walking tour, you follow a short stretch of the footpath through Piermont, a charming, small New York town on the western bank of the Hudson River that seems more suited for Vermont than the New York City suburbs.

That the nation's largest, most congested city should have a direct footpath to wilderness is no fluke. It reflects the vision of the region's avid walkers who formed into dozens of local clubs as early as the late 19th century and, perhaps, even earlier. In the early 1900s, walking had become so popular that the *New York Post* published a regular column on the subject, "The Long Brown Path," penned by Raymond Torrey. Torrey, revered by

▼

local walkers as an early pioneer, also helped write the *New York Walk Book,* the region's first comprehensive walking guide, published in 1923 and currently in its fifth edition in 1996.

In 1920, Major Welch, chief engineer of the Palisades Interstate Park Commission, established a trail conference to construct and maintain trails in the newly acquired Harriman Park northwest of New York City (*see* Experience 4, Dunderberg). Enlisting the help of local walking clubs, the group, which became known as the New York-New Jersey Trail Conference, worked for seven years constructing numerous blazed trails in the fledgling park. Considering its work accomplished, the group disbanded in 1927, but trail-building by local clubs continued. The popularity of walking gave rise to an anarchic development of trails throughout the region, some blazed one way, some blazed other ways, many not blazed at all.

The trail-building frenzy alarmed Torrey. He brought together the heads of the region's walking groups in the 1930s to revive the New York-New Jersey Trail Conference and bring order to the system of trails and blazes. It has functioned ever since, building and maintaining trails, facilitating communication between the area's numerous walking clubs, and working to preserve the region's wild lands.

The idea for the Long Path was born during the New York region's walking renaissance of the 1920s, the concept of Vincent Schaefer of the Mohawk Valley Hiking Club. Despite extensive preliminary planning, the idea eventually languished. It lay dormant until the 1960s, when local walkers Robert Jensen and Michael Warren revived the dream and began actively promoting the concept. By 1987, the trail was completed all the way to East Windham, New York, in the Catskills. and it has since been extended a short way further. Proponents hope to extend it to the Adirondacks by the year 2000.

Much of the Long Path followed on this walk parallels the

▼

crest of the towering Palisade cliffs south of Piermont through Tallman State Park. Probably the first white men to come to this area were Henry Hudson and his crew, who may have anchored the *Half Moon* in present-day Piermont at the mouth of a creek then called the Tappan Slote, now named the Sparkill. Early Dutch founded a settlement in the early 1600s near here, but they didn't remain for long. The Native Americans from whom they had bought the land grew fed up with white man's presence and destroyed the settlement in a regional uprising.

Another small settlement was established in the 1600s along the Tappan Slote. Here, a small boat could go inland several miles before hitting a waterfall, just far enough to transport produce from inland farms back to the river for shipment to New York City. During this early period, a black settler named Nicholas Emmanuel established a farm and gave rise to a long line of farmers and business people whose descendants survive to this day in and around the community. By the Revolutionary War, an active community sprang up alongside the creek, where a gristmill and other small enterprises prospered.

During the Revolution, the local population was divided in loyalty, and frequent attacks by the British, Tories, or Americans against local farms and businesses brought a virtual halt to the growth and prosperity. The small community had one of its finest hours in May 1783 when General George Washington and Sir Guy Carleton, commander-in-chief of the British forces, met here briefly before proceeding inland to Tappan, where the British formally surrendered.

Old maps suggest that much of the land covered by this walk was farmed during the colonial period and in the 19th century. Thankfully, the farm land of the Dutch settlers gave way to forest in the 19th century when farming shifted to less populated areas. It could have turned out quite differently. In 1832, Jeremiah Pierson and his son-in-law, Eleazor Lord, who lived in what is now Piermont, incorporated the New York and

▼

Erie Railroad and decided to establish the eastern terminal at the Piermont site. They believed that the hills directly across from New York City could not be cost-effectively bored for a tunnel and that the Sparkill Creek afforded good access to the interior. Lord had an estate on a hill above the village and had grand schemes to develop the region with housing and local industry. For the idea to work, the railroad had to provide easy access to docks along the river, so that passengers and freight could be easily transferred onto boats for the final journey into New York.

The name Piermont did not originate until after the construction of a huge pier, which sticks far out into the river. Lord apparently devised the name by linking the word pier to "mont," referring to the hill that rises above the town. With the construction of the huge pier and railroad came hundreds of workers who crowded the small village and erected shanty towns for shelter. The town reached the peak of its glory in 1851, when the train line to Lake Erie was complete, and such dignitaries as President Millard Fillmore, Secretary of State Daniel Webster, and hundreds of other big shots disembarked in the town to begin the inaugural rail journey to the Lake Erie.

The Piermont terminal enjoyed only a brief period of success. A rival railroad developer built a tunnel further south and opened a terminal directly across from Manhattan. The Piermont line almost immediately lost business but remained active for several years. In 1860, the town's population had reached nearly 2,500. Within a few more years, nearly half the people had left, and Piermont's days of industrial glory had passed forever.

Today, Piermont maintains much of its quaint 19th-century appearance undisturbed by industry. The downtown received a small facelift when the movie director Woody Allen made his movie, *The Purple Rose of Cairo,* and celebrities who live in the nearby exclusive enclave of Sneden's Landing sometimes can be seen frequenting the small village's restaurants and nightspots.

▼

GETTING THERE

By car:

From the New Jersey side of the George Washington Bridge, head north on the Palisades Interstate Pkwy. and get off at exit 4 for Rte. 9W. At the end of the ramp, turn left at the light onto Rte. 9W north. When you come to a fork, bear left onto Rte. 340, following a sign to Sparkill. Then bear right to follow Rte. 340 north, and proceed a short distance to Ferdon Ave., where you turn right. Proceed along the Sparkill Creek until it crosses a small bridge. Park on Piermont Ave. or at the main parking area several hundred yards north near the Hudson River.

By bus:

From the George Washington Bridge Bus Terminal at 178th St. (reachable by the Eighth Ave. subway line) in Manhattan, take Red and Tan Lines bus No. 9A (ask for bus schedule No. 9) to Piermont (about a 45-minute ride). The bus will let you off in downtown Piermont; there is no formal bus stop. For the return trip, simply flag down the bus at any safe place along Piermont Ave. (buses in Rockland County currently operate on the flag-down system). For the current schedule, call Red and Tan Lines at 201-384-2400 or 914-356-0877. For information about travel to or within Rockland County, you can call Transportation of Rockland at 914-634-1100.

Walk Directions

TIME: 1 1/2 hours
LEVEL: Easy
DISTANCE: 3 miles
ACCESS: By car or bus

This experience takes you to the cliffs above the Hudson River, offering wonderful views. Much of the walk follows the turquoise-blazed Long Path, which in some places follows the traces of old farm roads. Pick up picnic foods in

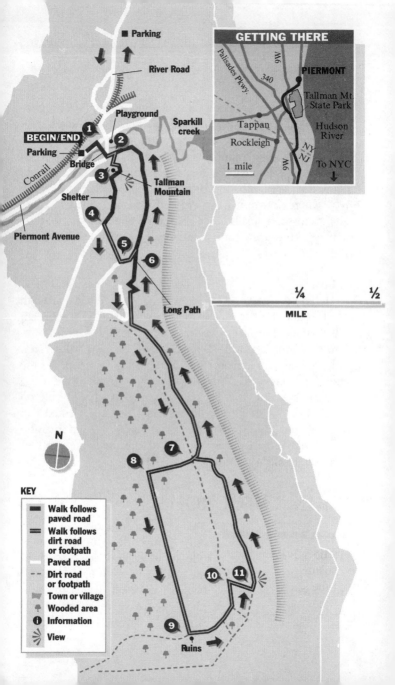

■ Parking

River Road

Playground

Sparkill creek

BEGIN/END

1

2

Parking

Bridge

3

Conrail

Tallman Mountain

Shelter

4

Piermont Avenue

5

6

Long Path

N

7

8

KEY

Walk follows paved road

Walk follows dirt road or footpath

Paved road

Dirt road or footpath

Town or village

Wooded area

ⓘ Information

View

10

11

9

Ruins

GETTING THERE

Palisades Pkwy.

9W

340

PIERMONT

Tallman Mt. State Park

Tappan

Hudson River

Rockleigh

NY / NJ

1 mile

9W

To NYC

¼   ½

MILE

▼

Piermont. Serious walkers can walk from Manhattan to Piermont by following the Long Path for 12 mi. On Manhattan's upper West Side, start at 178th St. and Cabrini Blvd. and follow the pedestrian walkway across the north side of the George Washington Bridge. Once you reach the New Jersey side of the bridge, go up the stairs leading to a park on the right. You soon will see the turquoise blazes for the Long Path, which you can easily follow through the woods along the Palisades.

TO BEGIN

Walk toward a tiny playground at the intersection of Piermont Ave., Ferdon Ave., and River Rd.

1. Just before the intersection, go right across a tiny bridge over Sparkill Creek. *This bridge was used by military troops in World War II to board ships bound for Europe from the pier in Piermont.* Cross the street and follow a bike trail sign onto a dirt road into Tallman Mountain State Park. You'll see a turquoise blaze on a telephone pole, indicating that you're on the Long Path. *Before entering the woods, stop to admire the old homes lining the marsh along the river.*

2. After you have followed the bike trail a short distance, follow the turquoise blazes to the right up a steep hill. It's a short but straight ascent to Tallman Mountain. *When the leaves have fallen, a look back will reveal more picturesque views of the old homes and marshland.*

3. At the top of the hill, you enter a large picnic area that could be busy on a warm weekend, but don't despair, you'll find solitude in the forests. As you follow the turquoise blazes along the paved road, you see the Westchester County villages of Irvington-on-Hudson, across the river toward the left, and Dobbs Ferry, toward the right. *The spires of the Lyndhurst man-*

▼

sion rise out of the trees just upriver from Irvington (see
Experience 2, Irvington-on-Hudson).

4. In a short distance, follow the turquoise blazes to the
left away from the paved road, downhill into the forest.

5. Cross an intersection of paved roads and proceed downhill on a little paved path that leads toward a park pool.

6. In a short distance, go right, following the turquoise
blazes into the forest. Follow the blazes as the trail bears left
uphill. At the top of the hill, you see beech trees with carvings
from the 1950s. The trail winds through a small picnic area, and
you see a paved park road on your right.

Follow the blazes to the left of a stone shelter. You must
keep looking for blazes in this stretch, because the trail zigzags
through a relatively open forest. After a short while, the trail
leads to the escarpment above the Hudson River. You're now
on an old farm road that could easily date to the 1700s.

7. Just after the trail veers sharply to the right, it crosses a
paved bike trail and leads onto an old berm, *which was part of
an oil-tank storage facility that a local industrialist planned to
build in this area earlier this century.*

8. The trail veers sharply left onto another berm, still following the turquoise blazes of the Long Path. *Through this
stretch you will notice numerous dikes and other odd earthworks
now covered by forest.*

9. When you reach a bike path, go left onto the path in
front of some ruins. You have now left the turquoise blazes of
the Long Path. *In the valley below to your right, mostly obscured
by forest, lies the historic and now exclusive enclave of Sneden's
Landing.* Follow the bike trail as it veers to the left. Ignore sev-

▼

eral unmarked trails that lead into the forest on your right.

10. About 100 yards after the bike trail has curved back north, go right on a footpath leading straight into the forest toward the cliffs above the river.

11. At a three-way intersection on the cliff top, go left. You shortly reach an overlook offering splendid views of the river, the villages of Irvington-on-Hudson, Dobbs Ferry, Hastings-on-Hudson, the city of Yonkers, and the George Washington Bridge far to the right. **Be very careful—the cliffs are particularly steep here.** Continue on the old footpath along the cliff top. *These lands undoubtedly were farmed as early as colonial days but have all returned to forest.*

After curving to the left, the old, unmarked path intersects the turquoise-blazed Long Path just before Point 7, its intersection with the bike path. Go right and retrace your steps to Point 6. From there, proceed straight down to the paved road at the riverbank. Go left and follow the path back to Point 2. From there, retrace your steps to your car.

PLACES ALONG THE WALK

■ **Tallman Mountain State Park.** This park offers walking/biking paths (including part of the Long Path) and picnic areas with views of the river and the Piermont Marsh, part of the Hudson River National Estuary Research Reserve. *Rte. 9W, Sparkill, NY 10976; tel. 914-359-0544. Open daily until sunset. Parking charge late Jun.-Labor Day when pool is open. About 5 mi. south of Piermont.*

OTHER PLACES NEARBY

■ **Hopper House.** The boyhood home of Edward Hopper features memorabilia and exhibits of work by local artists. *82 N. Broadway, Nyack, NY 10960; tel. 914-358-0774. Open Sat.-Sun. 12-5, Fri. 5-8. About 5 mi. north of Piermont.*

▼

■ **Hudson Valley Children's Museum.** Interactive exhibits and programs help children ages 1 through 12 explore a variety of topics in the arts and sciences. *Nyack Seaport, 21 Burd St., Nyack, NY 10960; tel. 914-358-2191. Scheduled to open in early 1996. Admission. About 5 mi. north of Piermont.*

■ **Nyack.** Well-known for its art and antique shops, quaint Victorian houses, and funky atmosphere, Nyack is home to a series of huge craft and antique fairs. *On Rte. 9W, about 5 mi. north of Piermont.*

■ **Paradise Boats Inc.** Rent canoes or take a guided tour of the salt marshes that line the Hudson River below the Palisades cliffs. *9 Paradise Ave., Piermont, NY 10968; tel. 914-359-0073. Open daily, weather permitting. Located behind the playground at the beginning of the walk.*

■ **Tappan.** The narrow streets of this tiny historic village take one back in time. This was the site of many dramatic events of the Revolutionary War, including the imprisonment and execution of Major John André, the British spy, and the formal surrender of the British at the end of the Revolutionary War. *About 3 mi. southwest of Piermont.*

DINING

■ **Xaviar's at Piermont** (very expensive). The exquisite contemporary American cuisine created by chef/proprietor Peter Xaviar Kelly has won the highest ratings for both this restaurant and its sister up north across the river, Xaviar's at Garrison (*see* Experience 5, Cold Spring). The prix-fixe meal includes four or five often spectacular courses. Jacket and tie and reservations are required. No credit cards. *506 Piermont Ave., Piermont, NY 10968; tel. 914-359-7007. Open Wed.-Sun. for dinner, Fri. and Sun. for lunch.*

■ **Freelance Cafe and Wine Bar** (expensive). Think of this cafe as a relaxed sibling to Xaviar's next door; they share the same chef/proprietor, Peter Xaviar Kelly, and even the same kitchen. Specialties include coconut shrimp as well as Pacific ahi tuna, served rare with wasabi. A line often forms before opening time on weekends. No reservations accepted; no credit cards. *506 Piermont Ave., Piermont, NY 10968; tel. 914-365-3250. Open for lunch and dinner Tue.-Sun. For dinner, get there before opening time: 5:30 on Fri. and Sat., 5 Sun.*

■ **Il Portico Ristorante** (expensive). Housed in a restored 1850s hotel that was once a stagecoach stop and recently received National Historic Landmark status, this restaurant offers excellent Italian cuisine in a romantic atmosphere. The menu emphasizes pasta and fresh seafood. *89 Main St., Tappan, NY 10983; tel. 914-365-2100. Open Mon.-Fri. for lunch and dinner, Sat.-Sun. for dinner. About 3 mi. southwest of Piermont.*

■ **Cafe Portofino** (moderate). This cozy, intimate Italian restaurant is a favorite with locals. Specialties include shrimp and scallops scampi and pasta with putanesca sauce. No reservations accepted. *587 Main St., Piermont, NY 10968; tel. 914-359-7300. Open for Tue.-Sun. for dinner.*

■ **Hudson House** (moderate). The upbeat nouvelle American menu has "a little bit of everything" including seafood and pasta. Everything is fresh, and the restaurant smokes its own salmon and chicken. *134 Main St., Nyack, NY 10960; tel. 914-353-1355; fax 914-353-1459. Open Tue.-Sat. for lunch and dinner, Sun. for brunch and dinner; Mon. for dinner, late May-Sep. About 5 mi. north of Piermont.*

■ **The Turning Point** (moderate). We include this listing primarily for the great entertainment: national-caliber acts, primarily folk, blues, Cajun, and jazz, in an intimate atmosphere. *468 Piermont Ave., Piermont, NY 10968; tel. 914-359-1089. Restaurant open daily for lunch, Wed.-Mon. for dinner, and Sun. for brunch. Coffeehouse usually open Wed.-Sun. evenings, but sometimes there are special acts. Call for schedule.*

LODGING

Unfortunately, this area has few inns or bed-and-breakfasts that meet our standards. *See* Experience 2, Irvington-on-

Hudson, and Experience 3, Rockefeller State Park.

■ **Blauvelt Bed & Breakfast** (inexpensive). Not exceptional, but a good value in an area where alternatives to sterile motels are scarce. This 30-year-old colonial, located on a quiet cul-de-sac in an old village, has two rooms: one large and bright with a queen-size bed; the other smaller, with twin beds. *10 Green Hedge Ln., Blauvelt, NY 10913; tel. 914-359-6583. Closed in Feb. Take Rte. 303 to Erie St; follow past Western Hwy. About 5 mi. northwest of Piermont.*

FOR MORE INFORMATION
Tourist Offices:
■ **Nyack Chamber of Commerce.** A comprehensive local guidebook is available. *Best Western Inn, 26 Rte. 59, Nyack, NY 10960; tel. 914-353-2221. Open Mon.-Thu. 10-3.*
■ **Rockland County Department of Tourism.** *11 New Hempstead Rd., New City, NY 10956; tel. 914-638-5800. Open Mon.-Fri. 9-5.*

For Serious Walkers:
Hook Mountain State Park and High Tor State Park offer excellent hiking opportunities on the hills that line the west shore of the Hudson River. Pick up the New York-New Jersey Trail Conference's packet of Hudson Palisades Trails. You can walk to Piermont on the Long Path from the northwest corner of the George Washington Bridge.

Sunnyside by the Tappan Zee

EXPERIENCE 2:
IRVINGTON-ON-HUDSON

The Highlights: The home of Washington Irving, a castellated mansion along the Hudson River, a unique riverside village with several dining choices.

Other Places Nearby: A riverside museum displaying the works of the Hudson River School, a Georgian mansion, the estate of the Rockefellers (*see* Experience 3).

As you walk up from the Hudson River on Irvington-on-Hudson's steep Main Street, the quiet of this pretty Westchester County village may come as a surprise to out-of-towners. You're only a 29-minute drive to Manhattan's West Side and a short drive to the Bronx border, but you'd swear you're in some charming isolated New England hamlet.

The action on Main Street usually occurs when a train from Manhattan pulls into the station and cars shuttle up and down to pick up passengers. Serious crime is rare, and local police officers seem to spend most of their time directing traffic after a train pulls in or when church lets out. Irvington probably has more raccoons than people, and you have to watch for deer on the roads at night, even on Broadway (Route 9), the main thoroughfare through the village.

▼

The area that would later be named Irvington was considered a neutral zone during the Revolutionary War, sandwiched between the northern Westchester stronghold of the patriots and the southern Westchester domain of the English and the Tories. Both sides carried out raids in the area, bringing misery and economic hardship to what had been a thriving farming community since the arrival of the first Dutch settlers in the 17th century. British raiders disembarked from a ship in the Hudson River, partly burning the house of Wolfert Ecker, a Dutch settler employed as a farmer and a cooper, and causing his relatives to leave behind all their possessions and run for their lives.

On this walking tour, you'll visit the house they fled, a place that would later become known as Sunnyside, the historic home of noted American author Washington Irving (after whom the village was later named). In 1835, Irving purchased a portion of the Ecker farm, including the war-burned rectangular farmhouse. The land, on the eastern bank of the Hudson River, abutted the property of his nephew Oscar Irving.

Washington Irving fell in love with Sunnyside because of its location: overlooking a section of the river called the Tappan Zee. "It is a beautiful spot, capable of being made a little paradise," he observed. "There is a small Dutch cottage on it that was built about a century since. I have had an architect there, and shall build a mansion upon the place this summer. My idea is to make a little nookery, somewhat in the Dutch style, quaint but unpretending."

Using the talents of landscape painter and neighbor George Harvey, Irving remodeled and enlarged the home. He created a wisteria-covered, stepped gable entrance and added a Spanish-style tower and old weathervanes that had once sat atop buildings in Albany and New York City.

Irving, who was in his early fifties when he bought the property, wanted to settle down after spending much of his life abroad. He had lived in Europe from 1815 to 1832, traveling in Spain, where he wrote the first English biography of

▼

Christopher Columbus, and working in England as a diplomat and in his family's export business.

The author first achieved literary acclaim as a humorist. In 1809, he penned a satire poking fun at the Dutch settlers, *Diedrich Knickerbocker's A History of New-York*. The satire was so well-read that the word Knickerbocker soon became synonymous with New Yorker, and today New York City's professional basketball team, the Knicks, retains the moniker.

Ten years after Irving wrote his successful satirical work, he published *The Sketch-Book*, a book that related England's Christmas customs in great detail and inspired Americans to follow them. The book contained legendary Hudson River Valley characters whom children and adults would speak of for generations: Rip Van Winkle, who fell asleep and missed the Revolutionary War, and Ichabod Crane, who was chased by a Headless Horseman over the hills of Sleepy Hollow (*see* Experience 3, Rockefeller State Park).

On your way to Sunnyside during this walking tour, you'll pass the home of millionairess Sarah Walker. Walker invented an anti-kink formula for the hair of black Americans, an idea that catapulted her from an income of less than $2 per day while washing clothes in 1907 to the status of the world's wealthiest black woman at the time of her death 12 years later.

You also will visit the gorgeous riverside estate that once belonged to railroad baron Jay Gould. A striking castellated mansion called Lyndhurst stands as the centerpiece of the estate and is open for tours. The mansion was built in 1838 by architect Alexander Jackson Davis, noted for designing villas with sweeping gardens in the Hudson River Gothic Revival style. The home's first owner was General William Paulding; then it was sold to merchant George Merritt in 1864. Merritt, who gave Lyndhurst its name, hired Davis to expand the mansion while retaining its architectural integrity. In 1880, Gould bought Lyndhurst as a summer home. Lyndhurst was his escape from the business world: He owned Western Union Telegraph as

▼

well as Union Pacific Railroad and the New York City elevated subway line.

On your return to Irvington from Lyndhurst, you can see the exterior of the architecturally renowned Octagon House. The five-story home is privately owned and visitors must stay off the property, but there's plenty to marvel at from a distance. Constructed in 1860 by a family member of the Armour meat packing company, it originally was built as a two-story house with a flat roof. In 1872 tea merchant Joseph Stiner bought the home and added an elaborate two-story dome topped by a multiwindowed cupola.

The cupola allows the home's residents to peer over the surrounding trees toward the Hudson River. A wide wrap-around veranda encircles the outside of the house, and there are a host of other fascinating architectural touches. The Octagon House is listed as a National Historic Landmark.

GETTING THERE

By train:

From Manhattan's Grand Central Station, take the Metro North Hudson River Line (212-532-4900) to Irvington-on-Hudson, about a 45-minute train ride along the banks of the Hudson River.

By car:

From Manhattan, take the West Side Hwy. north to the Saw Mill River Pkwy. Get off the Saw Mill at exit 17 (Ashford Ave., Dobbs Ferry, Ardsley). Turn left at the traffic light and proceed on Ashford Ave. into Dobbs Ferry. When you reach a major intersection with three gas stations on the street corners, turn right onto Rte. 9 (Broadway) and follow it 1 1/2 mi. into Irvington. When you reach a Texaco gas station at a traffic light, turn left in front of the gas station and head down Irvington's steep Main St. toward the Hudson River. Park at the bottom of the hill near the train station (there are free six-hour spots on both sides of the station).

▼

Walk Directions

TIME: 1 1/2 or 2 1/2 hours
LEVEL: Easy
DISTANCE: 3 1/2 or 5 miles
ACCESS: By train or car

This walk and its optional extension have only one tiring uphill stretch: from the train station up Irvington's Main St. Most of the walk is on the level dirt path of the Old Croton Aqueduct, which extends 41 miles from Croton, NY, to Manhattan, and which carried water to New York City residents from 1842 to 1890. Pick up picnic provisions at the Noble Cafe next to the Irvington station, or at one of the village's delis, including Geordane's at 61 Main St. The grounds of Sunnyside and Lyndhurst make fabulous picnic spots.

TO BEGIN

With the train station at your back, proceed uphill on the sidewalk on the left side of Main St. Pass numerous stores. Go by the library/town hall building and Irvington Middle School on your left.

1. Turn left a few steps past the school into the school's paved parking lot. Proceed through the parking lot and go to the right of basketball courts onto a dirt path. A cyclone fence is on your right. Continue straight on the dirt path (the Croton Aqueduct) through the trees and cross a paved road. Cross a second paved road and proceed straight on the dirt path. Cross a third paved road and then a fourth.

2. At the fifth paved road, go straight through the woods.

3. When you reach a dirt and gravel road, continue straight, ignoring a road going down to the left. Proceed straight alongside a stone wall that's on your right. Continue

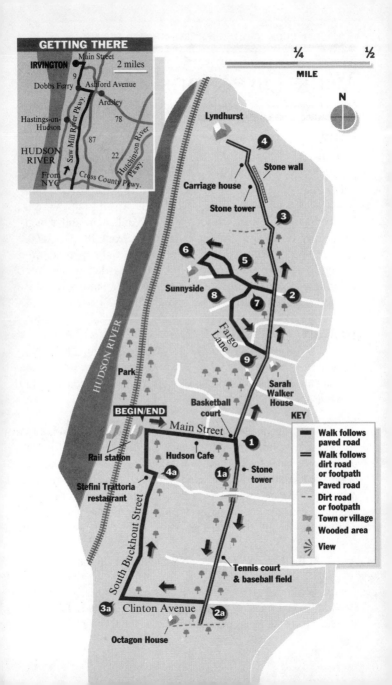

Main Street

IRVINGTON

2 miles

9

Dobbs Ferry · Ashford Avenue

Ardsley

Hastings-on-Hudson

78

87

HUDSON

RIVER

22

Hutchinson River Pkwy.

Saw Mill River Pkwy.

From
NYC

Cross County Pkwy.

¼   ½

MILE

N

Lyndhurst

4

Stone wall

Carriage house

3

Stone tower

6

5

Sunnyside

8

7

2

Fargo
Lane

9

Park

Sarah
Walker
House

KEY

BEGIN/END

Main Street

Basketball
court

1

Rail station

Hudson Cafe

4a

1a

Stone tower

Stefini Trattoria
restaurant

South Buckhout Street

Tennis court
& baseball field

3a

Clinton Avenue

2a

Octagon House

HUDSON RIVER

KEY

■ Walk follows
paved road

═ Walk follows
dirt road
or footpath

☐ Paved road

- - - Dirt road
or footpath

🏠 Town or village

🌲 Wooded area

View

▼

past a 15-foot-tall stone tower that's on your left. Go past the carriage house on your left and then pass a sign for the Lyndhurst estate on your left. Proceed about 40 yards on the grounds of the estate.

4. Turn left and proceed to the castellated mansion. *You must pay an admission to the mansion and the grounds. If you choose not to visit the home, you must stay on the dirt path and cannot wander on the Lyndhurst grounds.* After you have visited the mansion, retrace your steps to Point 4. Turn right onto the dirt path and retrace your steps to the paved road at Point 2. Turn right onto the paved road and head downhill with a brook to your right. Pass a Sunnyside sign on your right and then ignore a paved road on your left.

5. At the Y in the road (at the Historic Hudson Valley Sunnyside sign), bear to the right and follow the paved road through the gates into the grounds of Sunnyside. Follow the paved road as it circles to the left to the paved parking lot. Continue straight through the parking lot to a picket fence. Turn left at the fence and proceed about 35 yards to the front entrance of Sunnyside.

6. Turn right into the entrance and visit Washington Irving's home and grounds. *There is an admission charge.* When you're finished visiting the historic home, retrace your steps to the entrance (Point 6) and go straight through the parking lot. Exit the parking lot by following the paved road to the right. Follow the paved road as it bears to the right. When you reach an intersection, turn left onto a paved road and proceed uphill past the Sunnyside gates.

7. When you reach the next paved road on your right, turn right onto it. A short fire hydrant is on your right. Follow the road as it winds to the right (suburban houses are on both sides of the street).

▼

8. When you reach a junction (a dirt island sits in the middle of the junction), bear left and follow the paved road. Proceed on the paved road as it circles to the left and heads slightly uphill. Continue uphill on the road (Fargo Ln.). Ignore a paved road (Meadow Brook Rd.) on your left and proceed uphill with a white picket fence to your right. When you reach the end of the picket fence—just past the bicycle sign on your right—proceed about 15 steps forward.

9. Turn right and go through the gates onto the dirt path of the Croton Aqueduct. *The white mansion to your left is now private, but it once was owned by Sarah Walker, the inventor of anti-kink hair lotion.* Continue straight to the intersection of Aqueduct Ln. and Main St. (Point 1). *If you want to lengthen the walk and see the Octagon House, follow directions in the Optional Extension below.* Otherwise, turn right onto Main St. and proceed on the sidewalk downhill to the railroad station.

Optional Extension

At Point 1, cross Main St. and enter a public parking lot. Walk straight through the lot.

TIME: An extra 30 minutes
LEVEL: Easy
DISTANCE: 1 1/2 miles

1A. Step onto a dirt path (the Croton Aqueduct) and proceed to the right of a stone tower. Continue straight on the path as it rises high above houses on both sides. *To your right in the distance is the Hudson River. You are actually walking above an old one-lane tunnel through the aqueduct.* **Be careful to stay on the wide path—there's a steep drop to the ground on both sides.** Proceed straight past the tennis courts and the baseball field that are on your left. Cross over a paved road and continue straight on the dirt path.

▼

2A. Cross the next paved road (Clinton Ave.). Continue about 100 yards. Stop just before a dirt road that intersects the path you're walking on and look to your right through the trees at the Octagon House. *It's private and you can't visit its grounds, but, from this viewpoint, you can marvel at the house's unique architecture.* Retrace your steps back to the paved road, Clinton Ave. (Point 2A). Turn left and go down the paved road toward the Hudson River. Walk by the Octagon House on your left.

3A. At a stop sign, turn right onto paved South Buckhout St. Proceed straight with river to your left. Continue past the next stop sign, ignoring paved road (Station Rd.) to the right.

4A. At the next intersection, turn left and proceed down the paved road toward the river. On your left is Stefini Trattoria restaurant. Follow the road as it winds to the right in front of the train station. If you're heading south by train to the Bronx or Manhattan, go down the steps into a tunnel and cross under the tracks to the platform that's closest to the Hudson River.

PLACES ALONG THE WALK

■ **Lyndhurst.** Numerous special events—craft fairs, chamber music concerts, sunset serenades—add to the excitement at this Gothic revival mansion with magnificent riverside grounds. You can grab lunch in an historic carriage house or picnic on the lawn. *635 S. Broadway, Tarrytown, NY 10591; tel. 914-631-4481. Open daily 10-5 except Mon. May-Oct. First tour 10:30, last tour 4:15. Open Sat.-Sun. 10-5 Nov.-Apr. First tour 10:30, last tour 3:30. Carriage House cafe open Thu.-Sun. 10-3 May-Oct. Admission. On Rte. 9, just north of the Irvington border.*

■ **Sunnyside.** Led by guides in mid-Victorian garb, it's easy to drift back to yesteryear while touring Washington Irving's home. The lovely grounds are a great place to picnic on the high bluffs overlooking the Hudson. The visitors center includes a gift and book shop and a small theater documenting the famous

▼

author's life. *W. Sunnyside Ln., Tarrytown, NY 10591; tel. 914-591-8763, 914-631-8200. Open daily 10-5 except Tue. (Mar.-Dec.). Closed Jan.-Feb. Off Rte. 9, at Irvington-Tarrytown border.*

OTHER PLACES NEARBY

■ **Hudson River Museum.** The Hudson River School and the work of various local artists are displayed in this 1876 mansion. Try lunch on the riverside terrace—a fine way to slow down the day and enjoy food a quantum leap above that of many museums. The Andrus Planetarium is fun for young and old and features special laser-light shows for those who prefer their glimpse of the firmament accompanied by the space-rock thunder of Pink Floyd or the music of other rock musicians. *511 Warburton Ave., Yonkers, NY 10701; tel. 914-963-4550. Admission. Open Wed., Thu., and Sat. 10-5, Fri. 10-9, and Sun. 12-5. Off Rte. 9, about 5 mi. south of Irvington.*

■ **Newington-Cropsey Foundation Gallery.** Tucked away in a ravine near Hastings-on-Hudson's industrial waterfront, this complex of buildings in a mixture of elaborate architectural styles displays a large permanent collection of paintings by Jasper Cropsey, a leading 19th-century painter of the Hudson River School, and changing exhibits of other artists' paintings. The gallery's interior is as elegant as the exterior. *25 Cropsey Ln., Hastings-on-Hudson, NY 10706; tel 914-478-7990. Open by appointment only Mon.-Fri. 1-5. Closed Jan. and Aug. Off Southside Ave., across from the Hastings-on-Hudson train station; about 4 mi. south of Irvington.*

DINING

Besides the eateries listed below, Piermont's exceptional restaurants (*see* Experience 1) are directly across the river, and those in Tarrytown (*see* Experience 3) are a short drive away.

■ **Stefini Trattoria** (expensive). This intimate yet relaxed northern Italian restaurant specializes in seafood, particularly scampi and sole, and veal and chicken entrées. Look for veal Stefini: veal piccata with sun-dried tomatoes, prosciutto, and

▼

artichokes. The linguine in white clam sauce is terrific. *50 S. Buckhout St., Irvington, NY 10533; tel. 914-591-7208. Open Tue.-Fri. for lunch and dinner; Sat.-Sun. for dinner. Closed for lunch Jul.-Aug. Southeast of the Irvington train station.*

■ **The Hudson Cafe** (moderate). This historic restaurant with an old bar from a former casino in nearby Ardsley delivers more imaginative food today than ever before, while still offering inexpensive fare like a burger platter and a tasty chicken pot pie. Expect such specials as rabbit stew or lobster paella. On the regular menu, you'll find a variety of pastas, meat, seafood, and salads. Don't miss the flourless chocolate cake. *63 Main St., Irvington-on-Hudson, NY 10533; tel. 914-591-9850. Open daily for lunch and dinner, and Sat.-Sun. for brunch.*

■ **Station Plaza Cafe** (moderate). The warm atmosphere created by owner Nick D'Agostino can even make newcomers feel they're among old friends. A popular entrée on the new American menu is Norwegian salmon with walnut breadcrumb crust, served with a balsamic vinaigrette. The sweet potato seafood crow's nest filled with shrimps, bay scallops, and portobello mushrooms is an exclusive recipe. On Friday and Saturday nights, reservations are not accepted except for parties of five or more. *12 N. Astor St., Irvington, NY 10533; tel. 914-591-4444. Open daily except Mon. for dinner and daily except Mon. and Sat. for lunch. Across from the Irvington train station.*

■ **Noble Cafe** (inexpensive). Former warehouse space has been converted to an intimate cafe featuring inexpensive yuppie-type lunches such as a sandwich of mozzarella, roasted peppers, and fresh basil. A variety of salads and grilled individual pizzas are on the menu. A cup of cappucino will get you buzzing, if you're not already from the trains that pass by outside. *1 Bridge St., Irvington, NY 10533; tel. 914-591-2233. Open daily for breakfast and lunch; Wed.-Sat. for dinner. On the river side of the Irvington train station.*

LODGING

There are chain hotels in nearby Tarrytown, but accommo-

▼

dations with character are hard to come by in this suburban area. *See* Experience 3, Rockefeller State Park, for additional options.

■ **Tarrytown House** (expensive). Primarily a corporate conference center, this establishment is a curious blend of historic estate and modern resort. Most of the 150 guest rooms are relatively bland. If charm and style are important, request one of the ten rooms in the elegant, old King mansion; however, you won't be guaranteed it till a few days prior to your arrival. A full buffet breakfast is served in the Biddle mansion's riverview dining room. There is a swimming pool and two tennis courts. *E. Sunnyside Ln., Tarrytown, NY 10591; tel. 914-591-8200. Just off Rte. 9 (Broadway), at the Irvington border.*

■ **Krogh's Nest Bed & Breakfast** (inexpensive). The 1896 center-hall Victorian is modestly and comfortably furnished in colonial decor, including some antiques. The three guest rooms are small, but each has three exposures. The first-floor room is paneled with pine and has a double four-poster bed and a private bath. You may eat breakfast on the wraparound porch or on the patio. The house is visually secluded on one acre, including beautiful gardens. *4 Hillcrest Rd., Hartsdale, NY 10530; tel. 914-946-3479. About 7 mi. east of Irvington.*

FOR MORE INFORMATION
Tourist Offices:
■ **Irvington Chamber of Commerce.** *64 Main St., Irvington, NY 10533; tel. 914-591-6006. Open Mon., Wed., Fri. 9-5; Tue., Thu. 2-5; Sat. 9-1.*

■ **Town Clerk's Office.** *85 Main St., Irvington, NY 10533; tel. 914-591-7070. Open Mon.-Fri. 9-3.*

For Serious Walkers:
The Croton Aqueduct is a great walking trail that passes through several towns north and south of Irvington. For information, call the Old Croton Trailway State Park (914-693-5259).

The Land of
Ichabod Crane

EXPERIENCE 3:
ROCKEFELLER STATE PARK

We can only imagine the rigors faced by the early Europeans who first settled the Hudson River valley. After the stress of a long ocean voyage and the prospect of setting up a new life, they encountered a vast, virgin wilderness with strangely clothed inhabitants. The new

The Highlights: Stunning Hudson River views, colonial footpaths in legend-filled forests, the remains of a large riverside estate.

Other Places Nearby: The Old Dutch Church of Sleepy Hollow and its 350-year-old graveyard, the Rockefeller estate, a spectacular river-front park.

world undoubtedly played on the minds of these travelers, whose first explanation for the strange phenomena they encountered often included some aspect of the supernatural.

As 19th-century author Washington Irving tells us in his books, the early Dutch who settled the Hudson lands you travel on during this walking tour had particularly vivid imaginations, especially if you have a taste for the macabre. Irving passed through the Hudson River valley in his youth and fell in love with its charms. Years later, while living in London, he wrote his famous *The Legend of Sleepy Hollow,* borrowing, it is said,

▼

from stories he heard while visiting a friend on an estate near Kinderhook in the Hudson valley. One literary historian, however, has attributed much of Irving's legends to German tales the author read while living in London.

In either case, the visitor to Sleepy Hollow should have little trouble imagining the valley in Irving's time, because the land covered by this walk still maintains its quiet, rural character and has some of the same footpaths that were in use during Washington Irving's life.

The area known as Sleepy Hollow that is covered by this walk was first inhabited by Native Americans, part of the Weckquaesgeek and Sintsinct tribes. The tribes spent summers on the Hudson River shore enjoying its plentiful harvest of oysters, before moving inland during winter to sheltered valleys away from the wind.

The first white settlers came to the area in the 1600s, after the voyage of Henry Hudson up the river. Although the Dutch West India Company offered generous incentives to attract settlers from Holland, including near-feudal powers for people with sufficient resources, few people took the bait, and settlement remained sparse throughout most of that century. The lack of competition made it possible for a penniless Dutch carpenter, who eventually changed his name to Frederick Philipse, to amass an extraordinary domain covering almost half of present-day Westchester County.

In the late 17th century, he established a grist mill at the mouth of the Pocantico River, where river sloops could find harbor and transport animal pelts, grain, and other agricultural products down to New Amsterdam, which later became New York City. Early maps show that a number of tenant farmers rented land from Philipse in the area of the walk, so the fields and forests you cover probably have not changed much from that time. Gone are the few farmhouses that dotted the area, but some of the old farm roads remain.

▼

If the legends of these early settlers are true, you may have one of several supernatural encounters along your walk. When you're on the hilltop on a misty evening near the walk's Point 15, perhaps you'll catch sight of the Flying Dutchman, the specter of a ship said to sail silently up river in defiance of wind or tides, with a Dutch flag flying from its mast. Or you may see the ghost of a young Dutch partygoer named Van Dam on the river in a rowboat hopelessly looking for shore. Against the advice of friends, he had headed home from a party drunk at midnight on the Sabbath and was never seen again.

If you walk along the trail near Spook Rock, perhaps you'll see strange lights produced by the ghost of a Native American who comes in search of her lost husband and baby. The men who built the Old Croton Aqueduct, which you pass on the walk, were terrorized by ghosts they said haunted the Pocantico River valley near their camp.

As you walk along the river, you may be overcome by an unexplained drowsiness, if the stories of Washington Irving are true. It's the result of a spell cast by a Native American wizard to subdue an enemy tribe, and it explains why the valley here is called Sleepy Hollow.

Of course, Sleepy Hollow's most famous legend is the story of Ichabod Crane, who disappeared on his way home from a party late at night after encountering the Headless Horseman on a dark wooded trail. A setting much like the one described by Washington Irving can be found on Gorey Brook Road, one of the oldest roads in the area and just a few hundred yards from where Irving imagined Ichabod Crane made his fateful encounter. The setting has changed little in hundreds of years.

All of this magical land would have fallen into the hands of suburban developers, but not for the Rockefeller family, which began buying land here in the 1890s. Over the years, they created a vast preserve of manicured meadows and forests, crisscrossed with an impressive network of bridle paths. John D.

▼

Rockefeller built a great mansion he called Kykuit, which you can visit today, and his brother William constructed an impressive mansion called Rockwood Hall, which stood on sweeping grounds facing the Hudson River. All that remains of this mansion are the foundations and beautiful grounds, now open to the public. There is no prettier park along the Hudson River in southern Westchester, and its entrance is at the western end of Route 117, only a short drive from the main entrance to Rockefeller State Park.

GETTING THERE:
By car:

From New York City, take the Saw Mill River Pkwy. north to the Taconic State Pkwy. Just north of where the two parkways intersect, get off the Taconic at the exit for Rte. 117 (Bedford Rd.). At the end of the ramp, turn left and head west on Rte. 117. Continue until the road ends, bearing left past the exit for Rte. 9. At the end of the road, make a U-turn and proceed back on Rte. 117 eastbound to the Rockefeller State Park entrance.

If you want to cut 2 hours off the full walk (and begin your walk at Point 1 below), take the same Taconic Pkwy. exit, go left on Rte. 117, and then make the first left on Rte. 448. Make your first right and follow Sleepy Hollow Rd. for about 2 mi., bearing left at an intersection along the way. You can park along the road near the gates to the bridle paths just beyond an overpass for Rte. 117.

By train:

Take the Hudson Line of Metro North from Grand Central Station to the Tarrytown station. Call Metro North (800-638-7646) for information. You can get a taxi (call Knapp-McCarthy at 914-332-8294) from Tarrytown to the entrance to Rockefeller State Park. There is a phone booth you can use at the visitors center to call a cab for the trip back to town.

▼

Walk Directions

TIME: 1 1/2 to 3 1/2 hours
LEVEL: Easy to difficult
DISTANCE: 3 to 7 miles
ACCESS: By car or train

Most of the trails follow bridle paths, so the going is easy. There are numerous ways to shorten the walk. You can save almost 2 mi by parking at Point 1 and can lop off additional distance by going left at Point 6 and picking up the directions at Point 18. There are delicatessens and other places to get picnic supplies on Rte. 9 or on Main St. in Tarrytown.

TO BEGIN

Facing the visitors center, go right on the paved road heading uphill toward a metal barrier. Go around the barrier and continue straight on the unpaved Old Sleepy Hollow Rd. that heads gradually downhill. Follow this old road for almost 20 minutes, probably along the same path used by Dutch settlers centuries ago.

1. Cross the paved Sleepy Hollow Rd. and continue along a bridle path. **Be careful crossing the road; cars approach suddenly.** In a few minutes, you cross the Pocantico River. *Notice the old stone walls along the river, probably built in the last century or earlier to channel the water for a mill.*

2. When you arrive at a three-way intersection, go left.

3. In just a few dozen yards, you come to a four-way intersection. Go right on the bridle path leading uphill. *Remember this intersection, because you will pass through here on your way back.* The bridle path goes straight for a while, then winds as it gets steeper. *You may hear the sounds of traffic from Rte. 117 to your right through the forest.*

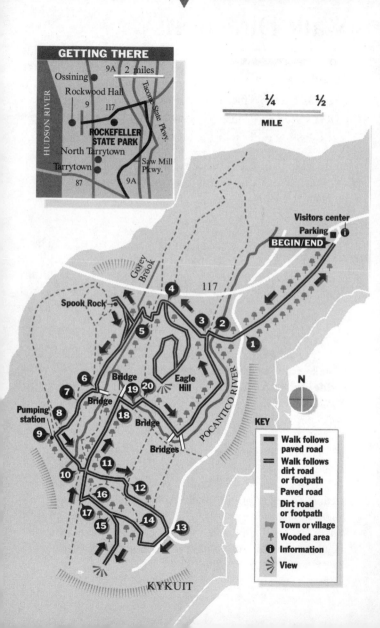

GETTING THERE

Ossining
Rockwood Hall
HUDSON RIVER
9A
2 miles
Taconic State Pkwy.
117
9
ROCKEFELLER STATE PARK
North Tarrytown
Saw Mill Pkwy.
Tarrytown
87
9A

¼   ½
MILE

Visitors center
Parking
BEGIN/END

Gorey Brook
Spook Rock
117
4
3 2
5
1
6
Bridge
19 20
Eagle Hill
7
Bridge
POCANTICO RIVER
18
8
Bridge
Pumping station
9
Bridges
N
11
10
12
16
17
14
15
13
KYKUIT

KEY

■ Walk follows paved road
= Walk follows dirt road or footpath
Paved road
Dirt road or footpath
Town or village
Wooded area
❶ Information
View

▼

4. You arrive at an intersection of four trails, with the four-lane Rte. 117 not far to your right. Go left onto the trail that heads up a hill. In less than 10 minutes, you come to the crest of Eagle Hill, where you see the stone mansion of Kykuit looming on a hill to your left, beautiful farmland and forests below, and the Hudson River and Tappan Zee Bridge beyond.

Continue along the bridle path as it loops around to the path that took you up the hill. Go left, retracing your steps to the intersection at Point 4. *Those looking for a short walk can go right and retrace their steps from here.* Otherwise, turn left onto the bridle path leading downhill. When you reach another bridle path, turn left again.

5. In a very short distance, you arrive at another bridle path, which you follow to the right downhill. In a few moments, you cross the remains of Gorey Brook Rd., one of the oldest roads in the forest, dating to the 19th century or earlier. The road is no longer used but is clearly visible here.

Follow the trail as it loops to the left. The brook is now on your left. *Legend says that a Native American maiden haunts the area around Spook Rock. If you'd like to try to pick up the vibes, make a right on the first path leading uphill. In about 100 yards, you arrive at a large, flat stone where the maiden is said to return in search of a lost husband and a child. (It's unlikely that you'll sense her ghost in the din of nearby Rte. 117.) If you visit this spot, retrace your steps downhill.*

Follow the trail along Gorey Brook. *Legend attributes its name to a battle between Dutch settlers and Native Americans which bloodied the tiny creek.* Gorey Brook shortly merges with the larger Pocantico River, which is on your left.

6. When you come to a three-way intersection, go right. Follow the bridle path a short way as it winds to the left.

Before continuing on, you may want to go left for a moment, down to the stone bridge over the river. It's a refreshing

▼

place for a rest and a good place to sense the spirits of Sleepy Hollow.

7. At a four-way intersection, take the trail to the left that leads uphill.

8. At the crest of the hill, don't follow the trail as it loops to the right; instead, go straight on a short, narrow path through the woods toward a stone pumping station.

9. Turn left in front of the pumping station, stopping to enjoy the view of Sleepy Hollow Cemetery and the forest far below the towering aqueduct. Follow the aqueduct over the Pocantico River.

10. As the aqueduct bears to the right to rejoin the hillside, make a left over an old stone wall through the brush toward a stone footpath that leads uphill. It is marked by a brown sign that says "Notice" in big letters. *You will pass by this intersection on your way back.* Follow the trail uphill. *You are now on private lands that are open to the public. Obey the simple rules stated on the sign. Beautiful views of field and forest unfold to your left. Watch for deer grazing in the fields and notice the bluffs of Eagle Cliff.*

11. Near the top of the hill, you reach a bridle path. Follow it straight downhill. *This may be one of the oldest roads on the walk, according to a copy of a map dating to 1725. The map shows a farm road here leading toward Sleepy Hollow Rd., where a schoolhouse once stood somewhere near the stone bridge at Point 13. Could this be the schoolhouse where Irving imagined that Ichabod Crane taught?*

12. At an intersection, go right, following the old farm road as it bears left between old stone walls. *You're surrounded by*

▼

beautiful fields, until recently under cultivation by Hudson Farms, a Rockefeller-owned dairy farm. Ignore a bridle path that's on your left. Continue straight toward a stone bridge that leads Sleepy Hollow Rd. over a bridle path.

13. At a three-way intersection in front of the bridge, go right. Follow the trail as it bears right up Cedar Hill, offering broad views of the farmland below and hills beyond. *At the top of the hill, the Kykuit mansion towers above on your right. In front of you, across the fields below, is Eagle Hill.*

14. At a three-way intersection, turn left, following the bridle path uphill.

15. When you reach a three-way intersection, go left uphill to get impressive views of the Hudson River, the hills across the river, and the Hudson Highlands way to the north. *At the crest of this hill, if you walk down to an old stone wall on your right, you get a glimpse of Manhattan on a clear day. There are many great picnic spots on the summit of Cedar Hill.* **Do not proceed downhill from here. It's private property.**

When you're done enjoying the views, retrace your steps and continue straight downhill past Point 15.

16. At a three-way intersection of bridle paths, go left down a path leading through the woods.

17. At the next three-way intersection, you arrive at Gorey Brook Rd., where you go right. *To your left, you see the aqueduct.* In a few minutes, you reach the intersection at Point 10 that you crossed earlier. Continue straight, ignoring another trail that descends toward the Pocantico River, which you see in the valley to your left. *You are once again walking on one of the park's oldest paths.*

▼

18. At the bottom of the hill, you reach a four-way intersection. Turn right. *A short distance ahead on your left is the beautiful stone bridge over the Pocantico River you visited earlier in the walk.*

19. In just a few minutes, go left and cross a bridge over the Pocantico River.

20. After a short distance, you reach another three-way intersection. Go right. Follow an old road for about 20 minutes as it winds along the rushing Pocantico River. *This road probably bore the wagons of settlers carrying crops to and from the grist mill up along the river not far from Point 3.* When you get to Point 3, continue straight. Go right at Point 2, and then retrace your steps to your car.

OTHER PLACES NEARBY

■ **Kykuit.** This mansion, high on a hill in North Tarrytown overlooking the Hudson, was home to four generations of Rockefellers, beginning with John D., founder of Standard Oil. Tours of the mansion (including a modern art collection), its splendid gardens, and its coach barn (housing vintage vehicles) are available only by making a reservation with Historic Hudson Valley. Your only chance of scoring a same-day opening is if you check with the Philipsburg Manor visitors center (*see* listing below), from which Kykuit tours leave. *C/o Historic Hudson Valley, 150 White Plains Rd., Tarrytown, NY 10591; tel. 914-631-9491. Kykuit is open Wed.-Mon., mid-Apr.-Oct. Admission. Visitors center is about 2 1/2 mi. southwest of Rockefeller State Park.*

■ **Old Dutch Church of Sleepy Hollow.** This is the church and graveyard mentioned in the story of the Headless Horseman from Washington Irving's *The Legend of Sleepy Hollow.* You may tour the church, built in 1685 by Frederick Philipse, and the graveyard. *N. Broadway, N. Tarrytown, NY 10591; tel. 914-631-*

▼

1123. Open Mon., Wed., Thu., Sun. 1-4 Jun.- Aug. Worship service Sun. at 10, from second Sun. in Jun.-Sun. in Sep. Open by appointment only early Sep.-May. On Rte. 9 opposite Pierson Ave. About 2 mi. southwest of Rockefeller State Park.

■ **Philipsburg Manor.** This restored colonial farm and working grist mill, originally established by Frederick Philipse in the late 17th century, is now operated as a "museum of living history," with tours conducted by interpreters in period costume. *Rte. 9, North Tarrytown, NY 10591; tel. 914-631-3992. Open Wed.-Mon. 10-5 (last tour at 4), Mar.1-Dec. 31. Admission. About 2 1/2 mi. southwest of Rockefeller State Park.*

■ **Union Church of Pocantico Hills.** This church's stained-glass windows by Marc Chagall and Henri Matisse were commissioned by the Rockefellers. *Rte. 448, N. Tarrytown, NY 10591; tel. 914-332-6659. Open Mon. and Wed.-Fri. 11-5, Sat. 10-5, and Sun. 2-5, Apr.-Dec. Call to make sure public hours not pre-empted by a church function. Admission. Worship services (nondenominational) Sun. at 8:30 and 10 Jul.-Aug., and at 9 and 11 the rest of the year. On Bedford Rd., next to Rockefeller State Park in Pocantico Hills.*

DINING

■ **Sonoma** (expensive). Still unknown to many locals, this relative newcomer arguably delivers the best food of any Westchester County restaurant. Expect big portions of nouvelle cuisine that bursts with flavor and thoughtful preparation. For an appetizer, try the pot stickers with lemon grass soy vinaigrette. Look for such main fare as roast chicken breast stuffed with spinach, goat cheese, and sun-dried tomato, served on a bed of fedelini. *Rte. 9A and Baltic Pl., Croton-on-Hudson, NY 10520; tel. 914-271-4100. Open Tue.-Sun. for dinner. About 12 mi. northwest of Rockefeller State Park.*

■ **Crabtree's Kittle House** (expensive). One of Westchester's finest restaurants, locals may quibble whether it has slipped a notch, but there's no denying it consistently deliv-

▼

ers high-quality food and a spectacular wine list in a restored 1790s carriage house. Expect ample portions of such inspired creations as loin of free-range Australian lamb with Yukon Gold roasted garlic puree or Montauk Point big-eye tuna with stir-fry vegetables and lime vinaigrette. *11 Kittle Rd., Chappaqua, NY 10514; tel. 914-666-8044. Open Mon.-Fri. for lunch; daily for dinner (including Sun. afternoon), and Sun. for brunch. On Rte. 117, about 10 mi. northeast of Rockefeller State Park.*

■ **Dudley's** (expensive). Dudley's was a speakeasy during Prohibition and retains an old American charm. The frequently changed "freestyle American" menu features specialties such as blackened swordfish with black beans, basmati rice, and arugula vinaigrette. *6 Rockledge Ave., Ossining, NY 10562; tel. 914-941-8674. Open Mon.-Fri. for lunch and dinner, Sat.-Sun. for dinner. Off Rte. 9, about 4 mi. north of Rockefeller State Park.*

■ **Goldie's by the Bridge** (expensive). This small restaurant offers views of the Hudson River and the Tappan Zee Bridge, a cozy, casual atmosphere, and an American "fresh market" cuisine that attracts a loyal following. One specialty favored by customers is an appetizer of baked brie with roasted garlic and fresh fruit; a popular entree is seared tuna with sesame herb crust and wasabe vinaigrette. *226 Beekman Ave., N. Tarrytown, NY 10591; tel. 914-631-9794. Open Mon.-Fri. for lunch and dinner, Sat.-Sun. for dinner. About 2 1/2 mi. southwest of Rockefeller State Park.*

■ **Main St. Cafe** (inexpensive). This is a good place to go for lunch or a casual dinner. In addition to your basic hamburgers and pasta dishes, you'll find more creative items such as linguine with spinach, salmon, sun-dried tomatoes, garlic, and olive oil. The 19th-century building has a quaint, appealing atmosphere. *24 Main St., Tarrytown, NY 10591; tel. 914-524-9770, 914-332-9834. Open Tue.-Sat. for lunch and dinner, Sun. for brunch and dinner. About 3 mi. southwest of Rockefeller State Park.*

▼

LODGING

■ **The Castle at Tarrytown** (very expensive). This turn-of-the-century stone castle has been converted to a luxury inn. Carefully renovated to retain the period ambience while providing all modern amenities, the inn has seven suites and one room, all with private baths. The rooms in the tower have the best views. *400 Benedict Ave., Tarrytown, NY 10591; tel. 914-631-1980. About 4 mi. south of Rockefeller State Park.*

■ **Alexander Hamilton House** (expensive). This seven-guest-room Victorian has an excellent Hudson River view, and many of the rooms and common areas are sensational. The library and the suites are huge, featuring attractive sitting areas and fireplaces. There are also more modest, moderately priced rooms, but you'll never forget the stained-glass, back-lighted Jacuzzi in the very expensive Master Suite or the sunlight dancing through the skylight of the Bridal Chamber. *49 Van Wyck St., Croton-on-Hudson, NY 10520, tel. 914-271-6737; fax 914-271-3927. About 10 mi. northwest of Rockefeller State Park.*

■ **Crabtree's Kittle House** (moderate). The suites are a bargain—spacious and nicely decorated. Recommended suite: 2F, a very large, bright blue room with plenty of charm. If it's filled, try to book 2G or 2J. But steer clear of many of the rooms like 1C and 2A, which need upgrading or updating. *11 Kittle Rd., Chappaqua, NY 10514; tel. 914-666-8044. On Rte. 117, about 10 mi. northeast of Rockefeller State Park.*

FOR MORE INFORMATION
Tourist Office:

■ **Sleepy Hollow Chamber of Commerce.** *80 S. Broadway, Tarrytown, NY 10591; tel. 914-631-1705; fax 914-631-1512. Open Mon.-Fri. 10:30-3:30. On Rte. 9.*

For Serious Walkers:

Rockefeller State Park has miles of additional trails, documented on a map available in the visitors center.

The Lost Railroad

EXPERIENCE 4:
DUNDERBERG MOUNTAIN

I f you walk along a trail on Dunderberg Mountain and the leaves rustle mysteriously on a calm day, you may be hearing the ghost of William T. Howell, an inveterate hiker who tramped over these lands at the turn of this century. Year after year, the legendary wanderer

> **The Highlights:** An abandoned mountain railroad, stunning Hudson River views, a Revolutionary War footpath.
>
> **Other Places Nearby:** A historic river cruiser, Revolutionary War forts and battlegrounds, a ghost town, excellent hiking.

and storyteller returned to this mountain above the Hudson River and did his best to explore its every corner. Few New Yorkers except hikers have ever heard of Dunderberg, but it has made a contribution to history and captured the spirits of diverse characters over the years who tried to pull some profit from it, material or spiritual.

Dunderberg rises nearly 1,400 feet above the west bank of the Hudson River, just to the south of the Bear Mountain Bridge. Its rugged, heavily forested ridge stretches for three miles from east to west, culminating at a towering cliff known as The Timp. The name Dunderberg probably comes from an

▼

old Dutch word meaning something like "thunder mountain." Dutch sailors might have given it that name for the way thunderstorms echoed over the highlands, a phenomenon they surely would have ascribed to supernatural forces. The name Timp may also have come from the Dutch, perhaps an adaptation of an old word describing a Dutch bread.

In a valley north of Dunderberg rests the ghost town known as Doodletown. Its abandoned fields, gardens, and foundations fill a picturesque valley whose view you will enjoy from atop Bald Mountain, one of several summits on Dunderberg. Only about 100 people lived in Doodletown at any one time since settlers first came in the 1700s, and it hardly changed until the last inhabitants left in the early 1960s and the Palisades Interstate Park Commission tore it down. You can visit the town's cemetery, hidden in the woods, but still cared for by descendants. (*See* For Serious Walkers.)

The name Doodletown evokes memories of the town's one great moment in history, when British troops marched through on an old woods road you will cross on this walk (today called the 1777 Trail) that connected Stony Point to points north. Their object was to surprise American forts Clinton and Montgomery, which guarded the mouth of the Hudson Highlands from the northern advance of the British navy. As British soldiers marched through the tiny hamlet, they might have taunted the locals by singing "Yankee Doodle Dandy," thereby giving the town its name. (More likely, this odd name predates the Revolutionary War and comes from some derivative of an old Dutch word.) The British soldiers succeeded in their mission, capturing both forts despite the brave opposition of people like legendary Molly Pitcher, who picked up the musket of her fallen husband in an effort to drive off the attack.

The few people who ever lived on Dunderberg Mountain put their homes alongside the old road that is now called the 1777 Trail. These hardy settlers probably made a living by

▼

chopping wood, grazing cattle, or pulling iron ore out of a few mines, including one you can see near the summit of Bald Mountain. Little remains of their efforts except old woods roads leading to nowhere, a few small pits and slag heaps, and a few signs of foundations scattered across the mountain's uneven ridge.

Everything would have turned out differently for Dunderberg if some late 19th-century developers had gotten their way. Brothers T. L. and H. J. Mumford had visions of an elaborate mountain retreat. Their promotional literature promised that it would be designed for "the toiling millions of people who take an outing once or often during the summer in search of the strengthening, invigorating, life-giving oxygen of pure air and the healthful stimulant of a radical change from the monotony of their daily toil." In 1889, they filed plans for the Dunderberg Spiral Railway, which would transport tourists by an incline railroad up to a summit restaurant and lodge, and then carry them down on a gravity-powered train covering more than 10 miles of switchbacks across the mountain's broad face. Stations along the way would allow passengers to disembark for picnics or overnight stays in rustic cabins or campgrounds.

Construction began early in 1890 and lasted less than a year, but deep tunnels were partially excavated and huge viaducts built into the mountainside. The developers must have been confident of completion, because work progressed simultaneously up and down the mountain. Despite sinking over $1 million into the project, the developers failed to raise all of the capital needed for the project, falling victim, perhaps, to the financial uncertainties of the time. The project went bankrupt, and many investors, suppliers, and workers suffered.

All but forgotten by the general public, the impressive remains, long enveloped by forest, have attracted curious hikers for nearly a century. One of the first was William T. Howell. Over the years, he explored and mapped the entire route of the railroad and developed a deep knowledge of the

▼

mountain's intricate terrain and the ways of its tiny population. Near a reliable spring shown to him by a woodcutter named Jim Stalter, Howell and friends stashed grills, buckets, and other utensils that they would pull out to prepare elaborate mountaintop dinners.

Although hiking had already become a popular activity during Howell's time, there was no specialized gear. Photos of Howell and his friends show them clad in suit and tie (even on backwoods trails) and using canvas knapsacks and shelters and elaborate cooking methods no hiker today would consider.

During his short life, Howell spent countless days and nights walking through the Hudson Highlands, writing of his adventures in a diary and capturing some of the scenery in his photos. In his spare time, he wrote articles for local newspapers, describing the places he visited and the lore that surrounded them, and led hikes for various walking groups, one known as the Fresh Air Club. He also explored many of the Revolutionary War traces that have now given way to forest, such as the ruins of Fort Montgomery, still visible in the forest but without so much as a trail to mark its presence.

Howell actively promoted efforts to preserve the treasures of the Highlands from development. "Most interesting of all, in the remoter hills and forests," he wrote, "are sleeping the almost forgotten, overgrown military roads, ruined mines and forges, abandoned farms, and other reminders of very early days in our national life." Thanks in part to the efforts of preservationists like Howell, you can explore much of these treasures in a land even more unspoiled than in the legendary hiker's time. Howell was surprised to find a deer track on Dunderberg Mountain. Today, if you're quiet, you might see a herd.

Howell's writings and activities gained him some renown in the world of early 20th-century naturalists. His untimely death from tuberculosis at the age of 43 prompted friends to collect his diaries and publish them under the title of *The Hudson Highlands,* which can still be found in area libraries.

▼

Although Howell will argue that you'd need a lifetime of walking to know the many hollows, rock outcroppings, and odd formations of this diverse mountain, this walk introduces the walker to many of its most impressive sites—two tunnels built as part of the railroad project, viaducts and extensive rock walls, old roads used by woodcutters, the historic 1777 Trail, an iron mine, and the scenic overlook at The Timp. From there, you can see Manhattan on a clear day, as well as the rugged mountains of the Ramapos to the southwest and the Hudson Highlands to the north and east.

GETTING THERE:

By car:

From the Bear Mountain Bridge, go about 3 1/2 miles south on Rte. 9W around Jones Point to an intersection with a little-used paved road that comes in from the left at a sharp angle. Park here along Rte. 9W or off the small paved road.

Walk Directions

TIME: 1 1/2 to 3 hours
LEVEL: Moderate to difficult
DISTANCE: 2 to 6 mi.
ACCESS: By car

You can take a long hike covering the entire mountain or a short walk to see the most impressive of the railroad remains. Pick up picnic provisions in Stony Point a few miles south on Rte. 9W.

TO BEGIN

Walk south a short distance along Rte. 9W along the right side of the road beyond the intersection. The river will be on your left. **Watch for fast-moving traffic.**

1. A footpath marked prominently with blue blazes enters the forest. In a few minutes, you reach a partially constructed

▼

stone tunnel, probably where visitors would have begun their journey up the mountain on the incline portion of the railway. *Notice that you are walking along the remains of a rail bed, probably the end of the gravity-driven train's long journey downhill.*

As you head up the mountain, cross another rail bed and then enjoy some views of the Hudson River. Shortly beyond the viewpoint, the trail cuts left up onto a rail bed, and then right up onto a another rail bed before going left a short distance. You quickly reach the entrance to a partially constructed tunnel that was part of the downhill portion of the track. As the trail continues, you follow an impressive section of rail bed through a rock cut and reach a stream. *The rail bed veers right to a great stone cut, the other side of the incomplete tunnel. Those out for a short walk can explore this area and retrace their steps back to the car.*

Otherwise, cross the stream and follow the blue blazes uphill, ignoring an intersecting unmarked woods road. The trail winds up through a rocky forest, eventually yielding more views of the Hudson.

2. You cross a very old path, the 1777 Trail, used by British troops to surprise Fort Montgomery.

3. The trail proceeds up and down along the ridge of Dunderberg Mountain until it intersects with the red-blazed Ramapo-Dunderberg Trail. Go left and follow the trail, now double blazed with blue and a red dot.

4. The trails arrive at the crest of The Timp, offering impressive views of the Hudson River north and south, the Ramapo Mountains, and even the skyline of Manhattan on a clear day. *This is a great place for a picnic, but you probably won't be alone here on a peak weekend in spring or autumn. Even on the busiest days, though, you can find a peaceful spot.*

▼

Retrace your steps to Point 3, and bear left on the rail blazed with the red dot.

5. Go straight across the 1777 Trail. Continue on to a small

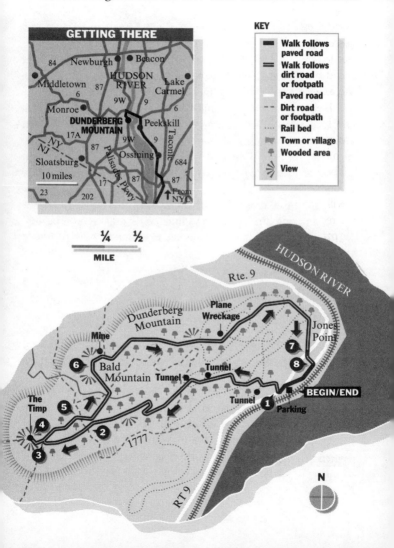

▼

stream, where you reach an old woods road. Stay on the trail blazed with a red dot.

6. You'll know you're at the summit of Bald Mountain when you reach an overlook offering views of abandoned Doodletown, the Hudson River, and the Highlands. The trail descends into the forest past an old pit on your right. About 30 feet to the left of the trail, just under the summit, is a slag heap and deep pit, left over from a mining operation. **Walk around the area with care.**

Follow the red-dot trail as it goes up and down over the various high points along the Dunderberg ridge, passing by a junction with a blue-blazed trail leading downhill to the left. About 20 minutes beyond that intersection, the red-dot trail crosses a rail bed, not far from the beginning of the long descent down the mountain. You can follow the rail bed around to the right, where it will eventually rejoin the red-dot trail, or continue straight on the red-dot trail past another viewpoint. *Just a short while later, the trail descends into a shallow ravine, where, to the left about 50 feet off the trail, lies the wreckage of a small plane that crashed on the mountain in the 1960s, killing the pilot. Somewhere around there, the mountain railroad planners envisioned the hilltop restaurant and inn at the terminus of the incline portion of the railway.* Continue straight on the blazed trail.

7. The trail arrives at a recently reconstructed portion of Rte. 9W. **Cross the metal barrier and road carefully.** Follow the red-dot trail downhill toward a paved road along the river.

8. When you get to this road, go right and walk up to the intersection with Rte. 9W and your car.

OTHER PLACES NEARBY

■ *The Commander* **Hudson River Cruises.** Experience the Hudson Highlands from the river on *The Commander*, a wooden passenger vessel built in 1917 and listed on the National Register of Historic Places. Full-day cruises depart from West Haverstraw; cruises lasting 1 1/2 hours leave from West Point. *Box 265, Highland Falls, NY 10928; tel. 914-446-7171. Scheduled public cruises run Mon.-Fri. and the first Sun. of the month, May 1-Oct. 31. Private charters are also available. Admission. W. Haverstraw is 6 mi. south of Dunderberg Mtn.; West Point is 6 mi. north.*

■ **Bear Mountain State Park.** One of the oldest parks in the region, this 5,067-acre park offers scenic vistas and a great variety of recreational opportunities, including boating, swimming, fishing, skating, and picnicking. Walkers have access to 200 miles of hiking trails. The Trailside Museum and Zoo offers indoor and outdoor nature exhibits. *Rte. 9W, NY 10911; tel. 914-786-2701. Open daily 9-4. On Rte. 9W, just south of Bear Mtn. Bridge. About 3 mi. north of Dunderberg Mtn.*

■ **Stony Point Battlefield.** This site of an important American victory in the Revolutionary War offers both history and spectacular scenic views. Staff members in period dress perform re-enactments of 18th-century army camp life, and there are tours of the museum and grounds. Picnic sites have great river views. *Park Rd., Stony Point, NY 10980; tel. 914-786-2521. Grounds open Wed.-Sat. 10-5 and Sun. 1-5, Apr. 15-Oct. 31. Museum closes 1/2 hour earlier. Open some holidays on Mon. and Tue. On Park Rd., off Rte. 9W. About 4 mi. south of Dunderberg Mtn.*

DINING

The selection of good restaurants and places to stay is slim. If none of the listings here suit you, you may want to check the listings in nearby Experience 5, Cold Spring, and Experience 6, Schunemunk Mountain.

■ **Fiesta Cancun** (moderate). Locals keep coming back for the restaurant's popular Mexican offerings. The Victorian exterior belies the exuberant, rustic Mexican decor of the interior,

▼

which includes windows painted in vibrant colors. The friendly Mexican owners create a warm and cheerful atmosphere. Try the *camarones* a la Cancun—shrimp and crabmeat in a creamy garlic sauce. In warm weather, you can sit on the terrace, which has a bit of a river view. *90 S. Liberty Dr. (Rte. 9W), Stony Point, NY 10980; tel. 914-429-9363. Open daily for lunch and dinner. On Rte. 9W, about 4 mi. south of Dunderberg Mtn.*

■ **Lynch's** (moderate). Don't come here for *haute* cuisine, but for good value and a friendly, casual atmosphere. The chef, a Culinary Institute graduate, supplements the basic Irish pub menu with creative specialties such as chicken with shiitake mushrooms and sun-dried tomatoes in scampi sauce over pasta. The 19th-century building was a speakeasy during Prohibition, and its tin ceilings and wainscoting add to the atmosphere. *Rte. 9W, Tompkins Cove, NY 10986; tel. 914-947-3363. Open daily for lunch and dinner. About 2 mi. south of Dunderberg Mountain.*

■ **Vincent's Landing** (moderate). This restaurant's location, tucked away in a very private nook on the banks of the Hudson River, is magical. Enjoy river views both from the dining room and, weather permitting, from the waterfront terrace. The menu features fresh seafood, as well as meats and pastas. The location and the high quality of the food make the trip through rather seedy Haverstraw worthwhile. *16 Front St., Haverstraw, NY 10927; tel. 914-429-3891. Open Wed.-Sun. for dinner early Apr.-Oct. Reservations essential on weekends. From 9W, turn east on Main St. and follow to the river. About 6 mi. south of Dunderberg Mtn.*

LODGING

■ **Bear Mountain Inn** (moderate). In an area with few lodgings, this old hotel offers plain but functional accommodations adjacent to great hiking. Ask for a room in one of the four stone lodges. *Bear Mountain State Park, Rte 9W, Bear Mountain, NY 10911; tel. 914-786-2731; fax 914-786-2543. Off*

▼

Rte. 9W, just south of the Bear Mtn. Bridge. About 3 mi. north of Dunderberg Mtn.

■ **Cove House** (moderate). This contemporary ranch house offers a nearly aerial view of the Hudson River from the guests' common living room, dining room, solarium, and deck. The largest guest room, the Queen Room, has not only the view but a large private bath and cathedral ceilings; it's worth the extra money. The two smaller rooms, which share a bath, are inexpensive. *Box 81, Tompkins Cove, NY 10986; tel. 914-429-9695. Call for directions. About 3 mi. south of Dunderberg Mtn.*

FOR MORE INFORMATION
Tourist Offices:
■ **Rockland County Department of Tourism.** *11 New Hempstead Rd., New City, NY 10956; tel. 914-638-5800. Open Mon.-Fri. 9-5.*

For Serious Walkers:
Just below Dunderberg is the ghost town of Doodletown, with its old cemetery, which makes for great exploring. Nearby Harriman State Park offers extraordinary hiking opportunities in the rugged Ramapo Mountains. Hook Mountain State Park and High Tor State Park also offer excellent hiking on the ridge of mountains that line the west shore of the Hudson River. Pick up the New York-New Jersey Trail Conference's packet of Harriman-Bear Mountain and Hudson Palisades Trails.

Ruins of a Lost Time

EXPERIENCE 5:
COLD SPRING-ON-HUDSON

Speak of ruins, and the traveler imagines places like Europe, Asia, and Latin America, certainly not the countryside around New York City. Yet, ruins there are, not as grand or impressive as better known monuments of the ancient world, but equally evocative of an era now gone.

The Highlights: Great Hudson River views, ruins of a once elegant estate, abandoned farms, old roads, a beautiful forest.

Other Places Nearby: Quaint villages, great hiking possibilities, a Buddhist monastery, the Boscobel restoration.

Just north of Cold Spring on the east bank of the Hudson River, sitting in a narrow valley separating rugged Breakneck Ridge and stately Mount Taurus, you'll walk through what's left of the once opulent Cornish estate and remnants of farms dating back to the early 19th century. Now almost swallowed by forest, these remains tell the walker a quiet story of life in another time.

With a railroad and a fast two-lane road now running along the Hudson, it's hard to imagine that the rugged country north of Cold Spring ever was considered remote. Yet, the upland val-

▼

ley traversed by this walk has never had more than a small population of Americans, even in colonial times. Before Europeans arrived, the land was inhabited by Native Americans of the Algonkian-speaking Wappinger tribe, of whom little is known.

The early Dutch settlers traveling upriver in the 1700s passed by the rugged lands of the Hudson Highlands in favor of land more suitable for farming farther north. The steep hills along the river north of Peekskill effectively blocked construction of roads for many years. Revolutionary War maps show the river's east shore road ending just north of Peekskill in what is now Garrison.

The earliest European settlers to the Hudson Highlands east of the river didn't come until 1687, when two Dutchmen acquired the land from the Wappingers. A few years later, the land was deeded to the Philipse family, and it became part of the huge Philipse patent, one of the largest in the Hudson Valley.

In 1715, an Englishman named Thomas Davenport built a home in what much later became Cold Spring. (Some people say that the town got its name from a freshwater spring located nearby that early sailors used on their river journeys and which may have attracted Davenport.) About the same time, a David Hustis came up from New York City to live in the Highlands along the "Path," a Native American trail (now Route 9) inland east of the river that settlers widened to become the postal route between New York and Albany. The wooded footpath followed on this walk through Breakneck Valley likely is the original east-west route cut by early settlers to connect the "Path" with the shores of the Hudson.

Sometime in the late 1700s or early 1800s, a member of the Hustis family set up a farm along this route a little west of the family's main domain. The walk takes you through this long-abandoned farm, now forest land, and another nearby farm. Today, little remains of these farms but a network of stone

▼

walls in the forest and the inexplicable depressions and overgrown mounds left over from their operations. Piles of rock at
various sites suggest the location of former dwellings but offer
no confirmation.

Only a few people inhabited these wilds lands until the early 1800s, when General Joseph Swift established the West Point
Foundry in a ravine near Cold Spring. Mines that you can still
see today some seven miles inland (*see* For Serious Walkers)
produced the ore, which laborers brought down on carts to the
foundry. Later, they built a gravity-powered railroad that led
downhill its entire length. The foundry played a prominent role
in providing armaments for the North in the Civil War, earning a
visit by President Abraham Lincoln. Little remains of the foundry
today. Cold Spring owes its existence to the foundry, whose
employees needed housing and places to shop and drink.

When the railroad along the river was completed in 1848,
a new wave of estates was built in the Hudson Valley by members of America's industrialist aristocracy. The river estates built
by wealthy families before then had used the Hudson River for
transportation; the railroad made the area much more accessible to New York City. Some of the mansions from the 18th,
19th, and even early 20th centuries have survived and are now
open to the public. The Cornish estate you'll visit along the
walk is one of those that did not survive.

In the 1920s, the estate, owned by wealthy industrialist
Edward Cornish, employed more than a dozen people, enjoyed
running water supplied by an elaborate system of dams in the
hills above, and was home to an impressive dairy farm, traces
of which you'll see beneath the forest canopy. You can find
remains of a swimming pool, a greenhouse, barbecues, and
gardens around the house. No one is quite sure when the
Cornishes abandoned the home, which burned down in 1956,
because the family did not mingle much with locals.

One of the great environmental battles of our time began
in Cold Spring in the early 1960s, when residents joined forces

▼

with other Hudson Valley inhabitants to oppose construction of a power plant on Storm King Mountain, across the river from Cold Spring. The Con Edison project would have cut huge holes into the mountain and erected an enormous facility on its north face. (At one point, another utility company envisaged a power plant in Breakneck Valley—the area covered by the walk.) After a tremendous legal and political battle, the project was halted, and today Storm King remains an unspoiled land of forests and rocky overlooks crisscrossed with hiking trails.

GETTING THERE

By train:

From New York City's Grand Central Station, take Metro North Railroad's Hudson Line train to Croton-Harmon and change trains for the local to Cold Spring. For information, call Metro North at 800-638-7646.

By car:

From New York City, take the Saw Mill River Pkwy. north to the Taconic State Pkwy. Take the Taconic north for about 35 minutes and get off at the exit for Cold Spring and Rte. 301. Turn left and head west on Rte. 301 into Cold Spring. At Rte. 9D, turn right and proceed north. In a short distance, park at one of the trail heads on Rte. 9D at Points 3 or 4 of the walk below.

Walk Directions

TIME: 3 hours
LEVEL: Moderate
DISTANCE: 5 miles
ACCESS: By train or car

This walk offers some of the most unforgettable scenery in the Hudson Valley, including views on clear days of the Catskill Mountains and the Manhattan skyline. The trail's uphill ascent is gradual for most of the way, but there are a few steep stretches. Those arriving by car reduce the walk by about 1 mi. by parking at Point 4 and follow the directions from there. People with only a little time will still enjoy a walk to the Cornish estate. Pick up sandwiches on Main St. in Cold Spring or on Rte. 9D, south of town.

TO BEGIN

When you get off the train, follow the platform that follows the tracks north to the station's exit. (If you arrived by car, follow the directions from Point 4 below.)

1. At the end of the platform, you see a kiosk with town information. Make a right onto Main St. and begin walking up the hill.

2. At Fair St., turn left and proceed along the street through the outskirts of Cold Spring. You pass the Riverview restaurant on your left.

3. Make a left onto Rte. 9D and walk carefully along the road. **Caution: This road is busy.** On your right, you pass a trail head for the white-blazed Washburn Trail, where you will exit on your return. *If you wish, you can enter the woods here and walk along an unmarked trail that leads to Point 4.*

4. In another few minutes, you reach a forest road marked by the remnants of a stone gate. Leave Rte. 9D and follow this road; it has no blazes, but its crumbling pavement offers a well-marked trail into the forest at the base of Mt. Taurus. This trail leads steadily but easily uphill. You are walking on the driveway of the Cornish estate, which follows the original river road. *Look for the foundations of old homesteads, dating back to the 19th century.*

5. The old road veers suddenly to the right, away from the river. Shortly after, you reach the elaborate, overgrown ruins of the Cornish estate. *You may want to take the time to explore the ruins, whose forested grounds still show signs of the estate's once splendid gardens.* After you're done, continue following the old road on its gradual ascent into Breakneck Valley. An impressive old stone wall lines the road for some time on your right. The

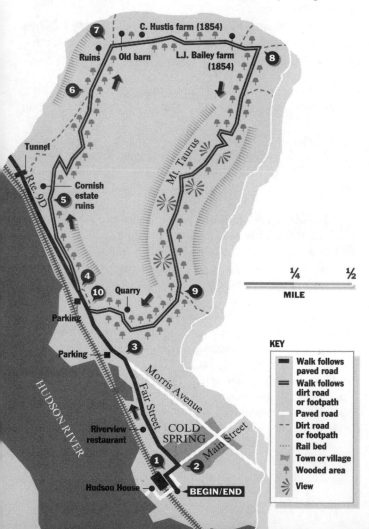

KEY

━━━ Walk follows paved road

═══ Walk follows dirt road or footpath

Paved road

--- Dirt road or footpath

···· Rail bed

Town or village

Wooded area

View

▼

road becomes gravel as it winds uphill, and you'll see an old cistern on your left before crossing the Catskill Aqueduct, which forms a marked hump through the forest.

6. In a few minutes, you reach the red-blazed Brook Notch Trail, on which you bear right. *The trail most likely follows the old road that connected the original Albany-New York Post Rd. and the Hudson River.* Within moments, you can see the impressive ruins of the Cornish dairy operations.

7. At an intersection with the blue-blazed Notch trail, turn right. Take time to explore the old farm before proceeding. *A tangle of trails fills the forest floor here; make sure you follow the blue-blazed trail up toward Mt. Taurus. It is well-marked but makes a sharp turn as it winds its way uphill.*

8. At the apex of the notch beneath Mt. Taurus and the unnamed hill north of it, folow the trail as it veers right and becomes the white-blazed Washburn Trail. As you proceed up the hill, you encounter increasingly impressive views in all directions. *On the right side of the trail, clear weather will permit views of Breakneck Ridge, Storm King Mountain, the Shawangunks (see Experience 7, Lake Minnewaska), and the ramparts of the Catskills (see Experience 8, Woodstock, and*

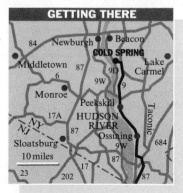

GETTING THERE

Experience 9, North/South Lakes). To the left, you get wonderful views of the Hudson River as it winds its way through the Highlands. On clear days, you can even glimpse the towers of Manhattan on the edge of the southern horizon. It was presumably from one of these

▼

overlooks that the 19th-century Hudson River School painter W. H. Bartlett made the sketches for a painting of Crow's Nest Mountain and Breakneck Ridge.

Follow the white-blazed trail as it frequently follows or crosses an old woods road, *perhaps built by wood cutters who deforested this entire region by the mid-1800s.*

9. Ignore an unmarked trail that veers left downhill and bear right following the white blazes. *As you descend, the trail skirts the top of a huge stone quarry that animated the hillside until the 1930s. At the base of the hill, you see only small remains of the huge apparatus constructed to bring the rock down to the river.*

10. At Rte. 9D, turn left. Retrace your steps back into town. If you parked at Point 4, make a right onto a footpath through the forest that you encounter a short distance before Rte. 9D.

PLACES ALONG THE WALK

■ **Village of Cold Spring.** The village's restored 19th-century Main Street offers a wide variety of antique, curio, and food shops. Make sure you stop by the gazebo at the foot of Main Street on the river to enjoy the dramatic view of Storm King Mountain and West Point to the south.

OTHER PLACES NEARBY

■ **Boscobel.** The riverside setting, gardens, and magnificent early 19th-century architecture make this a coveted stop on the trail of Hudson River valley mansions. Special events include a Shakespeare Festival in July, lawn concerts, and exhibitions of decorative arts. *Rte. 9D, Garrison, NY 10524; tel. 914-265-3638. Open Wed.-Mon. 9:30-5 Apr.-Oct., 9:30-4 Mar. and Nov.-Dec. Mansion tours start at 10. Admission. On Rte. 9D, about 3 mi south of Cold Spring.*

■ **Chuang Yen Monastery.** This majestic Buddhist

▼

monastery is a hidden treasure, situated on 125 acres off the Old Philipstown Tpke. (Rte. 301). Its library houses one of the world's largest collections on Eastern religions. The general public is welcome to attend English-language Buddhist religious services (meditation and discussion) as well as vegetarian brunches that are held on Sundays. *R.D. 2, Rte. 301, Carmel, NY 10512; tel. 914-225-1819; fax 914-225-1819. Main Hall (temple) open daily 5-5. Woo-ju Memorial Library open Mon.-Fri. 9-5 year-round, plus Sat. 1-4 spring, summer, and fall. Meditation service Sun. at 9; brunch Sun. at noon. On Rte. 301, about 10 mi. east of Cold Spring.*

■ **Clarence Fahnestock Memorial State Park.** This 6,800-acre park offers hiking trails, sites for picnicking and camping, and a beach on Canopus Lake for swimming and boating (rentals available). *Rte. 301, Carmel, NY 10512; tel. 914-225-7207. Park open daily year-round. Beach open weekends 9-7 in Jun.; daily Jul.-Labor Day. Campgrounds open May-Oct. About 8 mi. east of Cold Spring.*

■ **Foundry School Museum.** Headquarters of the Putnam County Historical Society, this museum is located in an 1828 schoolhouse. Permanent and temporary exhibits focus on aspects of local and regional history. *63 Chestnut St., Cold Spring, NY 10516; tel. 914 265 4010. Open Sun. 2-5, Tue.-Wed. 10-4, Thu. 1-4. Admission.*

■ **Manitoga.** Overlooking the Hudson River, the former home and environmentally designed landscape of industrial designer Russel Wright offers more than four miles of walking paths through forests and meadows in a "managed natural state." *Rte. 9D, Garrison, NY 10524; tel. 914-424-3812. Open daily Apr.-Oct., weekdays 9-4, weekends 10-6. Open weekdays 9-4 Nov.-Mar. Admission. Located 2 1/2 mi. north of Bear Mtn. Bridge. About 4 mi. south of Cold Spring.*

DINING

■ **Xaviar's at Garrison** (very expensive). The dining

▼

room, originally the ballroom of a Georgian-style mansion, has 25-foot ceilings and opens onto a terrace where one can dine in fair weather. Excellent contemporary American cuisine is served as six courses paired with six accompanying wines; the prix fixe menu is a value, considering the cost of the wine. You'll rarely be disappointed—this is one of the best restaurants in the Northeast. Jacket and tie required. No credit cards. *Rte. 9D, Garrison, NY 10512; tel. 914-424-4228. Open Fri.-Sat. for dinner, Sun. for brunch. Reservations required. On Rte. 9D, about 4 mi. south of Cold Spring.*

■ **The Bird and Bottle Inn** (expensive). Built in 1761 as a stagecoach stop on the old Albany Post Road, this well-known country inn offers American continental cuisine in an 18th-century atmosphere with beamed ceilings, candlelight, and working fireplaces. A delightful place for Sunday brunch. *Old Albany Post Rd. and Rte. 9, Garrison, NY 10524; tel. 914-424-3000. Open Wed.-Sun. for dinner, Thu.-Sat. for lunch, and Sun. for brunch. Call for seating times for Sat. dinner and Sun. brunch. Closed Wed. Jan.-Mar. On Rte. 9, about 6 mi. southeast of Cold Spring.*

■ **Plumbush Inn** (expensive). The former estate of a marquise, this impressive Victorian mansion set on five parklike acres has a number of individual dining rooms, each with its own individual decor; some have wood-burning fireplaces. The Swiss continental cuisine has received mixed reviews, but the ambience makes this restaurant popular with locals. *Rte. 9D, Cold Spring, NY 10516; tel. 914-265-3904. Open Wed.-Sat. lunch and dinner, Sun. for brunch and dinner. 3/4 mi. south of Cold Spring.*

■ **Riverview** (moderate). In addition to a creative selection of exotic pizzas baked in the visible wood-fired brick oven, this restaurant offers a trattoria-style menu including interesting appetizers, pasta, and fresh seafood. Indoors, the atmosphere is warm and Mediterranean; outdoors, in fair weather, the terrace gives great views of the river and Storm King Mountain. *45 Fair*

▼

St., Cold Spring, NY 10516; tel. 914-265-4778. Open daily for lunch and dinner except Mon. lunch. Off Main St.

■ **Karen's Kitchen** (inexpensive). The menu of this informal cafe is eclectic, creative, and health-oriented, including baked goods that are natural and homemade. Seasonal outside dining, weather permitting. A good place for walkers to pick up picnic provisions. *55 Main St., Cold Spring, NY 10516; tel. 914-265-1083. Open daily for breakfast, lunch and (early) dinner.*

LODGING

■ **Bird and Bottle Inn** (expensive). Step back in time to 1761, when this inn was built as Warren's Tavern, a stagecoach stop on the old Albany Post Road. The three rooms and cottage feature antique furnishings, fireplaces, and private baths. *Old Albany Post Rd. and Rte. 9, Garrison, NY 10524; tel. 914-424-3000. On Rte. 9, 6 mi. southeast of Cold Spring.*

■ **Hudson House** (expensive). Now a National Historic Landmark, this waterfront inn was built in 1832 and is one of the oldest New York hotels still in use. Although its rooms are small, six have excellent river views. Weekday rates are moderate; rates include continental breakfast weekdays, full buffet breakfast weekends. *2 Main St., Cold Spring, NY 10516; tel. 914-265-9355.*

■ **Pig Hill Inn** (expensive). All the antique furnishings are for sale in this 1830s brick townhouse. You can have your breakfast served in bed, in the dining room, or in the terraced garden in summer. Rooms in back are the most quiet. *73 Main St., Cold Spring, NY 10516; tel. 914-265-9247.*

■ **Three Rock** (expensive). How about a view of the Hudson River from your bed and your Jacuzzi? This B&B with spacious rooms is perched high on a bluff overlooking the river, yet is only a two-minute walk to the heart of the village. Weekends are heavily booked for weddings during spring and summer. Weekday rates are moderate, making it one of the

▼

best values in the area. *3 Rock St., Cold Spring, NY 10516; tel. 914-265-2330; fax 914-265-4412. Off Main St.*

■ **Plumbush Inn** (moderate). The former estate of a marquise, this Victorian mansion has two rooms and one expensive suite, all furnished with antiques and with private baths. The five-acre park-like setting provides a quiet, private environment. *Rte. 9D, Cold Spring, NY 10516; tel. 914-265-3904. Open Wed.-Sun. 3/4 mi. south of Cold Spring.*

FOR MORE INFORMATION
Tourist Office:

■ **Cold Spring Area Chamber of Commerce.** Leave a message with your address, and they'll send a list of latest travel services and attractions in the area. *Box 342, Cold Spring, NY 10516; tel. 914-265-9060.*

For Serious Walkers:

Spectacular walking options include Breakneck Ridge, Beacon Mountain, Fishkill Ridge, and the Appalachian Trail. Pick up the New York-New Jersey Trail Conference's set of maps for East Hudson Trails, which also includes walks to the old mines in Clarence Fahnestock Memorial State Park. On weekends, a Metro North train stops at the foot of Breakneck Ridge in the morning and afternoon, allowing hikers to do loop walks through beautiful, rugged land. Call Metro North at 800-638-7646.

A Forgotten People

EXPERIENCE 6:
SCHUNEMUNK MOUNTAIN

To New York metropolitan area residents, the New Jersey shore is synonymous with summer fun. Little do they know that their 20th-century ritual continues a tradition that began thousands of years before the arrival of

The Highlights: The site of an ancient Native American village, incomparable views, unique rock formations.

Other Places Nearby: Revolutionary War battle-grounds and encampments, a world-famous outdoor art museum, a crafts village.

the white man. Many Native Americans in the region wintered in sheltered inland valleys and summered on the shore to enjoy plentiful harvests of fish and shellfish and, perhaps, a dip in the cool, refreshing waters.

As you visit one of the Lenape winter homes on this walking tour in New York's Hudson Valley, it's difficult to imagine the pristine beauty enjoyed by the Native Americans before the arrival of civilization. But early accounts of western explorers suggest that the word "paradise" does not exaggerate. The words of Henry Hudson, on his first visit to this part of the New World, describe both the beauty and his intentions. These lands, he wrote, are "the finest for cultivation that I ever in my

▼

life set foot upon, and it also abounds in trees of every description. It's as pleasant a land as one can tread upon, very abundant in all kinds of timber suitable for ship-building and for making large casks. The people had copper tobacco pipes, from which I inferred that copper must exist there; and iron likewise, according to the testimony of the natives, who, however, do not understand preparing it for use."

You can no longer find many traces of the great Native American civilization. But this walk takes you where Native Americans lived for centuries and lets you appreciate the great diversity of nature so honored by the people who came before us. Somewhere on the north ridge of Schunemunk Mountain, where you will walk, was a Lenape village and fort that survived until well after the arrival of the white man—longer, in fact, than most Native American villages around New York. No traces of the village remain, but you can appreciate the unspoiled setting much as Native Americans did and walk on footpaths probably used for thousands of years before the arrival of the white man.

The Lenape were one of several Native American groups who lived in the New York region. Though the Lenape spoke a language related to those spoken by many other tribes, the northern Lenape who inhabited the area of Schunemunk Mountain probably could not have carried on a fluent conversation with Lenape in southern New Jersey. Perhaps the language discrepancy accounts for the various translations of Schunemunk Mountain, including "good fire place" and "place of excellent grapes."

Experts believe that the Lenape numbered in the tens of thousands when Henry Hudson came in 1609. By the Revolutionary War, the number of Native Americans dropped to the thousands, compared to 750,000 Europeans living in the New York area.

The Lenape usually lived during winter in small villages

▼

inland, in sheltered valleys in longhouses or in wigwams made of bark and grass. Some early accounts of settlers suggest that they built fortified positions on hilltops near their winter residences; there might have been such a structure on the northern ridge of Schunemunk Mountain where you will walk. In springtime, many would move to larger villages on the riverbanks and ocean shores, where they would fish, hunt, or plant squash, corn, and beans. In autumn, they prepared their harvests for winter storage and went back to their inland villages, storing food above them under the rooftops of their homes. The lives of the Lenape probably changed little for thousands of years.

The Lenape may have encountered some earlier explorers, but the one who brought the most change was Henry Hudson. Following his voyage in 1609, a growing number of settlers began to arrive in New Amsterdam and other Hudson Valley settlements. With them came diseases such as smallpox, measles, and syphilis, which decimated the Native Americans. Although the Dutch land-purchase policies were benign in comparison with those of the British, numerous clashes broke out between the newcomers and settlers, sometimes over issues as minor as the alleged theft of a peach by a Native American woman. Terrible atrocities were committed by both sides.

Killed by disease, pushed off their lands by first the Dutch and then the British, and made pawns of in the colonial wars, many Native Americans drifted west. Those who remained in the lower Hudson River valley by the time of the Revolution generally lived on the edge of white settlements. The village at Schunemunk Mountain was one of the last to be abandoned.

The people of this village figure in legends passed down by settlers and recounted in E. M. Ruttenber's *History of the Indian Tribes of Hudson's River,* published in 1875. In one story, a group of 17th-century traders landed at the mouth of a small creek (now known as Moodna Creek) that flows to the Hudson from the valley beneath Schunemunk Mountain. Enticed on shore by Native Americans, they were all killed, and the creek was dubbed Murderer's Creek. Later, a family by the name of Stacy settled nearby and became friendly with many of the Native Americans, including an elder known as Naoman. One day, the wife found Naoman moping about their home and finally got him to confess that the Native Americans planned to attack the white settlements that night. He warned the Stacy family to leave, making the woman swear that she would never reveal who had told her.

Other Lenape, suspicious that a traitor was in their midst, spotted the Stacy family as they began rowing across the river and took canoes out to catch them. After the family was forcibly brought back to shore, the Lenape demanded that the Stacys divulge their source. When the Stacys wouldn't speak, they threatened to kill the children. The Stacys remained silent, so the Lenape brought the children before the mother and raised a tomahawk above their heads. The children pleaded with her to save their lives. Just as the woman began to break down, Naoman spoke: "White woman, thou hast kept thy word with me to the last moment. I am the traitor." With that, he was struck down with a tomahawk. With him died the Stacy family as well, despite the heroism of Mrs. Stacy.

GETTING THERE
By car:

From the Tappan Zee Bridge, take the New York State Thrwy. north (I-87) and get off at exit 16 for Harriman, Rtes. 6 and 17 (signs also indicate Monticello and Liberty). After paying the toll, bear right following a sign for Harriman and Rte. 6 east, Rte. 17 south, and Rte. 32. At the light, make a right on Rte. 32 north toward Central Valley and Newburgh. In about 9 mi., you see a sign on your left for a Star Mountainville facility. Just a short distance north, make a left on Orange County Rte. 79. (It's opposite a right turn for Angora Rd.) Proceed for less than 1 mi., crossing a bridge over I-87, until you come to a large field and a trail entrance to Schunemunk Mountain (both

▼

on your left). Park along the road. Read the trail entrance sign carefully, because the trail crosses through private property on its way to the mountain.

Walk Directions

TIME: 2 to 3 hours
LEVEL: Moderate to difficult
DISTANCE: 4 to 6 miles
ACCESS: By car

Your hike up this mountain will be rewarded with stunning views to the west, north, and east, with particularly impressive views of the Shawangunk ridge and the Catskill Mountains. The trail uphill takes you along a rushing stream to a beautiful waterfall. You can shorten the walk by going to the first overlook just before Point 3 and retracing your steps, or by making a right at Point 3 and cutting over to Point 11. This shortened route provides you with much of the beauty without the physical exertion of the longer route, which leads up and down over the mountain's rocky ridge. Pick up picnic foods in Highland Falls on Rte. 32. The best picnic spots can be found at the numerous viewpoints on the top of the mountain.

TO BEGIN

Walk on the trail leading clearly across the field. It's the yellow-blazed Jessup Trail. The path skirts the forest on the right side of the field, offering a particularly pastoral scene in spring, summer, and fall. *Watch for a family of bluebirds that has returned to the area.*

The trail enters the woods and heads uphill, soon picking up the sound of rushing water from a stream on your right.

1. Follow the yellow-blazed trail as it turns right over railroad tracks **(beware of trains)** and into the forest to resume its course uphill. *Note the old stone walls marking old pasture land*

▼

now covered with forest. This trail may follow a path used by the Lenape to reach their village on the north end of the mountain. The trail passes by a small waterfall in a shaded spot offering a refreshing respite on a hot day.

2. At a junction with a red-blazed trail, go left uphill. In a short while, you get wonderful views of the Hudson River, the Catskills, the Shawangunk ridge to the north, and Black Rock Forest to the east. *Notice sprawling Stewart Airport to the north, one of the few airports with a small hill in the middle.*

3. Just a few minutes after the best views, the trail reaches a junction with a white-blazed trail, where you can go right if you want to shorten the walk. *You must watch for blazes carefully here, because many are painted on rocks or small stumps.* If you want to do the full walk, continue straight, following yellow and white blazes along the rocky ridge. *Watch your step and note the extraordinary conglomerate rock tinged with pink and embedded with quartz pebbles of all shapes. The rock was formed by the sediments of a shallow sound eventually uplifted to become highlands.*

4. You reach a junction of white and yellow trails, noted with a small sign that says "Sweet Clover Jct." Continue straight on the yellow-blazed trail, which continues along the ridge top. *If you want to shorten the trip, you can go left, descend until you cross the railroad tracks, and make a left on an unmarked trail that goes back to Point 1.*

5. In about 15 minutes, you reach another intersection, marked with a small sign that says "Dark Hollow Jct." Continue straight on the yellow-blazed trail that goes along the ridge.

6. In less than 10 minutes, you reach a rock slab where a pile of rocks and a hand-painted sign on the slab at your feet

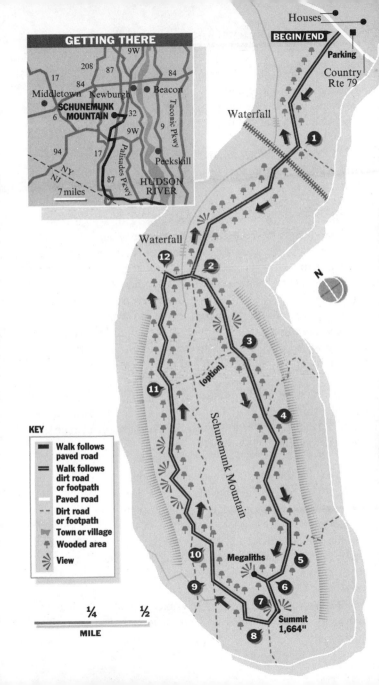

Houses

BEGIN/END

Parking

Country
Rte 79

Waterfall

GETTING THERE

9W

208 87

17 84 84

Middletown Newburgh ● Beacon

**SCHUNEMUNK
MOUNTAIN** ● 32

6

9W

9

94

17 Peekskill

NY

NJ

87

7 miles

**HUDSON
RIVER**

Palisades Pkwy

Taconic Pkwy

1

Waterfall

12 **2**

N

3

[option]

4

11

Schunemunk Mountain

KEY

▬▬ Walk follows
paved road

══ Walk follows
dirt road
or footpath

▭ Paved road

╌╌ Dirt road
or footpath

🛖 Town or village

🌲 Wooded area

🔆 View

10 Megaliths

9 **5**

6

7

8 Summit
1,664"

¼ ½

MILE

▼

point to the megaliths. Go right and descend a short distance to a collection of interesting rock formations offering wonderful views and a great place to picnic. Retrace your steps to the yellow-blazed trail and go right for a short distance.

7. You reach the summit of Schunemunk, marked on a rock with the elevation, 1,664 feet. *You get views in all directions but south.* Continue straight a short distance.

8. You arrive at a trail intersection with a sign reading "Western Ridge Jct." Go right on a blue-blazed trail, following the blazes carefully, because the trail weaves south and then north around a rock slab. Proceed carefully as it goes down a steep rock ridge into a shallow valley that is another of this mountain's unique features. *Native Americans undoubtedly found this a good place to hunt; the valley's steep walls would act as a natural pen, blocking an animal's escape route. Expect to find the conditions muddy on the valley floor, because a small stream floods in spring and creates a swamp that can last into summer.*

9. Just beyond the wettest spot on the valley floor, you reach a three-way intersection with the red-blazed Barton Swamp Trail. Go right, following the combination of blue and red blazes on the trail through the valley.

10. In a few minutes, your reach another three-way intersection. Go left on the blue-blazed trail that goes uphill onto the mountain's western ridge. Follow the trail carefully, which is marked with stone piles. At the top of the hill, go right on the turquoise-blazed Long Path. (*See* Experience 1, Piermont-on-Hudson.) Follow this trail north along the ridge and enjoy more splendid views to the west and the north.

11. You arrive at a three-way intersection marked "Sweet Clover Jct." Continue straight. *People who shortened the walk at*

▼

Point 3 will also pass through this intersection. Follow the turquoise trail carefully through this stretch because tiny footpaths head off in different directions to viewpoints looking east and west. The trail makes a sharp turn left and then right.

12. The turquoise-blazed Long Path arrives at a junction with a red-blazed trail. Go right following the red-blazed trail and descend carefully down the steep hill. You shortly arrive at the four-way intersection with the yellow-blazed Jessup Trail at Point 2. Make a left and proceed downhill back to your car.

OTHER PLACES NEARBY

If you're a Revolutionary War buff, you can visit many historic sites—too many for us to list individually. Contact Orange County Tourism (*see* Tourist Information) for details. Washington's Headquarters *(914-562-1195)*, which has a smashing river view, is in Newburgh; Knox's Headquarters *(914-561-5498)*, New Windsor Cantonment *(914-561-1765)*, and the Last Encampment of the Continental army *(914-561-5073)* are in New Windsor.

■ **Museum of the Hudson Highlands.** This regional natural history museum offers not only exhibits and nature trails but also a great variety of educational programs for children and adults on the ecology and natural history of the Hudson Highlands, cultural history (including Native American), and the arts. *Box 181, The Boulevard, Cornwall-on-Hudson, NY 12520; tel. 914-534-7781, 914-534-5506. Open Mon.-Thu. 2-5, Sat. 12-5, Sun. 1:30-5, Sep.-Jun.; Mon.-Thu. 11-5, Sat. 12-5, Sun. 1:30-5, Jul.-Aug. Look for blue-and-white museum signs on Rtes. 218, 9W, and 32. About 5 mi. northeast of Schunemunk Mtn.*

■ **Museum Village.** New York State's largest "living history" museum features costumed "villagers" and 40 buildings where you can see demonstrations and exhibits illustrating 19th-century life. Call for a schedule of special events, including re-enactments such as "Civil War Weekend." *Museum Village*

▼

Rd., Monroe, NY 10950; tel. 914-782-8247. Open Wed.-Fri. 10-2 (till 5 Jul.-Aug.), Sat.-Sun. 12-5, May-mid-Dec. Admission. At exit 129 on Rte. 17. About 9 mi. southwest of Schunemunk Mtn.

■ **Storm King Art Center.** The country's largest outdoor sculpture park features more than 120 contemporary sculptures, beautiful vistas, and a schedule of special events such as hikes and concerts in the park. *Old Pleasant Hill Rd., Mountainville, NY 10953; tel. 914-534-3190. Open daily 11-5:30 Apr. 1-Nov. 15 (open till 8 on Sat. Jun.-Aug.). Admission. Free 5-8 on Sat. Jun.-Aug. Off Rte. 32. About 5 mi. east of Schunemunk Mtn.*

■ **Village of Sugar Loaf.** For more than 250 years, artists and crafts makers have lived and worked in this crafts community. Visit studios, craft shops, and galleries, many in buildings one or two centuries old. *Chamber of Commerce, Box 125, Sugar Loaf, NY 10981; tel. 914-469-9181. Open Tue.-Sun. 11-5. From New York State Thrwy. (I-87), take Rte. 17 west to exit 126; follow signs to Sugar Loaf. About 15 mi. southwest of Schunemunk Mtn.*

■ **U.S. Military Academy at West Point.** Its site at one of the narrowest bends in the Hudson River gave West Point strategic importance during the American Revolution and continues to provide sweeping views of the river. Worth a visit both for its history and scenery, it offers tours, a museum, military band concerts, and other activities. Grounds include Fort Putnam, a Revolutionary War fort. *West Point, NY 10996; tel. 914-938-2638. Visitors center (Bldg. 2107) and grounds open daily 9-4:45; museum open daily 10:30-4:15. Off Rte. 9W, north of Highland Falls. About 10 mi. east of Schunemunk Mtn.*

DINING

■ **North Plank Tavern** (moderate). Winner of the Culinary Championships gold medal in 1994, chef Lucie Costa has gained attention from chefs nationwide for her "cuisine vigor," a gourmet cooking style using healthy foods while maintaining the classical French sense of taste and balance. For

▼

example, try the garlic soup or the seafood-stuffed Belgian endive. *18 N. Plank Rd., Newburgh, NY 12550; tel. 914-565-6885. Open for dinner Wed.-Sun. Aug.-Mar.; Thu.-Sun. Apr.-Jul. Closed mid-Jul. to mid-Aug. Off Rte. 9W, about 6 mi. north of Schunemunk Mtn.*

■ **Painter's Tavern** (moderate). The walls of this popular restaurant are jammed with a colorful display of art—all for sale. Located in a historic Tudor-style building, this tavern/inn offers an eclectic bistro menu of French, Japanese, and American *nouvelle* dishes. Specials range from grilled chile-lime chicken to pan-blackened swordfish. The two large rooms are often filled with a lively crowd and can be noisy. *266 Hudson St., Cornwall-on-Hudson, NY 12520; tel. 914-534-2109. Open daily for lunch and dinner, and Sun. brunch. Live jazz every other Thu. night. On Rte. 218 in Cornwall-on-Hudson (a different town than nearby Cornwall). About 5 mi. northeast of Schunemunk Mtn.*

■ **Sugar Loaf Inn** (moderate). The highly rated, creative New American cuisine is worth a drive to this small 1835 building in the quaint craft village of Sugar Loaf. At the time of our visit, a menu specialty was filet of salmon with a ginger and sesame-seed crust, served with a cilantro, white wine and butter sauce. The ambience is rustically romantic, with high ceilings revealing hand-hewn beams and an eclectic mix of chairs. *Kings Hwy., Sugar Loaf, NY 10981; tel. 914-469-2552. Open Tue.-Sat. for lunch and dinner; Sun. for brunch and dinner. On Rte. 13, about 15 mi. southwest of Schunemunk Mtn.*

LODGING

When planning your visit, try to avoid the week of West Point's graduation (usually early June), when the demand for lodging in the area outstrips the supply and can strain the temperaments of normally gracious innkeepers.

■ **Cromwell Manor Inn** (expensive). Elegance and tasteful restoration are the keynotes at this seven-acre estate that

▼

includes both a 1820s Greek Revival mansion with nine rooms and a 1764 house with four rooms. All rooms have recently renovated private baths and are furnished with period antiques; some have fireplaces. The estate includes gardens and meadows for your strolling pleasure, and it overlooks the 4,000-acre Black Rock Forest. Full breakfast included. Two large suites are very expensive. *Angola Rd., Cornwall, NY 12518; tel. 914-534-7136. Closed Dec. 23-28. Off Rte. 9W, west of Cornwall (a different town than nearby Cornwall-on-Hudson). About 6 mi. northeast of Schunemunk Mtn.*

■ **Sugar Loaf Village Bed & Breakfast** (expensive). You can enjoy antique atmosphere and your own Jacuzzi in this saltbox, whose original portion predates 1800 and features wide-board floors and exposed beams. Each of the two guest rooms has a private bath with single-person Jacuzzi and is decorated with Ralph Lauren fabrics. The downstairs room opens onto the deck and garden, while the upstairs room is cozily tucked under the eaves. Full breakfast on weekends, served in the breakfast room with its huge, old fireplace. *Box 23, Sugar Loaf, NY 10981; tel. 914-469-2717. Call for street address. About 15 mi. southwest of Schunemunk Mtn.*

■ **Painter's Tavern** (moderate). This newly opened inn, located in an old English Tudor-style building, has 10 rooms, all with private baths. At press time, the renovation (of 1960s-era rooms) was still a funky work in progress but promises to be creative; each room is painted and redecorated by a different artist. One, for example, has clouds painted on walls and ceiling. Breakfast not included, but Sunday brunch may be purchased in the inn's popular restaurant. *266 Hudson St., Cornwall-on-Hudson, NY 12520; tel. 914-534-2109. On Rte. 218 in Cornwall-on-Hudson (a different town than nearby Cornwall). About 5 mi. northeast of Schunemunk Mtn.*

■ **Wildflower** (moderate). This new colonial-style house, set on 2 1/2 acres of old farmland, has four guest rooms, two of which have private baths. All have queen-size beds, are deco-

▼

rated with country Victorian antiques, and share a common sitting room with a fireplace and a TV. The spacious Queen Anne's Room, which has a fireplace and a large bath with double sinks and a shower, is expensive. *399 Jackson Ave., New Windsor, NY 12553; tel. 914-496-0747. About 5 mi. north of Schunemunk Mtn.*

■ **Empty Nest** (inexpensive). Don't expect any antique ambience at this small, modestly furnished 1967 house, but be prepared to be coddled. This B&B has inspired raves for its outstanding service. The three small guest rooms share a bath and their own sitting room separate from the owners' quarters. Guests may also relax on the screened porch overlooking the meadows of the 165-acre family farm. Full country breakfast can be tailored to guests' dietary needs, including vegetarian. Moderately priced in fall. For an additional fee, owners will pick up and drop off at local train stations. *357 Lake Rd., New Windsor, NY 12553; tel. 914-496-9263. About 5 mi. north of Schunemunk Mtn.*

FOR MORE INFORMATION
Tourist Office:
■ **Orange County Department of Tourism.** Provides a comprehensive travel guide, information on B&Bs, and a calendar of events. *30 Matthews St., Ste. 111, Goshen, NY 10924; tel. 914-294-5151, 800-762-8687. Open Mon.-Fri. 9-5.*

For Serious Walkers:
Nearby Black Rock Forest's 4,000 acres of pristine woodland offer some of the best hiking in the region. For maps, consult the West Hudson Trails collection published by the New York-New Jersey Trail Conference.

Battle to Save the 'Gunks'

EXPERIENCE 7:
LAKE MINNEWASKA

L ooking to take a break from his farm work and head out on a traditional family outing, 19th-century Quaker farmer Alfred Smiley flipped a coin into the air—or so the story goes. Heads and the Poughkeepsie, New York-based family would travel to

The Highlights: Excellent Hudson River valley views, extraordinary rock formations, a serene mountain lake.

Other Places Nearby: The oldest street in America with its original houses, an arts and educational center, a canal museum.

West Point; tails and everyone was off to Paltz Point. The coin came up tails—a fortuitous toss that, unbeknownst to the Smileys, would lead to ownership of some of the nation's most spectacular mountain lands and a regional hotel and resort empire.

On this walking tour, you'll quickly understand why the Smileys decided to sell their farm once the family set eyes on the Shawangunk (pronounced *SHON-gum*) Mountains west of Paltz Point, near the present-day college town of New Paltz. The "Gunks," as they're affectionately known by rock climbers and other outdoor enthusiasts, tower more than 2,000 feet

▼

above the Hudson Valley and feature unique perpendicular rock formations composed of quartz pebbles and sand.

The 41-year-old Smiley convinced his twin brother Albert to join him in buying 300 acres of Gunks land, a tavern, and a lake for $28,000 in 1870. Though the twin brothers knew nothing about the lodging profession, they converted the tavern, situated atop Mohonk Mountain, into a hotel called the Mohonk Mountain House. The hotel, which is still in operation today, sat picturesquely next to small Mohonk Lake, and the setting attracted vacationers. The hotel's popularity rapidly grew, and the facility seemed to forever be expanding.

n 1876, Alfred and Albert took their families on a picnic to Peterskill Falls, located a few miles southwest of the Mountain House. Their horse-and-buggy driver mentioned that the mountain rising above the falls was home to beautiful Coxing Pond. The Smiley brothers let the driver take them there and were smitten by the sight. Surrounded by magnificent rock cliffs, Coxing Pond was bigger than Mohonk Lake, and its pristine, azure waters sparkled.

Alfred quickly found the property owner and negotiated a deal: 2,500 acres of land and the pond for about $3,000. Though Alfred liked the price, he didn't like the name of the pond and changed it to a Native American-sounding name, Minnewaska, the lake you circle in this walking tour. The name is fictitious and was not a part of any Native American tongue. After acquiring the land, Smiley arrived from Mohonk daily by carriage to oversee construction of a road to the lake and another resort, the Minnewaska Mountain House. The new resort opened in June 1879, and Smiley moved his residence there from Mohonk.

On horses and carriages guests shuttled back and forth between the Minnewaska Mountain House and the Mohonk Mountain House. Guests were allowed to eat their meals, which were included in the room rate, at either property. Liquor,

▼

dancing, and card-playing were forbidden, according to Quaker custom. Guests instead were encouraged to take nature walks, go boating and fishing, and enjoy the outdoors. A 10-minute prayer service was held daily after breakfast.

In 1887, Smiley opened another hotel, the Wildmere, on the shores of Lake Minnewaska and gave the Minnewaska Mountain House a new name, the Cliff House. The two hotels offered more than 350 rooms for vacationers and became known as the Minnewaska Mountain Houses.

A series of acquisitions increased Smiley's Minnewaska land holdings to 10,000 acres by the time of his death in 1903. Included in those 10,000 acres was Lake Awosting, the largest glacial lake in the Shawangunk Mountains.

Smiley's sons, and then a grandson, ran the popular Mountain Houses for the next 50 years. The health of the grandson, Alfred Fletcher Smiley, began to deteriorate, and business dropped off. Guests were staying fewer days, and the resort was saddled with increased costs.

Finally, in 1955, Smiley sold the resort to his right-hand man, Ken Phillips, and his wife, Lucille. In an attempt to generate more revenue in the mid-1960s, the Phillipses ended the long-standing liquor taboo, building a bar in the basement of the Cliff House. They also permitted, for the first time, motor boats on Lake Minnewaska and developed a golf course.

The Phillipses decided to turn the resort into a year-round destination, building ski slopes and a ski lodge. But the ad campaign to "Ski Minne" never paid off, and the Phillipses were $1.3 million in debt. The banks that had lent money to them scheduled an auction to sell off their property.

Just hours before the auction, the Phillipses agreed to sell Lake Awosting and about 7,000 acres to the Palisades Interstate Park Commission for $1.5 million. The bi-state (New York/New Jersey) agency had sought all the family's landholdings, but the couple insisted on keeping its two hotels, the ski lodge, and the land immediately surrounding Lake Minnewaska.

▼

The money received from the park commission wasn't enough to revitalize the two hotels, and the Phillips family couldn't get financing for their plan to turn the Minnewaska Mountain House into time-share condominiums. The parks commission bought another part of the land, and New York State obtained a conservation easement prohibiting major construction on 239 acres of land around Lake Minnewaska.

In 1978, after standing for 99 years, the Cliff House was destroyed in a fire of unknown origin. The house was uninsured, bringing no financial relief to the Phillipses.

Two years later the Marriott Corporation fell in love with the Minnewaska property. The giant hotel company acquired an option to purchase nearly 600 acres, including Lake Minnewaska and surrounding lands that were protected by the state easement. Marriott planned to construct a huge resort complex, including a 400-room hotel, 300 condominiums, a golf course, and an ice-skating rink.

The company's plans triggered one of the biggest wars between developers and environmentalists in the nation's history. Local residents formed an opposition group called Citizens to Save Minnewaska, and they were joined by other environmental groups. The coalition pointed out that Marriott's proposed golf course would violate the state's land easement, and they argued that there wasn't enough available water at Minnewaska for the planned hotel and condos. Despite the arguments, the park commission decided to amend the conservation easement, allowing Marriott to build its golf course, drill wells within the easement area, and increase the use of water from Lake Minnewaska.

The environmentalist refused to be defeated, soliciting donations and holding fund-raising rallies and benefit concerts. Musicians living near Minnewaska even produced a record album whose proceeds went to the anti-development cause.

Under the name Friends of the Shawangunks, Inc., the

environmentalists filed suit to stop the planned development. After a heated six-year battle, a federal appeals court ruled that the proposed golf course violated the terms of the easement. Marriott abandoned its development plans. In 1987, the state finally bought the rest of the land from the Phillips family.

Today, as you walk on the carriageways that were used to transport 19th-century vacationers to the resort hotels, you're the real winner in the long development battle. The land remains very much the way it was when the Smileys first bought it in the 19th century, and you're left in awe at the wonder of Lake Minnewaska and the surrounding Shawangunk Mountains.

GETTING THERE

By car:

From New York City, head north on I-87 (the NY State Thrwy.). Take the Thrwy. north to exit 18. Follow Rte. 299 west

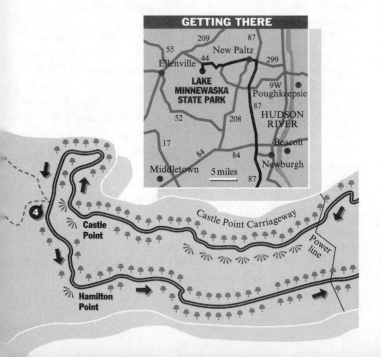

▼

to New Paltz. Go through the town and continue on Rte. 299 west until it ends. Turn right onto Rtes. 44/55 north. Turn left into Lake Minnewaska State Park. Proceed to the main parking area atop the hill, just north of Lake Minnewaska.

Walk Directions

TIME: 1 1/2 to 4 3/4 hours
LEVEL: Easy to difficult
DISTANCE: 3 to 9 miles
ACCESS: By car

Twelve-foot-wide carriageways that once were used to transport guests headed to and from the Minnewaska Mountain Houses make for easy walking, but the walk is rated difficult because of its length. You can shorten the walk substantially by following the directions in italics in Point 3. If you want to abbreviate the walk— but still see some of the spectacular viewpoints of the full walk—proceed for as long as you'd

KEY

▬	Walk follows paved road
═	Walk follows dirt road or footpath
	Paved road
- - -	Dirt road or footpath
	Town or village
🌲	Wooded area
🔆	View

¼   ½

MILE

like past Point 3 and then retrace your steps. There are picnic areas next to the lake at the beginning and the end of the walk; no picnics are permitted on the carriageways and trails. Buy provisions in New Paltz. The carriageways zigzag so frequently that the walking map below cannot show all the turns.

TO BEGIN

From the parking lot, face the picnic tables and follow a path to the right of the tables.

1. When the path ends at the rugged lake shore, turn right. After 20 yards, at the junction of two trails, bear left and take the lower of the two trails, following sign for Upper Awosting, Castle Point, Millbrook Mtn.

2. At the next junction by the shoreline, continue straight, following a sign for the red, yellow, and blue carriageways. At the next junction, bear left following a red-blazed trail. Follow the carriageway as it winds uphill. Ignore a road that intersects on your right. *In a minute, there will be a great view over the lake on your left.*

3. Just past the viewpoint, turn right onto Castle Point Carriageway and follow the blue blazes. Proceed uphill. *On your right is an incredible overlook that makes you feel like you're in the Rockies.* Continue straight. Ignore the yellow-blazed Hamilton Point Carriageway on your left. *If you want a very short walk, follow the yellow-blazed carriageway. You will pass Point 5 of this walk, where you continue straight. Follow the directions from Point 6 on.*

Otherwise, keep ascending on the blue-blazed carriageway and pass some great viewpoints on your left, including one that gives you a view in three directions. Follow the carriageway as it winds around a huge rock formation. **Beware of a steep cliff on your left.** Pass under a power line and notice the view on your left. Proceed past another great view atop a huge flat rock.

▼

Follow the carriageway path as it ascends above the rocky shelf. **Beware of crevices alongside the rock shelf.** *This is a great viewpoint and rest stop.*

Continue on the blue-blazed path. Finally, about two hours after you began the walk, you pass next to a huge boulder on your right and then reach Castle Point. *To the right ahead in the distance is Awosting Reservoir.* Proceed on the carriageway to the right, following blue and turquoise blazes. *Looking north you see great views of high mountains in the distance.* Descend downhill.

4. At a junction of trails (at this point you will have been walking for 2 1/2 hours since you left your car), turn left and follow the yellow-blazed Hamilton Point Carriageway. You are also following the turquoise blazes of the Long Path trail. In 5 to 10 minutes, you reach the rocky shelf of Hamilton Point. **Beware of the steep cliffs to your right.** Continue on. After about 3 1/2 hours since you began walking, you reach a roundabout aside a cliff. Follow either path. They merge after several yards.

5. After about four hours of walking, you reach a trail on your left (this is the carriageway for walkers who chose to abbreviate the walk in Point 3). Ignore it, as well as the sign pointing to Castle Point Trail. Continue straight.

6. In about two minutes, you reach a junction. Ignore the trail to the right toward Millbrook Mountain. Continue straight on the yellow-blazed carriageway.

7. At a trail junction, turn right and follow the red-blazed trail. You descend to the lake shore. Continue on the trail as it winds around the lake.

8. At the next junction, turn right following the red-blazed lower trail. *If you're looking for a picnic area, don't turn right and continue straight on the red-blazed upper trail.*

▼

9. At the next junction, turn right.

10. At a clearing next to a barn, turn left and follow the carriageway as it descends through the trees. Proceed under a wooden bridge spanning boulders.

11. At a road just before the park office, turn right. Continue down a dirt road, ignoring the red-blazed trail on your left.

12. At the next junction, turn left and proceed uphill, passing portable toilets on your right. Pass a ski rental shop that's on your left. Continue straight to the parking lot.

PLACES ALONG THE WALK

■ **Lake Minnewaska State Park Preserve.** You can swim at designated areas in Lake Minnewaska and Lake Awosting; at Minnewaska, scuba diving is also permitted. Besides hiking and walking, the park's carriageways are ideal for bicycling, horse-back riding, and cross-country skiing. Arrive early on summer weekends because parking is limited to 300 spaces. *Box 893, Rtes. 44/55, New Paltz, NY 12561; tel. 914-255-0752. Open daily. Summer hours: 9-9 mid-June–mid-Aug.; 9-8 mid-Aug.-Labor Day. Call for hours the rest of the year. Admission.*

OTHER PLACES NEARBY

■ **D&H Canal Museum.** A hands-on, pictorial museum portrays life on the Delaware & Hudson Canal during the 19th and 20th centuries. You can take a walking tour by five locks that have been designated a National Historic Landmark. *Box 23, Mohonk Rd., High Falls, NY 12440; tel. 914-687-9311. Museum open Thu.-Mon. 11-5 (Sun. 1-5) May 30-Labor Day and Sat.-Sun. May, Sep., and Oct. Admission. On Mohonk Rd., off Rte. 213. About 10 mi. northeast of Lake Minnewaska.*

▼

■ **Town of New Paltz.** Just north of this state college town's Main Street sits a fascinating historic district of stone houses built by Huguenots between 1692 and 1712. Called "the oldest street in America with its original houses," Huguenot Street includes such structures as the Jean Hasbrouck House, a fine example of Flemish stone architecture. *Stone houses open Wed.-Sun. 9:30-4, Wed. following Memorial Day weekend-Sep. 30. Call The Huguenot Historical Society (914-255-1660, 914-255-1889) for guided tours and off-season days and hours.*

■ **Unison Arts and Learning Center.** This arts center presents a wide variety of performances, programs, workshops, and exhibits. One recent night, Merry Prankster Wavy Gravy provided his psychedelic '60s comedy and insight. Another night, the Danny Kalb Trio played the blues. Request a complete schedule. *68 Mountain Rest Rd., New Paltz, NY 12561; tel. 914-255-1559. Events held year-round. Admission. On Rte. 6, north of Rte. 299. About 10 mi. northeast of Lake Minnewaska.*

■ **The Country Inn.** Owner Larry Erenberg operates one of the best beer bars in the world—in the middle of nowhere. On a wall scoreboard, Erenberg lists hundreds of top-quality beers, including many from esoteric micro-breweries, and they're all in stock. Erenberg has vast brewing knowledge, so make sure to follow his recommendations. Try the Rogue from Oregon or the Grant's Imperial Stout from Washington, D.C. *1380 Rte. 2, Krumville, NY 12461; tel. 914-657-8956. Open daily. Heading southwest from Stone Ridge on Rte. 209, turn right onto Rte. 2. About 20 mi. north of Lake Minnewaska.*

DINING

■ **Loup Garou** (moderate). Probably New Paltz's finest restaurant, this establishment specializes in French-Italian cuisine. Expect such dishes as shrimp Provençal, chicken piccata, and various pastas, including fettucine with shrimp and salmon and penne aglio olio (pasta with olive oil, roasted garlic, sun-

▼

dried tomatoes, and spinach). *46 Main St., New Paltz, NY 12561; tel. 914-255-2536. Open daily except Tue. for lunch and dinner, Sun. brunch. Live jazz Thu. On Rte. 299 in the heart of New Paltz. About 10 mi. east of Lake Minnewaska.*

■ **Clove Valley Trading Co., Ltd.** (moderate). This versatile restaurant, wine and beer bar, and gourmet food store appeals to many tastes. Breakfast is scrumptious, featuring such unique menu items as amaretto and almond pancakes. For lunch, about a dozen salads and gourmet sandwiches are offered. The soft track lighting puts you in the mood for such dinnertime appetizers as smoked trout or baked wedge of brie. Recommended entrees include green and white fettucini carbonara and scallops with basil, wine, and tangerine slices. *Rte. 213, High Falls, NY 12440; tel. 914-687-7911. Open daily for dinner and Tue.-Sun. for breakfast and lunch Memorial Day-Columbus Day. Open Wed.-Sun. for breakfast (beginning at 10:30 Wed.-Fri.; at 8, Sat.-Sun.), lunch, and dinner the rest of the year. About 10 mi. northeast of Lake Minnewaska.*

■ **Locust Tree Inn** (moderate). The food is decent, but you come to this 1759 inn next to a golf course for the ambience. Ask for a table in the old room downstairs. Notice the original stone floors, the carved moldings, and the fireplace. It's a good place for brunch with such menu items as French toast stuffed with cream cheese and a Western-omelet burrito. *215 Huguenot St., New Paltz, NY 12561; tel. 914-255-7888. Open Tue.-Fri. for lunch; Tue.-Sun. for dinner, and Sun. for brunch. Closed Feb. Off Rte. 299, about 10 mi. east of Lake Minnewaska.*

■ **Main Course** (moderate). In its deli/restaurant in a small shopping plaza, this caterer offers a wide variety of well-prepared and healthy foods. The eclectic dinner menu features contemporary American, Thai, Brazilian, and Mexican dishes. *232 Main St., New Paltz, NY 12561; tel. 914-255-2600. Open Tue.-Sun. for lunch and dinner, Sat. for breakfast, and Sun. for brunch. About 10 mi. east of Lake Minnewaska.*

■ **Main Street Bistro** (inexpensive). This almost-hippie,

almost-funky eatery serves good breakfasts, such as a pan-baked omelet on a bed of home fries or a spinach and tofu omelet. As reggae plays, you realize it delivers much more: the town's best beer list, an assortment of coffees, and lunch offerings like muffelettas and carcofi (supposedly a medieval recipe for deep-fried artichoke hearts with caper-lemon mayonnaise). *59 Main St., New Paltz, NY 12561; tel. 914-255-7766. Open daily for breakfast and lunch; Fri.-Sun. for dinner Apr.-Nov.*

LODGING

■ **Mohonk Mountain House** (very expensive). Though its heyday has long past, this legendary 275-room mountaintop resort remains a Shangri-La for walkers. The rooms are nothing to rave about and the old resort is somewhat tired, but—if you have the bucks—you are experiencing a National Historic Landmark whose surrounding lands can leave you breathless. Book a room with a fireplace, a private bath, and a view of magical Mohonk Lake. The 20 tower rooms are the most spacious and private; ask for one in the central building. *1000 Mountain Rest Rd., Lake Mohonk, New Paltz, NY 12561; tel. 914-255-1000, 800-772-6646. Off Rte. 299, on Mountain Rest Rd. About 10 mi. northeast of Lake Minnewaska.*

■ **The Inn at Stone Ridge** (expensive). Adjacent to a busy road, this 18th-century Dutch colonial mansion can still be a relaxing escape. The 9-guest-room mansion is on a 43-acre site and offers fine dining in its Milliways restaurant. The third-floor suite is the largest; Rooms 2, 4, and 5 are small but quiet. Only two rooms have private baths. Some inexpensive and moderately priced rooms are available. Stop at the antique pool table in the game room. *Box 76, Stone Ridge, NY 12484; tel. 914-687-0736. On Rte. 209, about 12 mi. northeast of Lake Minnewaska.*

■ **Audrey's Farmhouse** (moderate). This rustic B&B, a former general store, was built in 1740 and has great views of the "Gunks." You can feel its age as you enter the small, low-ceiling rooms, many without closets. The downstairs room is the most private, with its own bath and a mountain view. The owners' room, with a wood stove and a bath, can also be rented. Guests are welcome to bring dogs; the owner has two relatively mellow ones. *RD 1, Box 268A, 2188 Brunswick Rd., Wallkill, NY 12589; tel. 914-895-3440. On County Rd. 7, off Rtes. 44/55. About 8 mi. south of Lake Minnewaska.*

■ **Baker's B&B** (moderate). Built in 1780, this restored stone farmhouse on 16 acres has a good view of Mohonk Mountain and the rolling countryside. The third-floor attic room is the largest, with a private bath and a wood-burning stove. *24 Old Kings Hwy., Stone Ridge, NY 12484; tel. 914-687-9795. Off Rte. 209, 1 mi. south of intersection of Rtes. 209 and 213. About 12 mi. northeast of Lake Minnewaska.*

■ **Jingle Bell Farm** (moderate). The exterior appears ramshackle, but this small stone farmhouse with sheep out back and a quaint barn next door dates to 1776 and has plenty of Old World character inside. There's a charming breakfast room with a piano. The largest bedroom also features an old piano; it's located downstairs, but you must shower upstairs. The owner, who sang such commercial jingles as the famous line "Everything is better with Blue Bonnet on it," gave the B&B its name. *1 Forest Glen Rd., New Paltz, NY 12561; tel. 914-255-6588. Off Rte. 208, about 12 mi. southeast of Lake Minnewaska.*

FOR MORE INFORMATION

Tourist Offices:

■ **New Paltz Chamber of Commerce.** *257 1/2 Main St., New Paltz, NY 12561; tel. 914-255-0243. Open Mon.-Fri. 9-5.*

■ **Ulster County Public Information.** *244 Fair St., Kingston, NY 12401; tel. 914-331-9300, 800-DIAL-UCO. Open Mon.-Fri. 9-5.*

For Serious Walkers:

The Lake Minnewaska walk and other nearby trails can be found in the Shawangunk Trails four-map set published by the New York-New Jersey Trail Conference and the Mohonk Preserve.

The Times They Are A-Changin'

EXPERIENCE 8: WOODSTOCK

Woodstock's Overlook Mountain has attracted and inspired great artists for centuries. First, it mesmerized Thomas Cole and the Hudson River School of landscape painters. Then Ralph Whitehead set up the Byrdcliffe artists' colony at its base at the turn of this century. Finally, it

The Highlights: The Catskills' finest view, a town that symbolized a generation, excellent dining.

Other Places Nearby: Concert halls and art galleries, a unique bluestone sculpture, mountain lakes and a legendary resort site (*see* Experience 9).

turned on the creative juices of some of the most influential rock and roll talents—Bob Dylan, The Band, Van Morrison, Jimi Hendrix, and others—during the mid-1960s, a critical time in the birth of the Woodstock Generation.

When you reach the top of Overlook Mountain during this walking tour, you'll understand why the Impressionist Cole called it the finest view in the Catskill Mountains. Your mouth drops open in wonder at the magnificence of the rugged Catskills to the north, the awesome Shawangunk Mountains to the south, and the expansive Hudson River valley to the east. Cole, whose paintings made the Catskills famous, chose to

▼

come to Overlook on his last visit to the region in October 1847, a few months before his death.

Overlook's beauty was equally enticing to businessmen. Looking to imitate the success of nearby resorts, including the popular Catskill Mountain House, they built Overlook Mountain House near Overlook's summit in 1871. The new resort, whose ruins you will visit on this walking tour, boasted that it stood at the highest elevation of any New York state mountain house. It featured a mansard roof, gas lighting, telegraph service, and a waiter for each dining table. The rich and famous brushed shoulders with other guests, including a large contingent who believed the high mountain air could cure all that ailed them, and there was constant activity everywhere. At times, it resembled a freak show with trained-bear shows, high-jumping acts, one-man bands, and other performers trying to make a quick buck off hotel guests.

Business, however, did not always meet expectations, and management tried to hype the hotel, announcing that popular President Ulysses S. Grant would soon visit. When Grant finally arrived a few years later, the public had soured on his Administration, and his Overlook Mountain stay was a disaster. The President got drunk on the boat up the Hudson River and then kept drinking on the long stagecoach ride to the top of Overlook. He immediately had to be put to bed at the Mountain House, and the American temperance movement branded the resort an evil, booze-guzzling joint.

The resort lasted another 50 years or so before burning down in 1924, long after its heyday. It was being rebuilt when the stock market crashed in 1929, and the project was forever canceled.

Though the painters, entrepreneurs, and even President Grant left their marks, rock and roll will always be foremost in Woodstock and Overlook Mountain history because of a rain-drenched 1969 music festival that wasn't held anywhere near

▼

the town. Promoters of the festival, dubbed the Woodstock Music and Arts Fair, had originally wanted to stage the event in Woodstock and eyed land in the Hudson Valley east of Overlook. But town officials nixed the idea, saying that an adequate site wasn't available and that the road system couldn't handle a crush of rock fans.

Though the festival was eventually held far south in tiny Bethel, the continued use of the name Woodstock made sense. The cry of the nation's youth for peace, love, and liberation from the older generation meshed nicely with the beliefs of the Byrdcliffe arts and crafts colony at the base of Overlook Mountain—peace, an appreciation for music, and a resistance to conformity. For decades, musicians like Leadbelly, Pete Seeger, and Peter, Paul, and Mary, had visited Byrdcliffe and shared their muse despite being branded left-wingers or even communists by the conservative power structure in the federal government.

Yet no one would have thought of staging a Woodstock festival near Overlook Mountain if not for the impact of Dylan. The skinny, young folk-star-turned-rocker moved to Byrdcliffe a few years before the festival to escape the New York City limelight and wrote many of his best songs under the shadow of the mountain. Dylan energized Woodstock, attracting other major rock stars to the area and unintentionally creating a worldwide myth about the town being some kind of mecca for the younger generation.

Dylan holed up in a big, pink barn-like house in West Saugerties beneath the eastern slope of Overlook Mountain and cut some incredible sessions with The Hawks, a Woodstock-based group that for years had been Dylan's back-up band and would later blossom into The Band, one of the top groups in rock history. Each afternoon at 1, Dylan would meet The Hawks in the basement of the West Saugerties home they were renting; locals dubbed the home with the great Overlook Mountain view "Big Pink," and Dylan painted it on the cover of The Band's acclaimed first album, appropri-

▼

ately titled *Music from Big Pink* and featuring Dylan-penned songs from the sessions.

The Big Pink sessions of May through October 1967 also produced what later would be known as *The Basement Tapes*, regarded by some critics as the zenith of Dylan's prolific 35- year-plus recording career. Such Dylan classics as "I Shall Be Released," "Tears of Rage," "The Mighty Quinn (Quinn the Eskimo)," and a remarkable 150 or so other songs came out of the sessions. The songs largely shunned rock and were an amalgamation of folk, country, blues, and, at times, comedy. Dylan successfully improvised some on the spot while others took shape after he handed typewritten lyrics to the Hawks. The typewritten lyrics represented a departure from Dylan's usual songwriting technique of writing the music before the words.

The Basement Tapes were recorded on a low-fi, two-track reel-to-reel tape recorder, and Dylan apparently had no desire to release them to the public. For eight years the tapes remained unreleased, though their existence was known to rock fans and repeatedly talked about in the music industry. In summer 1969, a bootleg album, *The Great White Wonder*, snuck out, containing numerous songs from the tapes and giving birth to a bootleg record industry.

Dylan's Woodstock stay was also a conscious attempt to walk away from the caviar, money, marketing, and rock-star trappings and pressures. Radio stations throughout the world were continually playing his hit "Like A Rolling Stone," and the young generation was embracing his double-album rock masterpiece *Blonde on Blonde*. Dylan wanted none of the hoopla, looking only for introspection and seclusion next to Overlook Mountain. Still recovering from a 1966 motorcycle accident on Woodstock's Striebel Road, he watched his wife Sara give birth in 1967 to their first child, Jesse, and later a daughter, Anna.

After a post-*Blonde on Blonde* songwriting dry spell, the

▼

Big Pink sessions had sparked a creative rejuvenation. One month after the sessions, Dylan took off for Nashville with numerous Woodstock-penned songs in hand and, within six hours, had finished recording his monumental release *John Wesley Harding*. The lightning-quick album once more shocked music fans, who were still reeling from Dylan's conversion from folk artist to rock star, because it contained little rock and roll. The album had a folk underpinning with country and rock touches. But critics raved about the album's depth and insight, and applauded such notable songs as "All Along The Watchtower," "I'll Be Your Baby Tonight," and "I Pity the Poor Immigrant."

The hippies and flower children began flocking to Woodstock, and the curiosity-seekers showed up too frequently on the private road where Dylan lived with his family and other Byrdcliffe artists. Dylan moved his family out of the shadow of Overlook Mountain, south to Ohayo Mountain, which enjoyed a good view of Overlook. The curiosity-seekers kept coming, and Dylan was mortified by the prospect of hundreds of thousands headed for a music festival within an hour's drive of his home. He fled Woodstock two days before the festival and, unlike fellow superstars The Band, Jimi Hendrix, Janis Joplin, the Grateful Dead, The Who, Creedence Clearwater Revival, and Crosby, Stills, Nash, and Young, never set foot on the stage of the landmark festival. He'd been dubbed the poet of the Woodstock Generation— the musician whose lyrics stimulated the brain as well as the feet—but he was forced to run from his adoring fans.

Though Dylan's music had undoubtedly been influenced by Woodstock's lower-Catskill-Mountain setting, it was Van Morrison, another Ohayo Mountain resident, who released the quintessential Woodstock album, *Tupelo Honey*. Following on the heels of two other hit albums with songs written by Morrison in Woodstock—*Moondance* and *His Band and The Street Choir*—*Tupelo Honey* flashed beautiful, romantic images of Woodstock life. In "Old Old Woodstock," Morrison sang:

▼

"Goin' down to old, old Woodstock/Feel the cool night breeze/Goin' down to old, old Woodstock/Way behind the shady trees/Here I come a-slidin'/Way on over the ridge/See the water flowin'/Way beneath the bridge/And my woman's waiting/By the kitchen door/I'm driving along/In my old beat-up car/Going down to old, old Woodstock/Feel the cool night breeze/Goin' down to old, old Woodstock/Give my child a squeeze."

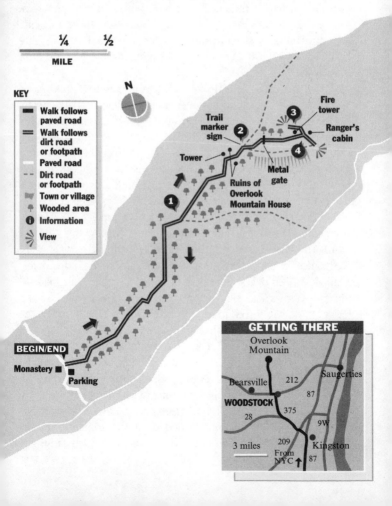

▼

In August 1994, Dylan returned to perform in the area where he gave his first child a squeeze. Possibly tying up some loose ends—his nonappearance at the original Woodstock Festival—he performed in nearby Saugerties at Woodstock '94, a three-day 25th anniversary concert. In typical Dylan fashion, he didn't say a word to the audience but gave a stirring performance on a giant stage just east of Overlook Mountain, singing 12 songs, including "All Along the Watchtower" and "I Shall Be Released," two songs he had written about 30 years before, in the shadow of the mountain.

GETTING THERE
By car:

From New York City, take the New York State Thrwy. (I-87) to exit 19 (Kingston). Follow Rte. 28 west toward Pine Hill. Turn right onto Rte. 375, following a sign for Woodstock. Turn left onto Rte. 212 and proceed into Woodstock. At the intersection just before the village green, turn right onto County Rd. 33, which is also Meads Mountain Rd. When you reach Lower Byrdcliffe Rd., continue straight on Meads Mountain Rd. Cross Glasco Tpke. and go 1 1/10 mi on the winding mountain road. Turn right into the Overlook Mountain parking area, located across the street from a Tibetan Buddhist monastery.

Walk Directions

TIME: 2 1/4 hours
LEVEL: Difficult
DISTANCE: 4 1/2 miles
ACCESS: By car

Unlike nearly all the loop walks in this book, you must retrace your steps to your car on this walk. The walk is on a firm, wide path with no difficult footing, but it is rated difficult because you ascend all the way to the mountaintop. Picnic on the rocky shelf overlooking the Hudson Valley. Provisions can be picked up at the inexpensive restau-

▼

rants in this chapter or at food markets along Rte. 212.

TO BEGIN

From the parking lot across the street from the monastery, walk several steps to an Overlook Mountain trail sign. Follow a wide dirt path and proceed uphill. The trail becomes steep and tiring for about 30 minutes. You come to a flat rock on your left that's ideal for resting. Walk about 10 more minutes uphill.

1. When you reach a trail intersection (a telephone pole with a red-blazed marker is on your right, though leaves may hide it from view), ignore the trail going off to the right and continue on the wide path uphill. Continue uphill for about 20 minutes. *On your right are the ghostly ruins of the 19th-century Overlook Mountain House. Inside the ruins of the main house on your right are photographs and descriptions of the resort in its heyday.* **Be very careful, because parts of the foundation are crumbling. Beware of dangerous drop-offs in the former resort's main lobby area; a fall off the deteriorating stairway or the wall-less perimeter could be fatal. Don't visit the ruins in the dark.** Proceed several yards beyond the ruins toward a trail sign on your left.

2. Ignore a blue-blazed trail going off to the left and continue on the wide dirt path uphill to the right. Pass by a metal gate with a stop sign and continue uphill. In several minutes you pass a huge rock formation on your left.

Pass a ranger's cabin that's on your right and continue on the dirt path as it winds to the flat rocks atop Overlook Mountain. Proceed to the right of a fire tower. When you reach the farthest leg of the tower, take about four steps.

3. Bear right to a rock shelf overlooking the Catskill Mountains. In the distance is Echo Lake, with towering Plattekill Mountain behind it. Retrace your steps to the ranger's cabin.

▼

4. Take one or two steps beyond the cabin's front porch and turn left onto a narrow dirt path leading through the woods. In a minute or two, you emerge from the woods into a clearing next to a cliff. **Beware of a dangerous drop-off along the ledge.** *Beneath you is a spectacular view of the Hudson River valley. Ahead to the right is the Ashokan Reservoir. Straight ahead and to the left is the Hudson River.*

Turn around and retrace your steps to the ranger station. *If you are a careful walker, you may opt instead for a **very dangerous** but astonishingly scenic walk alongside the cliff. **Don't try it at nighttime.** To walk along the cliff, turn right as you face the Hudson River and follow a very narrow path through short bushes. **Walk slowly because the ledge has eroded and its edge is next to your footsteps.** Follow the path for several minutes until it meets the wide path you took to ascend Overlook Mountain. Retrace your steps down to your car.*

If you elected to take the safer route, turn left at the ranger's cabin. Retrace your steps back to your car.

OTHER PLACES NEARBY

■ **Town of Woodstock.** Woodstock's always alive with art galleries, live music, good food, and interesting book stores and shops. The real fun is watching the characters lingering on the village green and the straight-out-of-Sputnik garb of so many who pass by. You'll now find hippies standing next to yuppies, too many weekend tourists, and mostly a whole lot of artsy, educated, and friendly people in a very scenic town.

■ **Maverick Concerts.** One of the nation's oldest chamber concert series, a new musical program is presented each summer and held in rustic Maverick Concert Hall. The series was founded in 1916 by Hervey White, who left the Byrdcliffe artists colony to form his own arts group. *Box 102, Maverick Rd., Woodstock, NY 12498; tel. 914-679-8217. Concert series: last week of Jun.-first week of Sep. Admission. Off Rte. 375.*

■ **Opus 40.** Harvey Fite took 37 years to create this "envi-

▼

ronmental" sculpture rising out of an abandoned bluestone quarry. Using Overlook Mountain as its backdrop, the sculpture consists of hundreds of thousands of tons of finely fitted bluestone, including a nine-ton monolith at its center. It's strange, it's different, and you can walk on it. *7480 Fite Rd., Saugerties, NY 12477; tel. 914-246-3400. Open Fri. and Sun. (and often on Sat.) 12-5 Memorial Day weekend-Oct. Admission. Off the Glasco Tpke., between Woodstock and Saugerties.*

■ **The Woodstock Guild.** This nonprofit arts group presents music, theater, visual arts exhibitions, and crafts demonstrations in the Kleinert James Arts Center and the Byrdcliffe Theater, located on the site of the original art colony founded by Ralph Whitehead. *34 Tinker St., Woodstock, NY 12498; tel. 914-679-2079. Guild office open Mon.-Fri. 9-5. Kleinert and James galleries open Thu.-Mon. 11-4.*

DINING

■ **Blue Mountain Bistro** (moderate). The decor is nothing to rave about, but you'll find exciting Mediterranean dishes such as bisteeya, a North African chicken pot pie with almonds, cinnamon, and saffron in a phyllo dough. Other specialties include seven-hour lamb (yes, cooked for seven hours) and salmon in parchment. Ask for a streamside outdoor table. *Box 22, 110 Mill Hill Rd., Woodstock, NY 12498; tel. 914-679-8519. Open daily for lunch and dinner Memorial Day-Labor Day. Open Tue.-Sun. for lunch and dinner the day after Labor Day-the day before Memorial Day. At the Woodstock Golf Club, at the intersection of Rtes. 212 and 375.*

■ **Café Tamayo** (moderate). In a 19th-century brick building in the heart of town, this eatery's ambience and food are delightful. It's fascinating to look up at the painted tin ceiling and watch the original fans whirling about, powered by a belt-and-pulley system. Stop at the mahogany bar before delving into the new American menu. Look for appetizers like shrimp dumplings and such entrées as confit of duck with red-onion

▼

marmalade. *89 Partition St., Saugerties, NY 12477; tel. 914-246-9371. Open Wed.-Sun. for dinner and Sun. for brunch. On Rte. 9W, 12 mi. east of Woodstock.*

■ **The Bear Cafe** (moderate). This modern cafe next to a stream manages to provide a warm, rustic feel and serves the best food in the immediate Woodstock area. Chef Eric Mann can send your taste buds into orbit with such entrees as crispy, fried soft-shell crabs with red lentils, green curry sauce, and minted yogurt, or New Zealand rack of lamb with pignoli nut crust and roasted garlic-mint-rosemary sauce. Don't miss the key-lime torte. *Box 366, Rte. 212, Bearsville, NY 12409; tel. 914-679-5555. Open Mon., Wed.-Sun. for dinner. 2 mi. west of Woodstock.*

■ **Gypsy Wolf Cantina** (moderate). This wood-paneled roadhouse serving tasty Mexican food has a serious wolf fixation. A life size wolf prowls above the front entrance and wolf masks hang everywhere. Blend that with a Christmas-lights, stained-glass psychedelic-Southwestern decor and it all becomes crazy but a lot of fun. The cooked-in-their-shells shrimp fajitas and the black bean soup are excellent. Look for specials like grilled Mako shark tacos. *261 Tinker St., Woodstock, NY 12498. Open daily for lunch and dinner. On Rte. 212 west of Woodstock, between Woodstock and Bearsville.*

■ **The New World Home Cooking Co.** (moderate). The eclectic menu features such risky combinations as Brie and pineapple quesadilla and mussels in chili paste. You can choose from various cuisines: If you want a Caribbean dish, try the jerk chicken; if you'd rather be in New Orleans, go with the Cajun shrimp. Many entrees are spicy, so you'll appreciate the excellent beer and wine list. Three small dining rooms display local artwork. *424 Zena Rd., Woodstock, NY 12498; tel. 914-679-2600. Open Mon.-Fri. for lunch and dinner; Sat.-Sun. for dinner. At Zena and Sawkill Rds., southeast of the town center.*

■ **Bread Alone** (inexpensive). This hip bakery woos customers with fabulous breads and other baked goods. The chocolate croissants and the scones are recommended. If you

▼

want a sit-down meal, eggs and home fries or a breakfast burrito should suffice. Salads and sandwiches are served for lunch and dinner. Sit back and listen to a hot Talking Heads song, and grab a copy of the *Woodstock Times* to find out what's happening in town. *22 Mill Hill Rd., Woodstock, NY 12498; tel. 914-679-2108. Open daily for breakfast, lunch, and early dinner (closes at 7 p.m. Sun.-Thu., 8 p.m. Fri.-Sat.). On Rte. 212.*

■ **Rashers** (inexpensive). Don't let the one-step-up-from-a-deli decor fool you: Some of Woodstock's best food is served here—at fabulous prices. From the strawberry lemonade to the linguine with baby scallops and cream in a goat-cheese sauce, everything is made with a sharp eye for detail and harmony of flavors. If you arrive between meals, don't despair: The items in the deli case—things like penne with wild mushrooms, spinach, and pistachio—are knockouts. At breakfast, try the brie omelette. *13 Tinker St., Woodstock, NY 12498; tel. 914-679-5449. Open Mon.-Thu. for breakfast and lunch until 5; open Fri.-Sun. for breakfast, lunch, and dinner until 9. On Rte. 212.*

LODGING

Many lodgings require a two-night stay on weekends but will relax the rule if you call late in the week and rooms are available. You can camp on Overlook Mountain, though there are no designated sites or facilities (call the Department of Environmental Conservation at 914-255-5453 for information). Camping is also permitted at nearby Kenneth Wilson State Park (914-679-7020, 914-255-5453) in Mount Tremper.

■ **Onteora, The Mountain House** (expensive). It's no exaggeration to say that this former summer home of mayonnaise mogul Richard Hellman has one of the most beautiful locations of any B&B in the world. The Catskill Mountain views in three different directions are spellbinding. The modern Adirondack-style lodge features a 20-by-40-foot living room with a cathedral ceiling and a huge stone fireplace. Four guest bedrooms have mountain views, but only the loft bedroom has

▼

a private bath. Don't miss the basement billiard room. *Box 356, Piney Point Rd., Boiceville, NY 12412; tel. 914-657-6233. Turn off Rte. 45 onto Cold Brook Rd., cross the town line into Olive, and proceed 1/2 mi. About 10 mi. west of Woodstock.*

■ **Ivy Farm Inn** (moderate). This country B&B with three guest rooms is a perfect place to relax. It has an inviting wrap-around porch with comfortable sitting chairs, a heated pool, and a well-maintained yard with a hammock. Each room contains antique furnishings, a private bath, and air-conditioning. Ask for the room with the skylight and queen-size bed. A full breakfast—sometimes featuring banana pancakes and lemon muffins—is served. *Box 51, 4262 Rte. 212, Lake Hill, NY 12448; tel. 914-679-9045. A few mi. west of Woodstock.*

■ **Mt. Tremper Inn** (moderate). This 12-guest-room 1850 Victorian mansion has a wraparound porch and an elegant country sitting room with a pump organ. Ask for the Wittenberg Room, a spacious suite with an antique couch and private bath. Many inexpensive rooms without private baths are also available. A full gourmet breakfast is served (on a veranda in the summer). *Box 51, Rte. 212 and Wittenberg Rd., Mt. Tremper, NY 12457; tel. 914-688-5329. Closed Mon.-Thu. Nov.-Apr. About 12 mi. west of Woodstock.*

■ **North Light Studio** (moderate). This simple, high-ceilinged art studio built by local painter Fletcher Martin makes for a cozy cottage and puts you into the artsy, yet tie-dyed, Woodstock mood. Conveniently located near the Overlook Mountain walk, the studio has a queen-size bed and a private entrance. There's a heated pool on the front deck with a view of Ohayo Mountain. Bring your own breakfast to prepare in the studio's kitchenette (unless you don't mind a day-old muffin stashed in your refrigerator by the proprietor). *224 Meads Mountain Rd., Woodstock, NY 12498; tel. 914-679-7839. From Woodstock village green, turn north onto Rock City Rd., which becomes Meads Mountain Rd.*

■ **Parnassus Square** (moderate). Like North Light Studio,

▼

this is another unconventional Woodstock lodging. A former crib for storing corn has been turned into a relatively spacious, rustic cottage with wood-paneled floors and ceiling fan. There's a double bed downstairs and another in an upstairs loft. A full breakfast is provided, but you'll have to prepare it yourself. There's no backyard to stretch out in; stop in at the friendly owners' art galley next door. *Box 241, Woodstock, NY 12498; tel. 914-679-5078. From the Woodstock village green, turn north onto Rock City Rd. and drive to Lower Byrdcliffe Rd. Turn left and make an immediate right into the parking area.*

FOR MORE INFORMATION
Tourist Offices:
■ **New York State Dept. of Environmental Conservation.** Contact this office for information about Overlook Mountain or the surrounding Catskills area. Written directions for various trails are available. *Region 3, 21 S. Putt Corners Rd., New Paltz, NY 12561-1696; tel. 914-256-3000.*

■ **Woodstock Chamber of Commerce.** *Box 36, Woodstock, NY 12498; tel. 914-679-6234. Information booth, just off the village green on Rock City Rd., open Thu.-Mon. 12-6 May 1-end of Dec.*

For Serious Walkers:
There are enough trails in the Catskill Preserve—including those in Experience 9, North/South Lakes—for a lifetime of walking. For information about the preserve, contact the Department of Environmental Conservation (*see* Tourist Offices).

■ **New York-New Jersey Trail Conference.** The trails to Overlook Mountain and other areas of the Catskills can be found in the hiking group's Catskill Trails five-map set.

The Catskill Mountain House

EXPERIENCE 9: NORTH/SOUTH LAKES

Most Americans regard 1963 as a tragic year because of the Kennedy assassination, but even historians forget that earlier that same year another part of the collective psyche was lost forever. At 6 a.m. on January 25, New York state officials put a torch to the remains of the legendary Catskill Mountain House, the resort that was the first of many deluxe hotels designed to lure urban Americans to get close to nature by vacationing in the countryside and the mountains.

> **The Highlights:**
> Unforgettable Hudson River valley views, the site of the historic Catskill Mountain House, two mountain lakes with sandy beaches and picnic areas.
>
> **Other Places Nearby:** A wondrous waterfall, a chairlift ride to the sky, the town of Woodstock (*see* Experience 8).

As the nation's first mountain resort, the Catskill Mountain House became the center of 19th-century vacation life and opened the door for the many hotels and resorts that transformed the Catskills into the country's most celebrated vacation destination of its time. Its location, which you'll visit on this walking tour, was the key to its success—a rocky shelf called

▼

the Pine Orchard above North and South lakes, looking out at a spectacular view of the Hudson River valley. The sight lines inspired great authors and artists for two centuries.

James Fenimore Cooper, one of the nation's leading 19th-century authors, gave it the highest praise, saying the Catskill Mountain House along with Niagara Falls and New York's Lake George were the most important sights in the eastern United States.

But it was painter Thomas Cole who let all America get a glimpse of this fascinating region. His landscape paintings romanticized and celebrated the Catskills wilderness, and they sold like wildfire to the American public.

n 1833, he stood on North Mountain and painted the inspiring Pine Orchard scenery in a work entitled *The Catskill Mountains*. The painting omitted the Mountain House and focused on the majesty of the landscape. Ten years later he returned to the same spot on North Mountain and painted *Catskill Mountain House*, one of his most romantic works.

Cole convinced other landscape painters to visit the Mountain House and settle in the area. The group of painters became known as the Hudson River School, a derisive label attached by a New York Tribune critic but a label that, to many others, signified America's first school of pure landscape painters. Before the Hudson River School, American painters had concentrated on portrait and historical paintings, with landscape a lesser concern.

The region around the Mountain House was also a favorite of many great Romantic writers, including Washington Irving and William Cullen Bryant. Cole introduced Bryant to the Catskills, and he, too, was stunned by its beauty, writing about the area's "sublime mountain tops, broad forests, and rushing waterfalls." The two went on all-day hikes and mountain climbs together and gave names—some of which still stand—to some of the geography they explored. Their camaraderie became symbolic of the unity of different art forms in the American Romantic movement.

▼

It wasn't only nature, though, that attracted people to the Catskill Mountain House. After taking a long boat ride and then riding four hours through the wilderness in a rickety stagecoach—including many precarious cliffside hairpin turns—guests marveled at the resort's elegance and extravagance. And they loved brushing shoulders with the artists and such celebrity guests as presidents Ulysses S. Grant and Chester A. Arthur, Civil War hero General William Tecumseh Sherman, and the Prince of Wales (who became King Edward VII).

But the late 19th and the 20th centuries were not kind to the Catskill Mountain House. The painters of the Hudson River School started heading west to the Rockies on the newly built transcontinental railroad, and many Americans came to the realization that the mountains out West were more spectacular and offered more adventure. The advent of the automobile and the airplane gave people more freedom to travel wherever they wanted and to travel greater distances. All the big Catskills hotels ran into financial trouble. The Mountain House was hard hit by the 1929 stock market crash and limped through the next decade in need of proper renovation. During World War II, vacations were not on many Americans' minds, and, in 1943, the Mountain House closed its doors forever.

After you leave the famed hotel's site on this walking tour, you'll head to the shore of South Lake, a body of water that, along with adjacent North Lake, mesmerized Cole. When the landscape painter first laid eyes on North and South lakes, he was inspired to write the following:

"Shut in by stupendous mountains which rest on crags which tower more than a thousand feet above the water, whose rugged brows and shadowy peaks are clotted by dark and tangled wood, they have an august aspect of deep seclusion, of utter and unbroken solitude, that when standing on their brink a lonely traveler, I was overwhelmed with an emotion of the sublime, such as I have rarely felt. It was not that the jagged precipices were lofty, that the encircling woods were of the

▼

deepest shade, or that the waters were profoundly deep; but that over all rocks, wood, and water brooded the spirit of repose, and the silent energy of nature stirred the soul to its utmost depths."

GETTING THERE

By car:

From New York City, take the New York State Thrwy. (I-87) to Exit 20 (Saugerties). Make the first left turn onto Rte. 32 north. Follow 32 north to Rte. 23A. Take Rte. 23A west towards Tannersville. Go through Palenville. Enter the Catskill Preserve and go 4 6/10 mi. In Haines Falls, turn right onto Rte. 18 following a sign for North/South Lake campground. Go 2 2/10 mi. to Scutt Rd., the street just before the entrance to North/South Lake State Park. Turn right onto Scutt Rd; turn right into a parking lot.

Walk Directions

TIME: 3 hours
LEVEL: Difficult
DISTANCE: 4 1/2 miles
ACCESS: By car

This walk requires no hiking skills but is rated difficult because of a few steep stretches. At one point, you have the option of boosting yourself up to step up on the trail or retracing your steps a short ways to avoid the small climb.

Tannersville, located 4 mi. west of North/South Lake park, is the best place for picnic provisions. Try the Last Chance Cheese and Antiques Cafe on Tannersville's Main St. There's also a general store on Rte. 18—about 2 1/2 mi. before the Scutt Rd. parking area—that has picnic and camping provisions.

TO BEGIN

Walk out of the parking lot and cross Scutt Rd. Proceed into the woods at a trail sign. Follow a well-worn blue-blazed trail as it winds through the forest. After about 20 minutes you

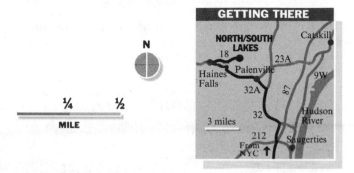

NORTH/SOUTH LAKES

Catskill

18

23A

Haines Falls

Palenville

9W

32A

87

Hudson River

3 miles

32

Saugerties

212

From NYC

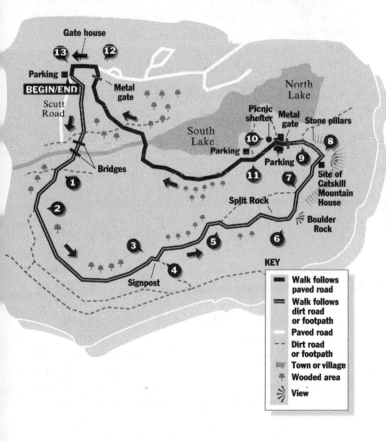

N

¼   ½

MILE

Gate house

13   12

Parking

BEGIN/END

Scutt Road

Metal gate

North Lake

South Lake

Picnic shelter   Metal gate   Stone pillars

10   8

Parking   9

11   7   Site of Catskill Mountain House

Bridges

1   Parking

2

Boulder Rock

Split Rock

3   5   6

4   **KEY**

Signpost

▬	Walk follows paved road
═	Walk follows dirt road or footpath
	Paved road
- - -	Dirt road or footpath
♣	Town or village
♠	Wooded area
≋	View

▼

reach a trail intersection. Continue straight following the blue blazes. Cross a wooden bridge. *Notice the brilliant moss-covered rocks in the stream.* Cross a second wooden bridge.

1. At a trail intersection, turn left and then make an immediate right turn onto an uphill red-blazed trail, following a sign to Sunset Rock, Inspiration Point, and Boulder Rock. Walk on this trail for 15 to 20 minutes.

2. At a trail intersection, ignore a yellow-blazed trail going off to the right and continue straight uphill on the red-blazed trail. Proceed on the trail as it levels off and then heads uphill.
About an hour after leaving the parking lot, you reach a trail on the right.

3. Turn right onto the trail and proceed about 15 yards to a trail marker signpost.

4. Bear left, ignoring the trail straight ahead and following a sign for Boulder Rock and North Lake. You're now on the blue-blazed trail. Walk several minutes and then ignore a narrow trail going off to the left. Follow the blue-blazed trail as the surface becomes flat rocks and then dirt again.

5. At a trail intersection, turn right onto a blue-blazed trail to Boulder Rock, ignoring the red-blazed trail straight ahead. **Be very careful as you walk along a rock shelf next to a ledge. The rocks can be slippery, and a slip off the cliff could be fatal.** You reach a boulder called Split Rock. **Again be careful as you proceed near the ledge and over large flat rocks.**

6. At another boulder in front of the blue-blazed trail turn left following the blue blazes. *Stop at a rock shelf alongside Boulder Rock to savor the view. There is a short uphill stretch ahead that may require you to boost yourself up while holding*

▼

onto a rock; to avoid it, retrace your steps to Point 5 and turn right onto the red-blazed trail. The red trail will meet the blue trail at Point 7 below. Otherwise, proceed uphill on the rocky trail as it winds through the forest and then ascends steeply.

7. When you reach the top of the hill, turn right and follow the blue-blazed trail. Step down carefully between rocks as the trail descends. *The rock shelf at the cliffside to your right makes a great picnic spot with a fabulous view.* Follow the trail alongside a cliff. The trail turns away from the cliff next to a huge rock on your left that's at a 45-degree angle; don't go straight. Instead, stay on the trail as it turns right, making sure that you're following the blue blazes. Next to a boulder that's on your left, sit down on a rock to get down.

Follow the trail as it bears left, with large rocks in the center of the trail. Proceed downhill. Continue on blue-blazed trail as it descends steeply through the trees.

8. When you emerge from the woods at a clearing next to the cliff, you've reached the site of the former Catskill Mountain House. *This is a great picnic spot; the view of the Hudson Valley is remarkable. Notice a sign on your right explaining some of the history of the Catskill Mountain House.* Turn left and follow a trail that leads through the trees away from the cliff toward high mountains in the distance. Ignore trails to the right, and continue past stone pillars.

9. When you arrive at a fork in the trail, ignore a path that's on your right and continue straight. Proceed into the hardwood forest and follow the trail as it winds to the left. Step over the flat rocks and ignore a path on your left that heads toward a mountain. Continue to walk straight and then pass a metal gate into a paved parking lot. Proceed through the parking lot toward the park's spacious covered picnic shelter.

10. Turn left in front of the picnic shelter and walk alongside a paved road toward a mountain that's in the distance.

11. At an intersection of paved roads, turn left. To your right are the bathing and picnic areas of South Lake. *This is a great place for a swim at a sandy beach with a mountain backdrop.* Walk on the grass alongside the paved road. Follow the road as it winds to the right to the shore of South Lake and then circles to the left away from the lake. Ignore dirt paths to the right and left. Continue alongside the paved road as it winds uphill. Pass a metal gate and a stop sign.

12. At an intersection of paved roads, turn left and proceed past a gate house out of the park. *If you need to use a telephone, several are on your right just before you leave the park.* Ignore a dirt road that's on your right.

13. At Scutt Rd., just past a North/South Lake sign that's on your left, turn left. Walk down Scutt Rd. to the parking lot on your right.

OTHER PLACES NEARBY

Besides the attractions listed below, Woodstock (*see* Experience 8) is only a short drive away.

■ **Kaaterskill Falls.** One of the Northeast's great natural wonders, this waterfall is well worth the 30-minute walk from the road. Tucked into the mountain landscape, the falls drop 260 feet and are higher than Niagara Falls. Thomas Cole first painted Kaaterskill in 1825 and a slew of other 19th-century painters, including Winslow Homer, followed. *Between Haines Falls and Palenville, about 4 mi. southwest of North/South Lake park. Parking area alongside Rte. 23A, 3 1/2 mi. west of 32A intersection in Palenville.*

■ **Hunter Mountain Sky Ride.** This popular ski resort uses its chairlifts for summer sky rides. The mountain views from the highest chairlift in the Catskills are superb. *Hunter Mountain Ski Bowl, Hunter, NY 12442; tel. 518-263-4223. Open Sat.-Sun. Memorial Day weekend-Jul. 1; daily Jul. 2-Labor Day, and Sat.-Sun. first weekend after Labor Day-end of fall foliage season. Admission.*

DINING

Besides the dining choices listed below, you can visit one of the restaurants in the Woodstock area (*see* Experience 8).

■ **Chateau Belleview** (moderate). Skiers love this French restaurant. In the summer, soak up the mountain view outside on the patio. Recommended appetizers include smoked salmon, carpaccio, and mussels. For entrées, you won't go wrong with beef simmered in red wine, steak with black and green peppercorn cream and brandy, or a soft-shell crab special. Order the cold raspberry souffle. *Rte. 23A, Tannersville, NY 12485; tel. 518-589-5525. Open daily for dinner except Tue. In summer, dinner is served beginning at 1 (at 3 on Sun.). About 5 mi. west of North/South Lake park.*

■ **Deer Mountain Inn** (moderate). At this lovely estate it may be hard to place owner-chef Danielle Gortel's European accent, but the Polish sausages on the appetizer menu should tip you off. Expect an interesting twist with the pork chops—a Hunter's sauce with bits of Polish sausage and Polish bacon. You'll find such specials as stuffed cabbage and pierogis, but there's plenty of other fare: sliced veal with mushrooms, shell steak, and poached salmon with mousseline sauce. *Box 443, Rte. 25, Tannersville, NY 12485; tel. 518-589-6268. Open daily for dinner except Tue. and Wed. Reservations required. About 5 mi. northwest of North/South Lake park.*

■ **La Griglia** (moderate). This northern Italian restaurant has an elegant dining area, smooth service, and good food. Try the shrimp stock soup with escarole and the penne pepperata, a pasta with a sweet pepper puree, sun-dried tomatoes, and basil. Recommended entrees are the filet mignon, roast duck, and rack of lamb. Locals love the all-you-can-eat gourmet Sunday brunch. *Rte. 296, Windham, NY 12496; tel. 518-734-4499. Open daily for dinner and Sun. for brunch Jul.-Aug., Christmas week, Jan.-Feb. Call for days open during the rest of the year. About 15 mi. northwest of North/South Lake park.*

■ **La Rive** (moderate). When you finally find this place down a bumpy dirt road in the middle of nowhere, you're confronted with a shack next to a big barn. Have no fear, you've come to a special hideaway with excellent food—a place you'll consider your own find for years to come. Sit on the creekside porch and savor the "gourmet continental cuisine" with French touches. Try the escargot, the shrimp and scallops Provencale, and the crème brûlée; look for the veal chop special. *141 Dedrick Rd., Catskill, NY 12414; tel. 518-943-4888. Open daily except Wed. for dinner first week of May-last weekend of Oct. Take Rte. 23 east toward Catskill and turn right onto Old King's Rd. Follow to Dedrick Rd. About 15 mi. east of North/South Lake park.*

■ **Last Chance Cheese & Antiques Cafe** (inexpensive). This attractively decorated cafe offers soups (try the pea soup), salads, sandwiches, and a few more substantial entrees like baby back ribs and barbecued chicken. The establishment, which also runs an interesting adjoining shop selling gourmet foods, prides itself on its 275 different kinds of beer, its 100 imported cheeses, and its espresso and cappucino bar. With hot music like B. B. King sizzling out of the speakers, it all adds up to a lot of fun. *602 Main St., Tannersville, NY 12485; tel. 518-589-6424; fax 518-589-6424. Open daily for lunch and dinner late Jun.-first week after Labor Day and Thanksgiving-end of ski season. Open Fri.-Mon. for lunch and dinner second week after Labor Day-day before Thanksgiving and end of ski season-late Jun. About 6 mi. west of North/South Lake park.*

LODGING

■ **Deer Mountain Inn** (moderate). Situated on a spectacular piece of property off a quiet road, this turn-of-the-century

▼

country estate is a great place to relax in the mountains. Take the time to sit out on the large outdoor deck next to the bar. Room 3, with a comfortable outdoor sitting area and a fireplace, is the most spacious. All seven rooms are modern and have private baths. *Box 443, Rte. 25, Tannersville, NY 12485; tel. 518-589-6268. About 5 mi. northwest of North/South Lake park.*

■ **Albergo Allegria** (moderate). Two 1876 cottages were joined and renovated into this lovely bed-and-breakfast inn with an impressive lobby area. Some of the original molding and doors were left intact. Room 7 has a view of Windham Mountain, but it's easy to get spoiled by the expensive suite with the Jacuzzi and king-size bed. A backyard deck peers over a stream where a Johnny Weismuller movie was shot. *Box 267, Rte. 296, Windham, NY 12496; tel. 518-734-5560; fax 518-734-5570. About 15 mi. northwest of North/South Lake park.*

■ **The Redcoat's Return** (moderate). The rooms aren't large at this English country inn surrounded by mountains in the heart of the Catskills, but they're bright and well-decorated. *Dale Ln., Elka Park, NY 12427; tel. 518-589-6379, 518-589-9858. About 12 mi. southwest of North/South Lake park.*

FOR MORE INFORMATION
Tourist Offices:
■ **Department of Environmental Conservation.** *Box 34, Haines Falls, NY 12436; tel. 518-589-5058. Open Mon.-Fri. 8-4:30 early May-late Oct. Call 607-652-7364 other months.*

■ **Greene County Promotion.** *Box 527, Catskill, NY 12414; tel. 518-943-3223, 800-355-2287. Open Mon.-Fri. 8-6; Sat.-Sun. 9-4. At exit 21 of New York State Thruway.*

For Serious Walkers:
For other walks in the North/South lakes area, buy the New York-New Jersey Trail Conference's Trail Maps 40 and 41.

A Romantic Landscape

EXPERIENCE 10:
THE MILLS ESTATE

The Mills estate is one of the few mansions along the east bank of the Hudson that remained on the river side of the railroad, which sliced through scores of others in the 1840s, cutting off their access to the water. At the Mills estate, now Mills Memorial State Park in Staatsburg, the lawn sweeps down unimpeded to the river's edge. Here, you have the rare opportunity to walk along the Hudson River for miles, following in the footsteps of the Native Americans who used these shores until some time in the 17th century.

The Highlights: A trail on the banks of the Hudson River, a neoclassical Beaux-Arts mansion, a 19th-century picturesque villa.

Other Places Nearby: The village of Rhinebeck, a variety of Hudson River estates, a plethora of charming, historic B&Bs and inns.

It is not surprising that this fortuitous site once belonged to the descendants of the Livingstons, a prominent family that was one of the largest landholders in the Hudson Valley. In 1792, the estate was purchased by Morgan Lewis, who was married to Gertrude Livingston and had served as quartermaster general of the Continental army during the Revolutionary War.

▼

The estate passed through generations of the family until it was inherited by Morgan Lewis' great-granddaughter, Ruth Livingston Mills, in 1890. At that time the estate consisted of 1,600 acres and an 1832 mansion, built on the site of Lewis' original farmhouse.

Ruth Livingston Mills was married to financier and philanthropist Ogden Mills, whose father had been one of the most successful "49'ers," making an enormous fortune in businesses associated with the California gold and silver rushes. Combining their family fortunes, the Millses led a high-society life as one of the "Four Hundred"—the top families in New York City's social world. In 1895, they commissioned the renowned architectural firm of McKim, Mead, and White to remodel and substantially enlarge the Staatsburg house to a stature befitting their lifestyle. The finished product was the neoclassical Beaux-Arts mansion you see today, with 65 rooms and 14 bathrooms.

The grounds of Mills State Park contain another, much smaller mansion—one that presents an interesting contrast to the imposing neoclassical Mills edifice. Just south of the Mills estate is The Point, also known as the Hoyt House. This property had been carved out of the original family estate and belonged to Ruth Livingston Mills' aunt Geraldine, another Livingston descendant, who was married to Lydig Hoyt. The Hoyt House, its outbuildings, and its landscaping were designed by Calvert Vaux in the mid 1850s. Although the house is now boarded up and the grounds are overgrown, they still represent a fine example of the "picturesque" style of the romantic movement in rural architecture and landscape gardening that flourished in mid-19th-century America, especially in the Hudson River valley.

The principles of this approach were defined and popularized by Vaux's mentor, Hudson Valley native Andrew Jackson Downing, in his highly influential book, *A Treatise on the Theory and Practice of Landscape Gardening,* first published in 1841

▼

and still in print. As it did in painting, literature, and other cultural expressions of the time, the romantic movement idealized nature in landscape gardening and architecture. According to this philosophy, humans' use of the land should be in harmony with nature. Downing's 1843 book, *Cottage Residences,* articulated the idea that a dwelling should blend in with—rather than dominate—its surroundings and that its positioning should maximize the site's aesthetic potential. The Point is an excellent expression of this approach. In his description of the house in his 1857 book, *Villas and Cottages,* Vaux explained how the stone to build the house was painstakingly selected to blend in with the landscape and how the site of the house was carefully selected so as to cut down as few trees as possible while commanding a good river view. When you visit it on your walk, observe the harmony of the house with its surroundings.

The romantic approach to the design of The Point also helped shape New York City's Central Park, which Vaux and Frederick Law Olmsted designed.

GETTING THERE
By train:
Amtrak operates direct trains from Penn Station in New York City to Rhinecliff, a trip of approximately 1 hour and 40 minutes. Depending on the time you travel, reservations may be required; call 800-USA-Rail for information and reservations. For local taxi service from Rhinecliff, call Horseless Carriage Cab Service (800-836-5466). You can also rent a car (delivered to the train station) from Northern Dutchess Rent-A-Wreck (914-876-7451; open Monday-Saturday) or Enterprise Rent A Car (914-336-4700).

By car:
Follow the New York State Thrwy. (I-87) north to exit 18 (Rte. 299 east) for the Mid-Hudson Bridge (Poughkeepsie). Cross the bridge and immediately take the exit

▼

for Rte. 9 north. Follow Rte. 9 nearly 10 mi., past Hyde Park, until you see on your left a sign for the entrance to Mills State Park. Turn left into the entrance and follow the narrow road through the golf course until its intersection with Old Post Rd. Enter the park's large stone gateway across the road and drive till you reach a 4-way intersection. Go right to park for the walk. You can also turn left to park near the mansion.

Walk Directions

TIME: 1 1/2 hours
LEVEL: Easy
DISTANCE: 3 miles
ACCESS: By car or train

For its first half, this walk takes you along the bank of the Hudson River, dipping down at points to water level. **Watch your step as you walk over tree roots and rocks; at times, there is a sharp drop near the edge of the path, so keep to the path and don't let children run ahead.** The second half of the walk is through gently sloping woodlands. You can picnic on a wide expanse of lawn, on rocks overlooking the river, or at picnic tables near the ruined foundations at the south end of the walk. Get picnic provisions in Rhinebeck. Grounds are open daily year-round.

TO BEGIN

From your car, walk to the 4-way intersection that you passed on the drive in. Make a right between the pillars (a left if you parked near the mansion) and follow the old paved carriage road (lined with maples) as it curves down past the sweeping lawn to the river. Stay on the road as it curves gently left. *Look up the hill to your left for a good view of the Mills mansion.* Ignore a path that goes down to the right to the old Mills dock and to a small building that was once a power station and now is a picnic shelter. Continue straight on the road.

▼

1. When you reach an intersection, bear right on a dirt road, ignoring a road to your left that leads to the site of the mansion's old greenhouses and a driveway straight ahead that led to the gardener's house. Bear right on the dirt road. *On your right is a good view of the cove and the river going north beyond the Esopus Meadows lighthouse, which was built in 1839.*

2. As soon as your view of the water begins to be obscured by a stand of trees, look to the right for a trail marker on a tree (two white disks, one with an encircled green leaf), and turn right onto a dirt footpath that follows the river through the edge of a hemlock forest. *Proceed to a rocky spit that extends into the river, where the Hoyts once had a dock. Take a minute to walk out onto the spit. The large building you see across the river to your left is the Mt. St. Alphonsus Seminary.* Go back to the trail and continue on south along the river, taking extra care where the edges of the trail have been eroded. *As you walk on a pebble beach past a tiny inlet, it's easy to picture a Native American canoe gliding in to shore.* Continue to follow the white disks, staying near the riverbank whenever the trail branches off.

Pass a small ruined shed, once a pump house for the Anderson estate, whose site you'll come to later. After you cross over an old stone wall, you come to the foundations of mid- to late-19th-century ice houses on your right; ignore a path that goes down to them. *Ice houses were used to temporarily store ice harvested from rivers and lakes before shipping it to market—until the advent of refrigerators made the industry obsolete.* You soon reach stone steps. Ignore the steps that go up to the left and, instead, walk down the steps to the right into a grassy area bordered by a split-rail fence. *Here there are picnic tables where you can sit and enjoy a view of the river. The tall stone walls that line the back of the grassy area are the remains of early-20th-century houses and terraced gardens that were demolished in the early 1960s.*

When you're ready to go on, continue on the white-blazed

▼

trail past more low foundations; you are still parallel to the river, though not quite as near. Continue until you reach the gazebo, part of an early 20th-century town park, and a parking lot.

3. Turn left and proceed away from the river, following the paved road uphill out of the parking lot. You soon ignore a dirt road that goes off to the right. *Looking to the left, you see stone walls through the trees—reminders of a time when this area was largely open fields.*

4. You reach a tall stone monument erected by Lewis Gordon Norrie in memory of the "happy youth" he spent on this land. Leave the paved road by turning left onto a blue-blazed dirt trail. Follow this trail a short distance, ignoring a horse trail that forks off to the left.

5. At an intersection, where ahead of you the paved road forks back to the main road, turn left and pass through or around a metal-pipe gate that marks the entrance to a gravel and dirt road. Proceed on this unpaved road, following blue blazes. *Note the bluebird boxes in patches of meadow to your right.* Almost immediately, you come to a dirt driveway on your left, leading to an abandoned stone building. *This was the water tower for the Anderson estate, a mansion whose site you'll pass shortly. The water was pumped up from the river via the pump house, which you passed earlier.* Take a few minutes to explore the water-tower site and return to the trail. Continue on the blue-blazed trail. *In one of the partially overgrown clearings to your left was the Anderson mansion. Not even the foundations remained after it was consumed in a fire.*

6. About 5 minutes after you left the water tower, you arrive at an intersection of dirt roads. Take the green-blazed trail that dips downhill to the right. *If you wish to shorten the walk, you can take the left trail, which takes you directly to the*

▼

Hoyt House. You then can rejoin the walk at Point 9 by turning left at the fork in the driveway and heading toward the brick buildings. If you shorten the walk, however, you'll miss the more dramatic approach to the house via its original, meandering driveway, a planned part of its picturesque landscape.

7. After walking a few minutes on the green-blazed trail, you come to a trail junction in the woods. Take a sharp left turn onto a red-blazed trail. Follow this trail downhill through a shady stand of hemlocks.

8. When you come to a T-shaped junction at the bottom of the hill, turn left. You are now on the original driveway to the Hoyt House. Ignore a dirt road that immediately forks off to the right. Pass some huge old trees and a lot of relatively young small ones. *Try to imagine what it must have been like to ride in a carriage through this landscape, before it was overgrown. Note how the driveway curves deliberately and gracefully around the hill.*

9. When the driveway forks, follow a road that curves uphill to the left, ignoring another road that leads straight ahead to brick outbuildings. *As you round the curve and reach the crest of the hill, you see the Hoyt House nestled in the remains of its romantic landscape. Take a few minutes to explore the grounds, noticing how the materials and positioning of the house help it blend into its site. The house is closed, but you are permitted to walk around it. Although trees now block much of the 180-degree river view, you can still get a sense of what a splendid site this was—and how Vaux made the most of it.* When you're ready, retrace your steps down the driveway to the fork. Turn left and go toward the brick buildings—two garages and a barn—that served the Hoyt House (though they were built at a later date). Pass by these buildings on your left and bear right on a dirt road. *On your right, notice the remains of the Hoyts' greenhouse and an older barn.* Follow

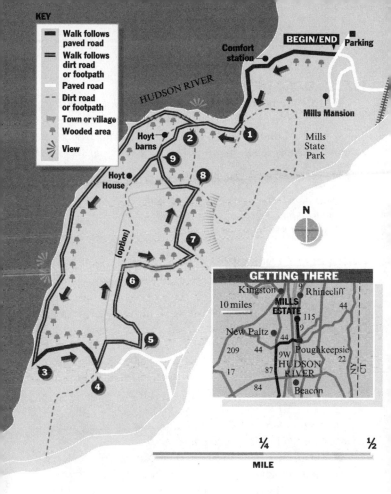

HUDSON RIVER

Comfort station

BEGIN/END ■ **Parking**

Mills Mansion

Mills State Park

Hoyt barns

Hoyt House

(option)

N

GETTING THERE

Kingston ● 9 Rhinecliff

10 miles · **MILLS ESTATE** · 115 · 44

New Paltz ● 44 · 9

209 44 9W Poughkeepsie

17 87 **HUDSON RIVER** 22

84 ● Beacon

¼ ½

MILE

the road as it curves down toward the water.

Now you're back on the road that you walked on earlier. Pass by the cove on your left and the old gardener's house on your right. *On the hill ahead, you can see through the trees a cylindrical stone water tower that was used at the Mills property.* When the road becomes paved and forks, bear to your left and follow the road (or cut across the lawn) to your starting point.

▼

PLACES ALONG THE WALK

■ **Mills Memorial State Park.** *Old Post Rd., Staatsburg, NY 12580; tel. 914-889-4646. Open daily sunrise-sunset.*

■ **Mills Mansion State Historic Site.** The Beaux-Arts mansion contains luxurious furnishings, primarily in the styles of 17th- and 18th-century France. *Old Post Rd., Staatsburg, NY 12580; tel. 914-889-8851. Mansion open Wed.-Sat. 10-5, Sun. 12-5, mid-Apr.-Labor Day. Open Wed.-Sun. 12-5 Labor Day-last Sun. in Oct. Shown only by guided tours, which begin every half hour until 4:30.*

OTHER PLACES NEARBY

■ **Montgomery Place.** If you had to pick just one Hudson River estate to visit, this would be our recommendation. It comes the closest to giving one a sense of what such an estate must have been like one or even two centuries ago. Its grounds, which are a beautifully preserved example of the romantic landscape, include picturesque trails originally laid out in the early 19th century. Splendid views of the Hudson River and the Catskills. *River Rd., Rte. 103, Annandale-on-Hudson, NY 12504; tel. 914-758-5461. Open daily except Tue. 10-5 Apr.-Oct.; Sat.-Sun. 10-5 Nov.-Dec. and Mar. Admission. Off Rte. 9G, about 11 mi. north of the Mills estate.*

■ **National Historic Sites.** The National Park Service administers three famous historic sites in Hyde Park: the home of Franklin D. Roosevelt, the Eleanor Roosevelt National Historic Site ("Val-Kill"), and the Vanderbilt Mansion. In addition to their historic interest, the FDR home and the Vanderbilt estate are worth visiting because of their location overlooking the Hudson River. For some of the best river views in the entire valley, go to the north of the Vanderbilt Mansion, or down to the estate's Bard Rock. *National Park Service, 519 Albany Post Rd., Hyde Park, NY 12538; tel. 914-229-9115. FDR Home and Vanderbilt Mansion open Wed.-Sun. 9-5. Eleanor Roosevelt Site*

▼

open 9-5, Wed.-Sun. May-Oct.; Sat.-Sun. Mar.-Apr. and Nov.-Dec. All grounds open daily year-round. Admission (to buildings). All sites are in the town of Hyde Park, about 4 mi. south of the Mills estate.

■ **Old Rhinebeck Aerodrome.** An unusual opportunity to see antique airplanes (from 1900 to 1937) on the ground and in the air. *Stone Church Rd., Rhinebeck, NY 12572; tel. 914-758-8610. The aerodrome and its air museums are open daily 10-5, May 15-Oct. 31. Air shows are held Sat. and Sun.; call for times. Individual barnstorming rides available before and after shows. Admission. About 9 mi. northeast of the Mills estate.*

■ **Wilderstein.** This Queen Anne mansion, which is undergoing restoration, is set in a landscape designed by Calvert Vaux. You can call or write for a trail map of the grounds. *Morton Rd., Box 383, Rhinebeck, NY 12572, tel. 914-876-4818. Mansion (1st floor only) open Thu.-Sun. 12-4 May-Oct.; open other days and months to groups, by appointment. Grounds and trails open daily year-round. Admission. Off Rte. 9, south of Rhinebeck; about 4 mi. north of the Mills estate.*

DINING

■ **Beekman 1766 Tavern** (expensive). You'll find both good food and historical ambience at this restaurant, located in what is reputed to be America's oldest continuously operated inn (yes, George Washington ate here). Chef-proprietor Larry Forgione, who also operates An American Place in Manhattan, creates a frequently changing American regional menu specializing in fresh seafood, such as traditional cedar-planked Atlantic salmon served with roasted corn pudding. *4 Mill St., Rhinebeck, NY 12572; tel. 914-871-1766; fax 914-871-1704. Open Mon.-Sat. for breakfast, lunch, and dinner, and Sun. for brunch and dinner. About 5 mi. north of the Mills estate.*

■ **Culinary Institute of America** (expensive). There are actually four separate restaurants at this famed school of the culinary arts: Caterina de Medici (serving regional Italian cuisine);

▼

Escoffier (classic French); American Bounty (contemporary regional American); and St. Andrew's Cafe (contemporary, health-oriented American). Each has an outstanding reputation and its own unique ambience. The food is prepared and served by students. *433 Albany Post Rd., Hyde Park, NY 12538; tel. 914-471-6608 for reservations; 914-471-9600 for information. Call for details about hours and reservations. On Rte. 9, about 8 mi. south of the Mills estate.*

■ **Bois d'arc** (moderate). This storefront restaurant in a small rural village has some of the best food in the county. Chef-owner Jim Jennings bought it from former owners Green and Bresler in 1994 and carries on the restaurant's excellent reputation. The "progressive American" menu features dishes such as corn pancakes with chunks of fresh lobster, garnished with creme fraiche, salsa, avocado, and red lumpfish caviar. *29 W. Market St., Red Hook, NY 12571; tel. 914-758-5992. Open Thu.-Mon. for lunch and dinner, and Sun. for brunch. May possibly close Mon. in winter. Near the intersection of Rtes. 199 and 9, about 9 mi. north of the Mills estate.*

■ **Calico Restaurant and Patisserie** (moderate). Don't be fooled by the postage-stamp size of this charming little storefront restaurant. Chef-proprietor Anthony Balassone, a Culinary Institute graduate, serves a diverse menu of "hearty" American food, using fresh local ingredients. Everything is made from scratch, even the sausages and the croissants. And keep the pastries in mind for breakfast, too (to eat there or take out). It's wise to make a reservation because there are only 6 tables. *9 Mill St., Rhinebeck, NY 12572; tel. 914-876-2749. Open Wed.-Sun. for breakfast (pastries only), lunch and dinner. On Rte. 9, about 5 mi. north of the Mills estate.*

■ **Portofino Ristorante** (moderate). Locals speak highly of the authentic regional Italian cuisine at this restaurant in the quaint and tiny hamlet of Staatsburg. The menu offers a full range of seafood, meat, and pasta dishes. A house specialty is the tortellini alla Portofino: shrimp, scallops, and clams sauteed in olive oil with garlic, broccoli, peas, sun-dried tomatoes, and mushrooms, and tossed with cheese tortellini and tomato-basil cream sauce. The ambience, just a cut above basic tavern, is not the restaurant's strong point. *57 Old Post Rd., Staatsburg, NY 12580; tel. 914-889-4711. Open daily except Tue. for dinner, and daily except Sun. and Tue. for lunch. Closed 2nd-3rd weeks Jan. Less than 1/2 mi. south of the Mills estate.*

■ **Foster's Coach House Tavern** (inexpensive). Foster's has been a local institution since the 1930s, when the original owner renovated a barn and gave the restaurant its signature horse-oriented decor. This is a good place to go for a quick burger or sandwich (the service is speedy). No reservations. *22 Montgomery St. (Rte. 9), Rhinebeck, NY 12572; tel. 914-876-8052. Open Tue.-Sun. for lunch and dinner. Closed during the Dutchess County Fair, usually the last week of Aug. About 5 mi. north of the Mills estate.*

LODGING

■ **Belvedere Mansion** (very expensive). After visiting a mansion or two nearby, perhaps you'd like to stay in one. This Greek Revival mansion, which was still undergoing massive renovation in 1995, offers a choice of six opulent rooms, all with private baths and some with river views. If you prefer coziness to elegance, you can stay in one of the ten less expensive "cottage" rooms in a detached building, but they're really small. Grounds include a swimming pool and a gazebo. *Box 785, Rhinebeck, NY 12572; tel. 914-889-8000. On Rte. 9, about 1 mi. north of the Mills estate.*

■ **Mansakenning Carriage House** (very expensive). Prices are in the stratosphere, but consider that this country retreat offers luxury accomodations. In the late-19th-century carriage house, each of the four tastefully renovated suites is spacious and has many amenities. Walkers can enjoy acres of woodlands. *29 Ackert Hook Rd., Rhinebeck, NY 12572; tel. 914-876-3500. About 5 mi. north of the Mills estate.*

▼

■ **Stanford White's Carriage House** (expensive). If your dream country weekend comes out of the pages of *Architectural Digest* rather than *Country Living,* this is the B&B for you. You won't find a scrap of Laura Ashley in the mostly white, casually elegant interior of this stunning brick carriage house, designed in 1892 by the renowned architect and recently renovated. Two of the smaller rooms (moderately priced) share a hall bath; a larger room has its own detached bath. The one enormous suite has not only a private bath and a sitting room but also its own kitchenette. The B&B sits on six secluded acres and has a small swimming pool. No credit cards. *252 Rte. 308, Rhinebeck, NY 12572; tel. 914-876-7257. Near the intersection of Rtes. 308 and 9G, about 7 miles northeast of the Mills estate.*

■ **Beekman Arms** (moderate). Said to be the oldest continuously operated inn in the country, the Beekman Arms is deservedly famous. But for all its antique ambience (wideboard floors and low ceilings), you need not worry about antique amenities. In 1995, all 13 rooms in the main inn were tastefully refurbished and their private baths fully renovated. Avoid rooms 34 and 35, whose windows are too close to the restaurant's ventilator. *4 Mill St., Rhinebeck, NY 12572; tel. 914-876-7077. At the intersection of Rtes. 9 and 308. On Rte. 9, about 5 mi. north of the Mills estate.*

■ **Delamater House Inn & Conference Center** (moderate). The inn encompasses seven buildings, four of which are historic. The best choice is the main Delamater House, an 1844 American Gothic gem. Its seven rooms all have private baths and are beautifully furnished in period style. The other three 19th-century buildings are also nice, each with its own ambience; some rooms have working fireplaces. *Rte. 9, Rhinebeck, NY 12572; tel. 914-876-7080. Delamater House Inn and the Beekman Arms are operated jointly; sometimes the phone number for one will be answered at the other. When making reservations, make clear which lodging you desire. Near the intersection*

▼

with Rte. 308, about 5 mi. north of the Mills estate.

■ **Veranda House** (moderate). In this 1845 Federal-style B&B, the tastes of the owners, an artist and an architectural historian, are reflected in the pleasing mix of antique furnishings and contemporary art. All four guest rooms have private baths or showers. *82 Montgomery St., Rhinebeck, NY 12572; tel. 914-876-4133. On Rte. 9, about 5 mi. north of the Mills estate.*

FOR MORE INFORMATION

Tourist Offices:

■ **Dutchess County Tourism Promotion Agency.** Ask for six pamphlets outlining historic county driving tours. *3 Neptune Rd., Poughkeepsie, NY 12601; tel. 914-463-4000, 800-445-3131. Open Mon.-Fri. 9-5.*

■ **Rhinebeck Chamber of Commerce.** *Box 42, 19 Mill St., Rhinebeck, NY 12572; tel. 914-876-4778. Volunteers will respond to telephone inquiries.*

For Serious Walkers:

Walkers interested in further exploring the trails in this area can obtain a map from the park office (914-889-4646). The white-blazed trail along the Hudson River links with the Hyde Park Trail, which takes walkers to parks and historic sites in Hyde Park. For a map, call the National Park Service (914-229-9115) or the Hyde Park Recreation Department (914-229-8086).

A Living Exhibit

EXPERIENCE 11:
STISSING MOUNTAIN

The topography of this northern Dutchess County area may be familiar to millions of people who have never set foot here. For four decades, New York City's American Museum of Natural History has displayed a set of exhibits and dioramas featuring Stissing Mountain in its New York State Environment Hall.

The Highlights: A 360-degree view of portions of five states from a fire tower atop a 1,400-foot mountain.

Other Places Nearby: Rolling hills and horse country surrounding the village of Millbrook; the enchanting Innisfree Garden; vineyards for wine-tasting, charming B&Bs and world-class country inns.

Why Stissing Mountain? For one thing, its geology is interesting and unusual. The mountain is an isolated chunk of Precambrian gneiss, the oldest type of rock in New York State (possibly as much as two billion years old) that somehow got separated from the Hudson Highlands. Stissing Mountain is surrounded by much younger rock, formed in part by sediment left behind when the area known as Pine Plains was a shallow arm of the ocean. As you walk up the mountain on this walking tour, you'll cross bare patches of the primordial rock.

126

▼

The area is also a good case study of what happens when a glacier retreats. About 10,000 years ago, the Wisconsin Glacier melted, dumping rocks and gravel and scratching deep grooves on the rock it scraped across. Great chunks of ice broke off and melted slowly as the waters deposited sand and gravel around them; the resulting impressions formed ponds or lakes known as kettles. You can see several of these kettles, including Thompson Pond, as you look down the eastern slope of Stissing Mountain to the valley below.

Although the mountain's geological history is well-documented, less is known about its role in human history. Little is known of its use by Native Americans, although a number of explanations for the derivation of its name are linked to the Mahican tribe. According to one legend, Stissing is named for an old Mahican named Teesink, or Tishasink, who was said to have lived in the notch between Stissing Mountain and Little Stissing Mountain. Another tale has it that the Mahicans saw in the outline of the ridge the profile of a reclining tribe member, feather and all, and they named him Teesink. And at least one source says Stissing means "Big Rock" in the Mahican dialect.

In the 1740s, Moravian missionaries established a mission in the nearby hamlet of Bethel, a part of Pine Plains, for the purpose of converting the Mahicans. Records indicate that the Mahicans used a trail over Stissing Mountain, but no one knows exactly where it was. Legend says that the mountain was used during the Revolutionary War as a hiding place by Tories. Later, during the 19th century, the mountain was clear-cut; its trees were dragged out by horses and oxen and burned for charcoal, which was then shipped down to local foundries for the production of iron. Many portions of the trail you will walk on are old logging roads.

After the decline of the county's iron industry, the wood was no longer needed for charcoal. Individual farmers, however, continued to own woodlots on the mountain, harvesting the

▼

wood for firewood; some woodlots are still owned and used as such today. Your walk is entirely surrounded by trees, but you'll notice that most of the growth is relatively new, due to extensive logging earlier this century and before.

Atop Stissing Mountain's north peak is a 90-foot fire observation tower that allows you to climb above the tree canopy for a smashing 360-degree panorama. The tower was built in 1934 by the Civilian Conservation Corps and was used for fire spotting until 1973, when that function was taken over by airplanes. The fire ranger on duty lived for months at a time atop the mountain, spending his days at the top of the tower and his nights in a small cabin in the woods nearby. The last fire ranger who lived there, a one-armed man, is said to have painted the entire tower by himself. Scheduled to be removed in 1986, the tower was saved by a local citizens' group, Friends of Stissing Landmarks.

Although not as popular as the "Gold Coast" bordering the Hudson River, this part of Dutchess County has over the years attracted relatively large numbers of the wealthy, seeking country retreats in picturesque surroundings, particularly in the area around Millbrook. In the late 19th and early 20th centuries, tycoons such as Henry Flagler (an oil baron who also made millions developing Florida) built mansions on large estates. One such estate, created around the turn of this century by Charles Francis Dieterich, became a sort of mecca for hippies in the 1960s, when it was the home of psychedelic pioneer Dr. Timothy Leary. You can still see the dramatic stone gatehouse of that private estate just east of the village of Millbrook on Route 44.

The area's beauty and expanses of open space (not to mention the potential for privacy) still attract the rich and famous, including Mary Tyler Moore, Daryl Hall, Kevin Bacon, and most recently, Liam Neeson and Natasha Richardson. Of the area's famous residents, the late James Cagney was one of the best known.

▼

GETTING THERE
By car:

From New York City, take the Henry Hudson Pkwy. north to the Saw Mill River Pkwy. north. Connect to the Taconic State Pkwy., which you take northbound. Get off at the Poughkeepsie/Millbrook exit and turn right onto Rte. 44 east. Follow Rte. 44 less than 1 mi. to the intersection with Rte. 82 north (just before the state trooper barracks). Turn left onto Rte. 82 and follow it north about 7 mi. to the village of Stanfordville. (In Stanfordville, there are several places to pick up picnic supplies.) Look for the Stanfordville Town Hall on your right. From the town hall, drive 3 mi. north on Rte. 82 and turn left onto Stissing Rd. About 1/3 mi. down Stissing Rd., bear right, ignoring the unmarked road that forks off to the left. You immediately come to another intersection, where you bear left onto Mountain Rd., which is also marked Dead End.

Follow Mountain Rd. 1 1/2 mi. to its end, and park in the turnaround. Do not block the private driveway that ends at the far side of the turnaround. (The property owner's generosity makes public access to the trail possible.) A new entrance to the Stissing Mountain trail is currently being blazed. It will begin at the Hicks Hill Rd. Multiple Use Area and will pass by a waterfall. Call the New York State Department of Environmental Conservation at 914-831-3109.

Walk Directions

TIME: 3 hours
LEVEL: Moderate
DISTANCE: 5 miles
ACCESS: By car

This path takes you through woodland, gradually ascending the mountain to one peak, then along a ridge to the north peak where the fire tower stands. You can picnic on one of the many rocks at or near the top, though there's no view except from the fire

▼

tower. Climbing all 106 stairs to the observation platform is not for those with vertigo, but you don't have to go all the way up to get above tree level and obtain a partial view. At intersections throughout the trail's length, it is blazed with yellow juice can tops, though sometimes you must look hard to find them. Usually, they'll be on one or two trees after, as well as at, a junction. Please stay on the marked trail to avoid trespassing on private property. Be careful here during hunting season; inquire at Dutchess County Tourism Promotion Agency for dates. (At other times, you may hear occasional sounds from a nearby skeet-shooting range: Don't be alarmed.)

TO BEGIN

Stand in the turnaround with your back to Mountain Rd. Avoiding the chained road with a stop sign directly in front of you, enter the trail that goes off to your right.

1. After walking less than 150 feet, you arrive at yellow plastic disks and a wooden trail box on your left, where you may sign the trail log if you wish. (If you don't immediately reach this spot, you're on the wrong trail.) Follow the yellow-blazed trail, ignoring the numerous trails that fork off. *The main trail is usually the obvious choice, because the other paths are more overgrown. If, after any fork, you don't shortly see one or two yellow blazes, go back and look down the alternative path to be sure you made the right choice.* As the trail rises, you begin to cross some large patches of bare rock, the exposed "bones" of the mountain. *Note some depressions on each side of the trail. These holes are said to be the remains of charcoal-burning pits.*

After about 15 minutes from the start, the trail gets steeper. After another 10 minutes or so, the trail levels off and dips temporarily. It then ascends to the right, eventually opening to a glade filled with ferns in summer.

The trail then undulates up and down for a bit. You may have to make your way around or over some large fallen trees.

After you've been walking a little over an hour from the start, the trail gets significantly steeper, and you may think you're almost at the top; you may even glimpse sky through the trees over the crest of the mountain. Indeed, you are almost at one

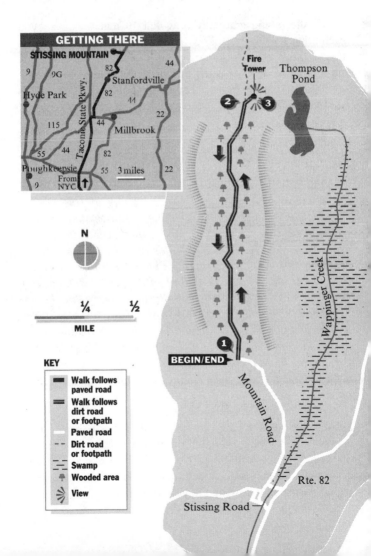

GETTING THERE

STISSING MOUNTAIN

Stanfordville

Hyde Park

Taconic State Pkwy.

Millbrook

Poughkeepsie

From NYC

3 miles

N

¼   ½

MILE

KEY

- Walk follows paved road
- Walk follows dirt road or footpath
- Paved road
- Dirt road or footpath
- Swamp
- Wooded area
- View

Fire Tower

Thompson Pond

Wappinger Creek

Mountain Road

Rte. 82

Stissing Road

BEGIN/END

▼

summit of the mountain, but now you have to turn and follow the ridge of the mountain to reach the fire tower. Keep following the yellow-blazed trail. When the trail starts to go downhill a bit, don't be alarmed. You're almost there.

2. After going gradually downhill 10 minutes or so, you reach a junction. Don't follow the yellow-blazed trail that goes straight ahead and steeply downhill. Instead, take a sharp right and follow the yellow-blazed trail that goes uphill to the right. Some of the yellow blazes that mark the correct trail at this point will be labeled with the letter T (for tower).

3. In another few minutes, after you have wended around or over some rocks, you reach a fire tower. Climb the 106 wooden steps to the top. At the top of the tower, take some time to enjoy the 360-degree view, unparalleled in the region. *On a clear day, you can see portions of five states: Connecticut, Massachusetts, Vermont, Pennsylvania, and, of course, New York. To the east, notice the Taconic Mountains; to the south, the Hudson Highlands and the Bear Mountain Bridge; to the west, the Catskills; and to the north, the towers of the Empire State Plaza in Albany (if it's very clear). Looking down to the northeast, you see the rural village of Pine Plains; to the east, Thompson Pond and Stissing Lake, two glacial kettles. In addition to forests, there are miles of farmland in the fertile plain and valley—countryside that probably looks much the same as it did a century ago. If you're lucky, you may also get a glimpse of one of the golden eagles that nest in the nearby preserve.*

To return, make your way back to the yellow-blazed trail. Retrace your steps, taking care to turn left at the T-shaped junction at Point 3. Going downhill the way you came up, some of the yellow blazes will be labeled with the letter S. The trail down the mountain is actually easier to follow than it was coming up. Just keep following the yellow blazes.

▼

OTHER PLACES NEARBY

In addition to the Cascade Mountain Winery (*see* Dining), you can visit two others in the area: Clinton Vineyards in Clinton Corners (914-266-5372) and Millbrook Vineyards in Millbrook (914-677-8383).

■ **Innisfree Garden.** This unique landscape was composed by artist Walter Beck according to Oriental principles of design, using rocks, water, and other natural features to achieve harmony, balance, and exceptional beauty. The result is similar to a three-dimensional landscape painting. The grounds, which include a 40-acre lake, waterfalls, streams, and trails, have a serenity and magic you won't want to miss. *Tyrrel Rd., Millbrook, NY 12545; tel. 914-677-8000. Open Wed.-Fri. 10-4, Sat.-Sun. and legal holidays 11-5 May 1-Oct. 20. Admission. On Tyrrel Rd. 1 mi. from Rte. 44; about 11 mi. south of Stissing Mtn.*

■ **Mary Flagler Cary Arboretum.** Part of the New York Botanical Garden's Institute for Ecosystem Studies, this 1,924-acre arboretum includes an extensive perennial garden and other horticultural displays, as well as two nature trails. Although there is no admission charge, visitors are requested to pick up a permit and a map at the Gifford House Visitor and Education Center. *Rte. 44A, Millbrook, NY 12545; tel. 914-677-5359. Grounds open daily except holidays 9-6 May-Sep.; 9-4 Oct.-Apr. Gifford House open Mon.-Sat. 9-5, Sun. 1-5 May-Sep.; Mon.-Sat 9-4, Sun. 1-4 Oct.-Apr. About 10 mi. south of Stissing Mtn.*

■ **The Village of Millbrook.** This small village is worth a stop just for its picturesque looks and its many antiques shops. In the heart of the county's rolling hills, it's an easy drive to many other attractions. *On Rte. 44, about 12 mi. south of Stissing Mtn.*

■ **Wethersfield.** This 1,400-acre hilltop estate, residence of the late investor and philanthropist Chauncey Stillman, can give you a good sense of the lifestyle of the very wealthy in the horse country of Dutchess County. In the house, there's an outstanding collection of antiques and art, including paintings by

Degas and Cassatt. Stillman also collected (and drove) carriages, which you can view in the carriage house. The grounds contain formal gardens and offer panoramic views. *R.R.1, Box 444, Amenia, NY 12501; tel. 914-373-8037. Open Wed. and Fri.-Sat., Jun.-Sep. Gardens open 12-5. House and carriage house shown by advance reservation only. Admission. About 6 mi. east of Stissing Mtn.*

DINING

■ **Old Drovers Inn** (expensive). In continuous operation since 1750, when it was a stopover for cattle drovers, this award-winning inn is a romantic country getaway, heavy with historic atmosphere and charm, especially in the original Tap Room, with its low-beamed ceiling and fireplace. Kemper Peacock and Alice Pitcher, owners since 1988, have raised the level of the cuisine to new heights. You'll enjoy Old Drovers classics, such as their cheddar-cheese soup and turkey hash, along with inventive dishes such as chilled grape soup and Thai-spiced lobster. *Old Rte. 22, Dover Plains, NY 12522; tel. 914-832-9311. Open Fri.-Sun. for lunch, and daily except Wed. for dinner. Old Rte. 22 is off Rte. 22, south of Dover Plains. About 21 mi. southeast of Stissing Mtn.*

■ **Simmons' Way Village Inn & Restaurant** (expensive). The menu includes such sophisticated creations as sun-dried tomato and brie soup and chicken with pesto butter and bacon. The wine list is impressive. Of the inn's two dining rooms, we prefer the large, rear one with a cathedral ceiling and skylights. *33 Main St., Millerton, NY 12546; tel. 518-789-6235; fax 518-789-6236. Open Wed.-Sun. for dinner, and Sun. brunch. About 12 mi. northeast of Stissing Mtn.*

■ **Troutbeck** (expensive). The four-star restaurant at this country inn and executive hideaway is open to the public only on weekends (reservations are essential), but it's a special treat worth planning for. Chef Paul Bernal, a James Beard guest chef, creates an outstanding menu including such imaginative dishes

▼

as Norwegian salmon filet with pesto, roasted red pepper, and Boursin, served with asparagus and tomato coulis. A five-course prix-fixe dinner is an option that's a good value. *Leedsville Rd., Amenia, NY 12501; tel. 914-373-9681, 800-978-7688; fax 914-373-7080. Open Fri. for dinner, Sat. for lunch and dinner, and Sun. for large "bruncheon." Off Rte. 343, between Sharon, CT, and Amenia; about 15 mi. southeast of Stissing Mtn.*

■ **Allyn's Restaurant** (moderate). The 200-year-old structure housing this country restaurant was originally built as a church. Four large fireplaces make this an especially cozy place to dine in cold weather. The American contemporary cuisine features fresh regional produce. Try the loin of local farm-raised venison, served with organic greens and lingonberries. There's an extensive wine list. *R.R.1., Box 91A, Rte. 44, Millbrook, NY 12545; tel.914-677-5888. Open daily except Tue. for lunch and dinner, and Sun. for brunch. Call to find out whether also open on Wed. Jan.-Mar. About 10 mi. southeast of Stissing Mtn.*

■ **Cascade Mountain Winery & Restaurant** (moderate). The American regional menu focuses, as much as possible, on local foods: grilled, boneless breast of chicken filled with local herb-and-garlic goat cheese, for example. You can eat in the cozy, rustic dining room or on the deck overlooking a meadow and an old orchard. *Flint Hill Rd., Amenia, NY 12501; tel. 914-373-9021. Open daily for lunch and Sat. for dinner Apr.-Jan. 1. Restaurant closed Jan.-Mar. Wine-tasting 10-6 daily. Call for directions. About 7 mi. east of Stissing Mtn.*

LODGING

■ **Old Drovers Inn** (very expensive). We'd be remiss if we didn't include this renowned country inn, even if it is a bit far from Stissing Mountain. Nearly 250 years old, its four rooms feature wide-board floors and antique furnishings, and all have private baths. The large, barrel-ceiling meeting room holds two double beds and a sitting area with working fireplace. Guests can also use the library and the parlor. Midweek rates include

▼

continental breakfast; the more expensive weekend rates include full breakfast and dinner in the inn's excellent restaurant (*see* Dining). *Old Rte. 22, Dover Plains, NY 12522; tel. 914-832-9311. Old Rte. 22 is off Rte. 22, south of Dover Plains. About 21 mi. southwest of Stissing Mtn.*

■ **Troutbeck** (very expensive). Weekdays, it's a classy executive retreat. Weekends, it's a world-class country inn, genteel but unpretentious, and a true escape on 442 acres (with river, trails, and gardens). There are 36 bedrooms, with 31 baths, spread among the three buildings. Rooms in the main stone mansion are furnished in traditional style; some contain a canopy bed, and some have a sun porch and a fireplace. Rate includes three meals in the inn's award-winning restaurant (*see* Dining) and an open bar. Amenities include two swimming pools and a tennis court. *Leedsville Rd., Amenia, NY 12501; tel. 914-373-9681, 800-978-7688; fax 914-373-7080. Open for individual bookings Fri.-Sat. nights only. Off Rte. 343, about 15 mi. southeast of Stissing Mtn.*

■ **The Mill at Bloomvale Falls** (moderate). At this B&B, a restored 18th-century stone mill, you can enjoy the sight and sound of a waterfall from three of the rooms and from the romantic courtyard patio (whose stone walls are the remains of the original 1760 mill). All four rooms share 2 1/2 baths. The Gold Room, in the rear corner of the house with the sluice running directly beneath its windows, is especially popular; it and the Red Room are expensive. Ask about weekday discounts. Full breakfast included. *Box 860, Millbrook, NY 12545; tel. 914-266-4234. On Rte. 82, about 7 mi. south of Stissing Mtn.*

■ **The Pines** (moderate). You get historic ambience and good value at this enormous 1878 Victorian, set on nearly five quiet acres in a small rural village. All hardware and woodwork is original. The six guest rooms are furnished with a mix of antiques and furniture styles. Most are large and all have sinks, though not all have private baths. The one suite is expensive. Expanded continental breakfast is served in the

▼

dining room. Guests also have use of two parlors and four porches (complete with rockers). *5 Maple St., Pine Plains, NY 12567; tel. 518-398-7677. At the corner of N. Main St. in Pine Plains, about 5 mi. north of Stissing Mtn.*

■ **A Cat in Your Lap** (inexpensive to moderate). The charming main house, built in 1840, offers two small, cozy rooms, each with private bath. Both have use of the living room and its working fireplace. The 1890 barn houses two spacious, moderately priced studio suites, each simply furnished with a private bath, a fireplace, and a small kitchen. *Old Rte. 82 and The Monument, Millbrook, NY 12545; tel. 914-677-3051. At the crossroads of Old Rte. 82 and Rte. 343, about 12 mi. south of Stissing Mtn.*

FOR MORE INFORMATION
Tourist Offices:
■ **Dutchess County Tourism Promotion Agency.** Ask for pamphlets on historic driving tours. *3 Neptune Rd., Poughkeepsie, NY 12601; tel. 800-445-3131. Open Mon.-Fri. 9-5.*

■ **Millbrook Business Association.** You can find brochures at their unmanned Tourist Information Center. *Box 1013, Millbrook, NY 12545; tel. 914-677-3225. Tourist center is in the foyer of the Millbrook Gallery, at the corner of Franklin Ave. (Rte. 44) and Church St. Leave a phone message if you want a brochure.*

For Serious Walkers:
The Harlem Valley Rail Trail, under construction in 1995, will follow the old railroad bed from Amenia to Millerton, and eventually north into Columbia County. For the latest developments, call the Harlem Valley Partnership for Economic Development at 914-877-3738.

A Sunken Forest Next to the Sea

EXPERIENCE 12: FIRE ISLAND

It rarely receives such acclaim, but Fire Island is one of the most spectacular geographic attractions in the entire country. Though it's only a quarter-mile wide, the 32-mile-long barrier island off the southern shore of Long Island consists of wide sandy

The Highlights: Great ocean beaches, magical maritime forests, ferry boat rides.

Other Places Nearby: A spacious bayfront state park, a lovely arboretum, good restaurants.

beaches and unique maritime forests wedged between fragile sand dunes. New York City is less than 40 miles away, yet, as you will learn on this walking tour, Fire Island remains a remote destination that has preserved its natural beauty by prohibiting roads for automobiles and by constantly rebounding from tropical storms and the daily battering of the Atlantic Ocean.

Former parks commissioner Robert Moses fought for a long time to alter this idyllic land. Moses, who is credited by some for aggressively pursuing acquisition of state park lands and keeping them out of the hands of developers, was never looked at as an environmentalist by Fire Island residents. His grand plan was to build a bridge to link Fire Island with the Long Island mainland and to construct a road down the middle

▼

of the narrow barrier island. Such a roadway system would enable Fire Island to be enjoyed by millions in the New York metropolitan area, he reasoned.

Fire Island residents furiously opposed the plan, envisioning a constant parade of automobiles that would destroy the natural wilderness. The impact, they said, would not only spoil the beaches and sea but also the island's rare vegetation, including the holly groves that proliferate next to dense oak and hardwood forests.

n September 1938, a devastating hurricane struck Long Island, and Fire island was one of its many victims. Giant waves slapped across the thin barrier island, washing away hundreds of summer homes and creating new inlets between the bays to the north and the ocean to the south.

Moses thought the time again was ripe to hatch his roadway plan. Fifteen days after the the storm had unleashed its fury, Moses proposed a new $15 million plan that called for construction of a highway, three drawbridges that would connect Fire Island to Long Island, two new beachfront parks, and an enormous boat channel that would run the length of Fire Island. The sand that would be dredged to build the channel would be used to form the base of the highway.

Such a plan, Moses said, would anchor Fire Island to Long Island, rebuild its beaches, and protect Long Island from future storms. In addition, the huge project would create jobs, boost property values, and make it easier for Fire Island residents to commute to work on Long Island and in New York City.

"Don't do us any favors," was the cry of most Fire Island residents. Locals rallied behind the editorials of the *Babylon Leader* newspaper which was based on Long Island's southern shore just across the bay from the western end of Long Island. The newspaper declared that Moses's plan to save Fire Island would destroy it and that past history showed Fire Island

▼

beaches would naturally rebuild themselves after storm damage. Fire Island's devastated sand dunes could also be rebuilt inexpensively by planting vegetation that would catch the sand, the newspaper said.

The opposition forces triumphed. The Suffolk County Board of Supervisors turned down Moses's plan saying it was too costly. An angry Moses predicted that Fire Island would be washed away within months.

Well, it's still standing there, looking as beautiful as ever despite further efforts by Moses in the 1950s and 1960s to implement development plans. Except for a road that connects, yes, Robert Moses State Park on the island's western tip to the mainland, there are no roads on Fire Island. The 17 summer resort communities that exist on the island depend on ferry service from mainland Long Island and are isolated from one another. If you want to travel between the communities, you must walk, use a boat, or take a water taxi (which operates only a handful of months during the year).

Most of the land is now protected from development by the federal government which has designated the land Fire Island National Seashore. This walking tour takes you to two of the national seashore's most spectacular areas: Sailors Haven, which contains the Sunken Forest, and Watch Hill.

The dense trees and vines in the shady Sunken Forest come as quite a surprise for first-time visitors who expect little cover from the sun near a barrier island beach. As you walk on the boardwalk that leads through the trees, you immediately realize that the 36-acre Sunken Forest is a magical wonderland, a forest so compact and surreal that it seems like a place that must have been created for a Hollywood set.

But, no, this is the real thing, and there's no forest in the country quite like it. Pruned by driving winds and salt-filled air, the trees and other vegetation grow only to the height of the nearby dunes and then grow horizontally. Two-hundred-year-old holly trees stand next to sassafras, tupelo, cedar, oak, and

▼

other hardwood trees, and tangled vines of grapes and catbrier jut out in every direction. Thick patches of poison ivy menace all who intrude this jungle-like setting, but the ivy's brilliant red color adds a lively and warm painter's touch in the fall. Deer bound through the forest; fox, raccoons, weasels, and mice scurry about, and birds flutter from tree to tree.

But the striking aspect is the quiet of this wondrous forest so close to the roaring ocean breakers. With tall dunes nearby and the Sunken Forest's thick canopy of gnarled trees providing natural soundproofing, you can't hear the sound of the 10,000 waves that daily pound the shore and carry away about a half million cubic yards of sand westward each year. In the off-season, this peaceful forest may often be yours to walk alone.

About seven miles east of Sunken Forest sits the very different but also fascinating landscape of Watch Hill, which you can reach by ferry from Patchogue or by hiring a water taxi at Sailors Haven. Located at the western border of the seven-mile Otis Pike Wilderness Area, Watch Hill consists of wild salt marsh and dense groves of pitch pine and holly, sandwiched between the bay and the ocean. A boardwalk that has been restored since a vicious northeaster storm ripped it apart in 1991 takes you over the marsh and then through a woodland filled with short shadblow trees to a great ocean viewpoint and, eventually, the soft sandy shore by the crashing breakers.

GETTING THERE
By train:

To get to the Sunken Forest from Manhattan, take the Long Island Railroad (718-217-5477) from Penn Station to Sayville. Grab a local taxi such as Colonial Car Service (516-589-3500) for the five-minute ($2-$3) ride to the ferry terminal where you catch the ferry to Sailors Haven. For the ferry schedule, call Sayville Ferry Service (516-589-0810). Ferries operate mid-May through the third Sun. in Oct. The round-trip fare is $8.

▼

To get to Watch Hill from Manhattan, take the Long Island Railroad from Penn Station to Patchogue. Walk south past Division St. and proceed several hundred feet on West Ave. to the ferry terminal. For the ferry schedule, call Davis Park Ferry Company (516-475-1665). Ferries operate mid-May through mid-Oct. The one-way fare is $5.50.

By car:

From Manhattan to Sayville (where you catch the ferry to Sailors Haven), take the Long Island Expwy. (I-495) east to exit 59. Turn right onto County Rd. 93 south (don't go north toward Ronkonkoma). In a few minutes, you follow the road as it veers to the left (you're now on Lakeland Ave.). Cross Rte. 27 (Sunrise Hwy.). Cross the railroad tracks into Sayville (Lakeland Ave. becomes Railroad Ave.). Turn left onto Main St. (Montauk Hwy.) and then immediately bear right on a road to the right of a town monument displaying an eagle atop a globe. At the first light, turn right onto Foster Ave. Turn left onto Terry St. Follow the green signs for the ferry. At the Cull House restaurant, make a right turn onto River Rd. Park in the parking lot on the right ($7 daily) or in the next lot down the street, which has a cheaper rate.

From Manhattan to Patchogue (where you can catch the ferry to Fire Island's Watch Hill), take the Long Island Expwy. (I-495) east to exit 61. Turn right and head south for more than five miles on Rte. 19. Cross a bridge over Rte. 27 (Sunrise Hwy.). Go through three traffic lights. Get in the left lane. When the road splits, follow the road to the left onto Lake St. At the next fork, stay to the right, following a sign to Watch Hill. Cross Main St. and get in the left lane. Cross the railroad tracks and then cross Division St. Proceed several hundred feet on West Ave. To your right is the ferry terminal that will take you to Watch Hill.

The ferry terminals in Sayville and Patchogue are about 6 mi. apart.

▼

Walk 1 Directions

TIME: 1 hour
LEVEL: Easy
DISTANCE: 1 1/2 mi.
ACCESS: By car or train,
and ferry

TO BEGIN

Get off the ferry and go toward Fire Island National Seashore Visitors Center. Turn right before the front steps of the visitors center and follow the boardwalk several steps to an intersection. Don't turn left; instead, continue straight across the boardwalk.

1. Walk on a narrower boardwalk with a sign "Trail to Sunken Forest." Continue on the boardwalk as it curves through the woods. **For environmental reasons, walkers are prohibited from straying from the boardwalk.** In about five minutes, you pass over a freshwater marsh with a great view of the Sunken Forest. *Deer are abundant in this area.*

2. In another 10 minutes, turn right when you reach a wooden deck with trees growing between the planks. Exit the deck and follow a boardwalk heading to the right. In a few minutes you pass through a salt marsh and reach the Great South Bay. *There's a turnoff to the right that offers a great view and a park bench to relax on.* Continue on to the left. Follow the boardwalk as it turns to the left away from the bay. Pass a seating area on the right and continue on as the boardwalk winds through the forest. Head uphill until the boardwalk emerges at a clearing overlooking the Atlantic Ocean. *To your right is the community of Point O' Woods.* Cross over the sandy trail nicknamed the Burma Rd. and head toward the ocean. Pass outhouses on your left. *Notice how the pine trees to your left grow horizontally instead of vertically.*

3. At the next intersection, turn left onto a boardwalk.

▼

Cross again over the sandy Burma Rd. Pass "Sunken Forest" sign on your left. Turn left and walk up stairs. Turn right and follow the boardwalk on your left uphill. Step up to the benches at a viewing area. *This viewpoint is the highest point on Fire Island.* Don't proceed down the steps to the left; instead, turn around and retrace your steps past the sign that's now on your right. Again cross the sandy Burma Rd. At the next intersection (Point 3), continue straight and follow the boardwalk uphill toward the ocean. Proceed across the beach toward the water.

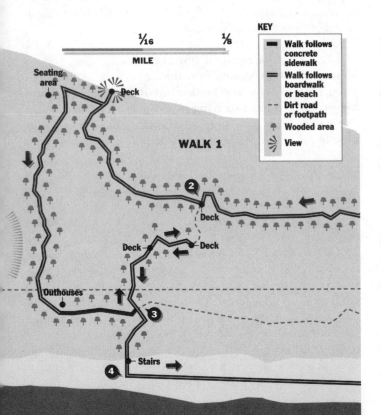

KEY

██ Walk follows concrete sidewalk

═ Walk follows boardwalk or beach

-- Dirt road or footpath

Wooded area

View

WALK 1

ATLANTIC OCEAN

▼

4. At the water's edge, turn left and head east on the beach. *The community in the distance is Cherry Grove.*

5. In about 15 minutes, turn left and head across the beach toward a large brown "Fire Island National Seashore" sign atop the dunes. Ascend the stairs and pass the sign on your right. Cross a sidewalk and continue on a boardwalk. Pass bathrooms on your left and continue on the boardwalk to the ferry dock.

Walk 2 Directions

TIME: 45 minutes
LEVEL: Easy
DISTANCE: 1 1/2 miles
ACCESS: By car or train, and ferry

TO BEGIN

Get off the ferry and pass Watch Hill Visitor Center. Head down the dock.

1.. At the end of the dock before a "Watch Hill" sign, turn left and walk on a wooden boardwalk. Ignore a boardwalk on the right and a dock to the left.

2. At a park maintenance office on your right, turn left and head down another dock with the water to your left. *Notice a picnic area with charcoal grills that's on your right.* Continue down the dock as it angles to your left.

3. After a few hundred yards, just before a maintenance shack ahead on your left, turn right onto a wooden boardwalk heading over a salt marsh.

4. In a minute, turn left at a boardwalk intersection and pass a park bench on your right. Continue on the boardwalk over water at the edge of the marsh. Pass another bench on your left. Pass two more benches at an enclosed area to your left. Follow the boardwalk as it turns right. Continue on as it

▼

turns left and then right. *You're passing by short shadblow trees.* Follow the boardwalk as it winds and then turns 90 degrees to the right. *On your right are holly trees.* Follow the boardwalk as

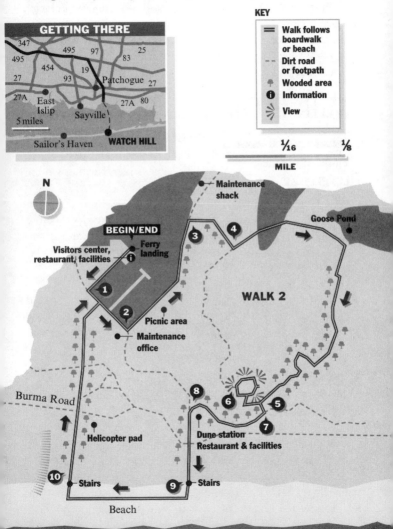

KEY

══ Walk follows boardwalk or beach

- - - Dirt road or footpath

🌲 Wooded area

ℹ Information

⤡ View

GETTING THERE

347
495   495   97   25
27   454   93   19   83
27A   East Islip   Sayville   Patchogue   27
5 miles   27A   80
Sailor's Haven   **WATCH HILL**

1/16   1/8

MILE

N

Maintenance shack

Goose Pond

BEGIN/END

Ferry landing

Visitors center, restaurant, facilities   ℹ

1
2   ③   ④

WALK 2

Picnic area

Maintenance office

Burma Road

8

6   5

7

Helicopter pad

Dune station
Restaurant & facilities

10   Stairs   9   Stairs

Beach

ATLANTIC OCEAN

▼

it turns 90 degrees to the left and then winds through the marsh. *Rabbits and wild geese frequent this area.*

5. At a boardwalk intersection, turn right and head uphill. Follow the boardwalk as it again turns to the right. Ignore a boardwalk to the left and continue straight up the stairs. Take about 15 steps and stop at the bench area on your right. *This is a great Atlantic Ocean viewpoint.* Continue on, turn left, and proceed down the stairs. Pass a bench on your right.

6. At an intersection, turn left and head uphill. Turn right before the stairs. Follow the boardwalk as it turns 90 degrees to the left. At the next intersection (Point 5), turn right.

7. Take a few steps and turn right again. Pass a few picnic tables on your left. Ignore a boardwalk to your left heading to the group campsite. Continue on toward a dune station.

8. At an intersection just before the dune station, turn left and head uphill past bathrooms, telephones, and a first-aid station. Go straight up a boardwalk ramp and cross over the sand dunes to the right and the left. *Stay on the boardwalk—poison ivy grows atop the dunes. The area to your left is the only federal wilderness area in New York State.* Descend downstairs toward the beach. **For environmental reasons, please stay off the dunes and the dune grass.**

9. Turn right and walk west down the beach. *Ahead in the distance is the community of Davis Park.*

10. After about 200 yards, turn right. Head up the stairs climbing over the dunes and away from the ocean. Follow the boardwalk downhill toward the National Park Service facilities and Great South Bay. Pass a wooden helicopter landing pad on your right that's used for medical emergencies. At an intersection, continue straight. Ignore a boardwalk to the left unless you want to head for Davis Park. Continue on, ignoring the next boardwalk on your left. **The National Park Service requests that visitors stay away from their facilities on your left and your right.** Continue on the boardwalk as it turns to the right toward the ferry dock.

OTHER PLACES NEARBY

■ **Bayard Cutting Arboretum.** Besides a fine collection of plants and trees, this 690-acre arboretum features several scenic walking trails. You can walk along the Connetquot River to a bird sanctuary and visit woodland, meadows, and marsh land. *Box 466, Oakdale, NY 11769; tel. 516-581-1002. Open Wed.-Sun. 10-5 during Daylight Savings; 10-4 rest of year. Admission (no charge on weekdays the day after Labor Day-Mar. 31, or on weekends Nov.-Mar.). Off Montauk Hwy. in Great River, about 7 mi. west of Sayville ferry terminal.*

■ **Fire Island Lighthouse.** You can visit the visitors center in the keeper's quarters next to the 19th-century lighthouse. For a lighthouse tour, call the Park Service in advance. *Fire Island National Seashore, Fire Island, NY; tel. 516-289-4810 (park headquarters), 516-661-4876 (lighthouse office). Visitors center open Wed.-Sun. 9-5:30 Jul. 4-Labor Day; Sat.-Sun. 9-5:30 the rest of the year. Cross the Robert Moses Causeway to the western end of Fire Island and park in field 5. Walk 1/2 mi. east to the lighthouse.*

■ **Heckscher State Park.** This 1,700-acre park jutting out into Great South Bay is a summertime favorite of Long Islanders. You can swim in the bay or in an ocean-view swimming pool. A paved path is available for cyclists, and there are 69 campsites. *Box 153, East Islip, NY 11730; tel. 516-581-2100. Open daily sunrise-sunset. Park office in field 1 open Memorial Day-Labor Day 8-6; 8-4 the rest of the year. Admission. On Heckscher Pkwy., about 13 mi. west of Sayville ferry terminal.*

▼

DINING

Sailors Haven has a snack bar and a picnic area. If you're looking for more substantial fare, you must return to the Long Island
mainland or walk on Fire Island about a half mile east to the gay
resort community of Cherry Grove. You can catch a ferry to Sayville
from Cherry Grove which, unlike the Sunken Forest, has frequent
service. Watch Hill has a restaurant listed below and a snack bar.

■ **Seashore Inn.** This dockside Fire Island restaurant cooks
such well-prepared standards as roast Long Island duck, shrimp
scampi, stuffed flounder, and filet mignon. A variety of pastas
round out the menu. *Box 128, Blue Point, NY 11715; tel. 516-597-
6655. Open Fri.-Sun. for dinner Memorial Day-mid-June; open
Tue.-Fri. for dinner and Sat.-Sun. for lunch and dinner mid-June-
Labor Day. Bar open through mid-Oct. Adjoining snack bar open
daily for lunch mid-May-mid-Oct. At Watch Hill Marina.*

■ **Le Soir** (expensive). In a Tudor-like building, this classic
French restaurant with friendly hosts and fresh flowers on the
table has a skillful hand with seafood. The menu includes such
specialties as lobster with whiskey sauce and a fabulous appetizer of sautéed crab cakes. *825 Montauk Hwy., Bayport, NY
11705; tel. 516-472-9090. Open Tue.-Sun. for dinner. About 4
mi. northeast of the Sayville ferry terminal.*

■ **Top of the Bay** (expensive). Sitting next to the Great
South Bay in a gay resort community, this restaurant has excel-
lent water views and good seafood with a southwestern flair.
Expect about eight seafood specials daily, as well as steak and
chicken. Come early for a table on the outside patio *Box 4134,
Cherry Grove, NY 11782; tel. 516-597-6699. Open daily for din-
ner and for Sun. brunch first week of May-first week of Oct. On
Dock Walk, next to the Cherry Grove ferry terminal.*

■ **Cafe Joelle on Main St.** (moderate). The decor isn't
impressive, but you'll love the creative meals and the lengthy
list of wines by the glass. You can order a burger for dinner but
will be a lot happier with a fresh pasta or a seafood dish. The
seafood ravioli and the penne California—artichoke hearts, sun-

▼

dried tomatoes, shiitaki mushrooms, basil, and garlic—won't disappoint. *25 Main St., Sayville, NY 11782; tel. 516-589-4600. Open daily for lunch and dinner; Sun. brunch. About 2 mi. north of the Sayville ferry terminal.*

■ **Cilantro's** (moderate). An eclectic, often brilliantly executed American menu with plenty of Italian touches pleases patrons at this small South Shore eatery. Reserve a corner table in the soft-pastel interior dining room, away from the bar. Keep an eye out for such entrees as roasted Long Island duck with a merlot and green peppercorn sauce and pesto-seared salmon. *154 Montauk Hwy., Blue Point, NY 11715; tel. 516-363-0500. Open daily except Mon. for dinner. About 4 mi. east of the Sayville ferry terminal or 4 mi. west of the Patchogue ferry terminal.*

LODGING

Sailors Haven and Watch Hill are daytrip destinations. There are no lodging options and no quality lodgings near the mainland ferry terminals. About a half-mile walk east of Sailors Haven in Cherry Grove, some accommodations—catering primarily to a gay clientele—are available (for information, call the tourism bureau below).

FOR MORE INFORMATION
Tourist Offices:

■ **Fire Island National Seashore.** *120 Laurel St., Patchogue, NY 11772; tel. 516-289-4810. Office open Mon.-Fri. 8-4:30. South of Montauk Hwy., off West Ave.*

■ **Fire Island Tourism Bureau.** The office handles telephone and written inquiries for information. *49 Main St., Sayville, NY 11782; tel. 516-563-8448.*

For Serious Walkers:

Besides a seven-mile wilderness walk from Watch Hill east to Smith Point, there's a one-mile boardwalk trail at Smith Point and a four-mile walk east from Smith Point to Moriches Inlet. The hearty can walk the entire 32-mile length of Fire Island.

In the Footsteps of Walt Whitman

EXPERIENCE 13:
WHITMAN HOUSE

Many places on Long Island inspired the writing of America's great poet Walt Whitman, but none was more meaningful than West Hills. Whitman was born there on May 31, 1819, and later fell in love with its nat-

The Highlights: The home of Walt Whitman, landscapes that inspired the poet, Long Island's highest point, excellent dining.

Other Places Nearby: An attractive harborside village with a whaling museum, President Theodore Roosevelt's mansion, the Vanderbilt mansion and planetarium.

ural beauty. He admired the tall trees, apple orchards, cornfields, and pastureland that stretched for miles.

Your walk begins at the old wooden farmhouse where he lived until just before his fourth birthday. "O to go back to the place where I was born,/To hear the birds sing once more,/To ramble about the house and barn and over the fields once more,/And through the orchard and along the old lanes once more." The author of those passionate lines in the poem "A Song of Joys" would be shocked today to find a shopping mall in his name on a commercial strip adjacent to his home. Thankfully, the wooden farmhouse is removed from the bustle,

▼

and this walking tour leads you into a peaceful county-run forest that has withstood decades of surrounding development.

You follow Whitman's footsteps to the top of 401-foot Jayne's Hill, Long Island's highest natural point, from which Whitman enjoyed sweeping views. "I write this back again in West Hills on the high elevation of Jayne's Hill which we have reached by a fascinating winding road," wrote an elderly Whitman during one of his last visits to the hilltop. "A view of 30 or 40 or even 50 or more miles, especially to the east and south and southwest; the Atlantic Ocean to the latter points in the distance—a glimpse or so of Long Island Sound to the north." Today, leaves of tall trees that have grown next to the hill block much of the view in summer, and you'll need a crystal-clear day—and a rabbit's foot—to spot the distant ocean. But it's still a fascinating historical spot and a nice introduction to the wonders of the soft, sand-bottomed forest you are about to explore. You weave your way around oak, maple, beech, ash, and long-needled pine trees and can stop at a riding stable for a horseback ride through the forest.

Whitman's family left this land for Brooklyn, where Walt attended public schools until the age of 11 and started work as a printer's apprentice the following year. He returned to Long Island in 1836 to teach in rural schools in Woodbury and Huntington, living with families in the school districts. Two years later he started editing *The Long-Islander* newspaper and began working in the presidential campaign of Martin Van Buren.

Between 1842 and 1848, he bounced from newspaper to newspaper in New York City. He served as an editor for such papers as *The New York Mirror, The Tattler, The New York Democrat, New York Sun,* and the *Brooklyn Daily Eagle,* where he was fired for his anti-slavery views. He departed for a three-month stint down south at the *New Orleans Crescent* before returning to New York to dabble in several jobs: building contractor, real estate speculator, manager of a stationery and printing store, and freelance writer.

Finally in 1855, he published the first edition of *Leaves of Grass,* his first poetry book. The 83-page book contained a dozen poems and a picture of Whitman but included no author's name. An even greater oddity—one that turned off many literary critics of the era—was that none of the poems rhymed.

The unconventional book spoke mostly about the lives and occupations of the everyday man as well as the direction of democracy in America. It angered many readers by promoting equality of the sexes and equality of the rich and the poor. But many critics were even more incensed by his glorification of the naked body. His former paper *The Long-Islander* called *Leaves of Grass* a "dirty book," citing the sexual content in some of the lines.

Most bookstores refused to carry it, but Whitman was not deterred. He sent a copy to the most renowned U.S. poet of the time, Ralph Waldo Emerson, though the two had never met. Emerson fell in love with Whitman's poetry. In a private letter to Whitman, Emerson praised *Leaves of Grass* as "the most extraordinary piece of wit and wisdom that America has yet contributed." Whitman, ever the self promoter, hustled to put out a second edition. Without receiving permission, he published Emerson's letter to stimulate sales and convince the critics of the importance of his works. Emerson was furious, but Whitman continued to promote.

He eventually would produce nine editions of *Leaves of Grass,* each with different poems included inside. During his lifetime, his poetry became known throughout America and England, but it never made Whitman wealthy. He constantly had to fight a backlash from critics who deemed several of his poems obscene. While working as a clerk in the Department of the Interior's Indian Affairs Bureau in 1865, he was fired by Interior Secretary James Harlan for being the writer of an "indecent" book.

But Whitman's works withstood the test of time, and he

▼

became known after his death as, arguably, America's greatest poet, as well as the poet of democracy. Millions have been moved by the sheer beauty of his writing and by his fervent love for the geography of Long Island, including the land you are passing through during your walking tour.

GETTING THERE
By car:

From New York City, take the Long Island Expwy. (I-495) east to exit 49. Follow Rte. 110 north for 1 8/10 mi. Turn left at a brown sign for the Walt Whitman Historic Site onto Old Walt Whitman Rd. Ahead on your right is the Walt Whitman Birthplace parking lot.

Walk Directions

TIME: 2 1/2 hours
LEVEL: Easy
DISTANCE: 4 1/2 miles
ACCESS: By car

You can cut off 1 2/10 mi. of the walk by driving from the Walt Whitman Birthplace parking lot to the end of Reservoir Rd. If you choose to drive, follow the directions below to Point 3 and park your car on the road near the ranger station. You can picnic atop Jaynes Hill or at picnic tables next to the riding stables in Point 14. Picnic provisions can be bought at numerous stores on busy Rte. 110. For information about horseback riding, call 516-854-4949.

TO BEGIN

Walk out of the parking lot and turn left onto Old Walt Whitman Rd.

1. Make the first right turn onto West Hills Rd.

2. Turn left onto Reservoir Rd.

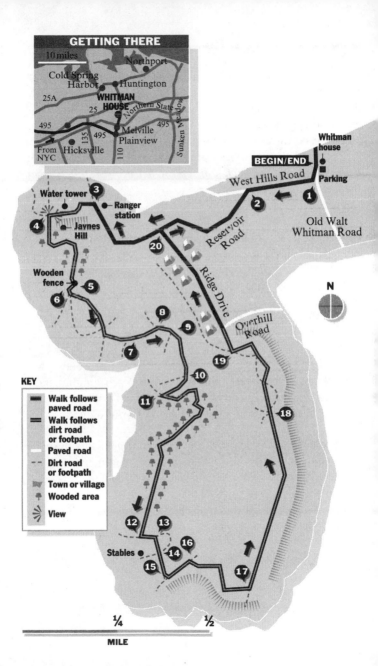

10 miles

Northport

Cold Spring
Harbor

Huntington

25A

WHITMAN
HOUSE

Northern State

25

495

Melville
Plainview

495

From
NYC

Hicksville

135

110

Sunken Meadow

Whitman
house

BEGIN/END

Parking

West Hills Road

1

2

Old Walt
Whitman Road

Water tower

3

Ranger
station

Reservoir Road

4

Jaynes
Hill

20

Wooden
fence

5

Ridge Drive

6

8

9

Overhill
Road

7

19

10

11

18

KEY

Walk follows
paved road

Walk follows
dirt road
or footpath

Paved road

Dirt road
or footpath

Town or village

Wooded area

View

N

12

13

16

Stables

14

15

17

1/4

1/2

MILE

▼

3. When you reach a ranger station on your right just before the paved road ends, turn left onto a blacktop path that ascends the hill. Continue through a gate and follow a grass-and-pebble trail uphill. Pass a water tank on your right and proceed toward a boulder at the top of Jaynes Hill. Stop at the boulder. *You're now standing at the highest point on Long Island. There's a view when the leaves have fallen from the trees.*

4. Turn left at the boulder (ignoring the trails straight ahead and to the right) and follow a narrow trail downhill. You are following the red-dot trail (a red dot inside a white circle). At one point ahead, you duck underneath branches and vines.

5. After walking about seven minutes since leaving the boulder atop Jaynes Hill, turn right onto a dirt path.

6. At a junction of three paths, turn left and proceed down a white- and red-blazed trail. When you reach another trail, continue straight on the white- and red-blazed trail past a sign (with a symbol for a walking path) that's on your right.

7. When you reach the next trail, turn left onto the trail and head uphill. Ignore a trail on your right and then a trail on your left. Continue on the white- and red-blazed trail.

8. At a junction of two trails, turn right following the white and red blazes.

9. About 20 yards ahead, turn left and follow white and red blazes.

10. At a junction of trails, follow the trail to the left downhill.

▼

11. In about a minute, when the trail curves sharply to the right, turn left into dense woods. Follow the white and red blazes marked on a small tree and pass a sign (with a symbol for a walking path) on your right. Follow the trail uphill and then proceed for about 10 minutes as it snakes through the woods.

12. At a junction of trails, turn left. Walk about 20 yards.

13. Turn right and walk past another walking-path sign. Follow the white and red blazes.

14. At a junction of trails, continue straight. Ignore a trail to the right heading to stables, unless you'd like to rent a horse or visit a picnic area (the walk to the stables or the picnic area takes about two minutes).

15. At a junction of trails, bear left. Immediately, you reach another junction. Turn left onto a wide path. Ignore a narrow path to the left that heads into the woods. Continue uphill.

16. At a junction, follow the trail to the right as it proceeds sharply uphill.

17. At a junction, turn left and follow the red-cross trail (red cross inside a white circle).

18. At a junction, follow the trail to the right uphill. Ignore a narrow trail on your left and then another branching off to the right. Continue straight on the widest trail. It soon goes downhill. At a junction, bear right following the red-cross trail. Continue straight. Ignore a trail to the left, indicated by a brown sign with a white arrow.

19. At a trail junction, turn right. Follow a wide dirt path until it ends at a paved road. Continue straight onto the paved

▼

road (Ridge Dr.). Pass Overhill Rd. and proceed straight on Ridge Dr. *You've now emerged from the woods, with residential houses on both sides of the street.*

20. When you reach Reservoir Rd., turn right and retrace your steps to Walt Whitman's house. (Turn left instead, if your car is parked near the ranger station.)

PLACES ALONG THE WALK
■ **Walt Whitman Birthplace.** This simple wood-beam farmhouse is hidden on a relatively quiet street near a bustling shopping mall named after the poet. A new visitors center with a permanent Whitman exhibit is scheduled to open in spring 1996. The center will feature bimonthly entertainment: poetry readings, dance, and music. *246 Old Walt Whitman Rd., Huntington Station, NY 11746-4148; tel. 516-427-5240. Open Wed.-Fri. 1-4; Sat.-Sun. 10-4.*

OTHER PLACES NEARBY
■ **Coe Hall and Planting Fields Arboretum.** An early 20th-century, Tudor-revival 65-room mansion sits on 400 acres of sweeping lawns, cultivated gardens, and woodlands. Many of the more than 400 species of trees and shrubs have been imported from Europe and Asia. Mozart and Beethoven festivals are held annually, and a concert series that has featured such artists as Judy Collins, Aaron Neville, Michael Feinstein, and the Preservation Hall Jazz Band is presented July-September by Friends of the Arts (516-922-0061). *Planting Fields Rd., Oyster Bay, NY 11771; tel. 516-922-9201. Arboretum open daily 9-5. Coe Hall open daily 12:30-3:30. Admission. North of both Long Island Expwy. exit 41N and Rte. 25A (N. Hempstead Tpke.). About 18 mi. northwest of Walt Whitman Birthplace.*

■ **Cold Spring Harbor.** This historic village next to Long Island Sound has funky stores selling antiques, books, and other wares. Its whaling museum contains a 30-foot whaleboat.

▼

Cold Spring Harbor Whaling Museum (516-367-3418) open daily 11-5 Memorial Day weekend-Labor Day; open Tue.-Sun. 11-5 the rest of the year. The village is on Rte. 25A, about 8 mi. northwest of Walt Whitman Birthplace.

■ **Old Bethpage Village Restoration.** This restored 15-building village depicts a pre-Civil War rural Long Island community. You visit an old church, an inn, a schoolhouse, blacksmith and hat shops, and assorted homes. Various festivals are held throughout the year, and historically correct 19th-century baseball games are played on certain days. *Round Swamp Rd., Old Bethpage, NY 11804; tel. 516-572-8401; fax 516-572-8413. Open Wed.-Sun 10-5. Last ticket sold at 4. Call to check winter schedule. Admission. 1/2 mi. south of Long Island Expwy. exit 48; about 6 mi. southwest of Walt Whitman Birthplace.*

■ **Sagamore Hill National Historic Site.** This 23-room Victorian mansion was President Teddy Roosevelt's summer White House from 1901 to 1909. Determined to have a good home for his daughter, Roosevelt paid $16,975 to build the house in 1884. An avid hunter, Roosevelt mounted numerous animal trophies on the walls. *20 Cold Neck Rd., Oyster Bay, NY 11771; tel. 516-922-4447; fax 516-922-4792. Park open daily 9-dusk; house tours daily 9:30-4:30, 9:30-4 in winter. Closed Mon.-Tue. Jan.-Apr. Admission. North of Rte. 25A, about 13 mi. northwest of Walt Whitman Birthplace.*

■ **Suffolk County Vanderbilt Museum and Planetarium.** There's plenty to see at this North Shore site: the 21-room Spanish-revival-style mansion of yachtsman William Vanderbilt, a museum with more than 17,000 animal and marine specimens, and a planetarium with a 16-inch telescope. *180 Little Neck Rd., Centerport, NY 11721; tel. 516-854-5555. Open Tue.-Sat. 10-5, Sun. 11-6 late Jun.-Labor Day; Tue.-Sat. 10-4, Sun.12-5 the rest of the year. Admission. 1 1/2 mi. north of Rte. 25A; about 12 mi. northeast of Walt Whitman Birthplace.*

DINING

■ **P. G. Steak House** (very expensive). You come to this

▼

traditional New York steak house to order one of three choices featured in a large rectangular box in the middle of the menu: single steak, steak for two, or steak for three. After you've devoured a succulent Porterhouse slab underneath former Mets shortstop Buddy Harrelson's autographed picture, you can relax in the relatively intimate dining room and ease into something maybe a bit lighter: cheesecake or pecan pie with whipped cream. *1745 E. Jericho Tpk., Huntington, NY 11743; tel. 516-499-1005. Open Mon.-Fri. for lunch and dinner, Sat.-Sun. for dinner only. About 7 mi. northeast of Walt Whitman Birthplace.*

■ **Panama Hattie's** (expensive). Chef Blake Verity succeeds brilliantly with his eclectic nouvelle cuisine dishes in this chic black-leather-seat eatery. His team of eight cooks does wonders with fish and game, and the presentations are spectacular. The menu changes weekly, but look for a Dungeness crab ravioli appetizer and such entrees as rack of lamb with pumpkin gnocchi and salmon with portobello crust atop a cranberry bean and cabbage cassoulet. Leave some room for the mouthwatering desserts. *872 E. Jericho Tpk., Huntington Station, NY 11746; tel. 516-351-1727, 800-439-3463. Open Mon.-Sat. for lunch and dinner; Sun. for brunch and dinner. About 6 mi. northeast of Walt Whitman Birthplace.*

■ **Canterbury Ales** (moderate). The walls of this British-style pub and restaurant are adorned with the autographed cartoons of the creator of "The Lockhorns" strip, the late Bill Hoest, whose son is the owner. Bill Hoest Jr. has a classy tap featuring Fullers, a traditional British ale, and gorgeously smooth Watney's Cream Stout. The food leaves the Brits in the dust, with attractively presented specials as well as burgers and other standard fare. Keep an eye out for special pastas and a tasty veal chop. *314 New York Ave., Huntington, NY 11743; tel. 516-549-4404. Open daily for lunch and dinner. About 5 mi. north of Walt Whitman Birthplace in the heart of Huntington.*

■ **The Crossroads Cafe** (moderate). An ugly exterior is forgotten when you discover the creative continental American

▼

cuisine inside. The seasonal soups burst with flavor, and the pastas are winners. For appetizers, look for oysters "a la Roberto" (oysters with zucchini, white wine, and parmesan cheese) and grilled Cajun shrimp. Stellar entrées have included salmon filet with horseradish crust, veal chop, and various lamb dishes. Desserts are outstanding, including the chocolate mousse. *26 Laurel Rd., East Northport, NY 11731; tel. 516-754-2000. Open Mon.-Sat. for lunch and dinner; Sun. for dinner. About 9 mi. northeast of Walt Whitman Birthplace.*

■ **Trattoria Grasso** (moderate). The quarters are small, so book in advance at this popular restaurant. Regulars keep returning for the fresh pasta and risotto dishes. The kitchen tries to keep the fare on the light side. The owners also operate a like-named restaurant in Cold Spring Harbor (516-367-6060). *9 Union Pl., Huntington, NY; tel. 516-351-1200. Open Tue.-Fri. and Sun. for lunch and dinner, Sat. for dinner only. Closed for lunch in summer. Off New York Ave. (Rte. 110 north becomes New York Ave.), about 6 mi. north of Walt Whitman Birthplace.*

■ **Los Compadres** (inexpensive). Don't come with any pretensions to this bright, red-brick Mexican restaurant with a yellow awning. Just take a seat at one of the four Formica tables, grab a soda (including exotic south-of-the-border concoctions) out of the refrigerator, and use your plastic cutlery to devour delicious, often poorly presented, home-cooked chow. You can expect first-rate tamales, chimichangas, guacamole, salsa, and warm chips. *243 Old Walt Whitman Rd., Huntington Station, NY 11746; tel. 516-351-8384. Open daily for lunch and dinner. Across the street from Walt Whitman Birthplace.*

LODGING

Chain hotels are the only choice in the immediate area around the Walt Whitman Birthplace. If you're looking for lodging with character, head for Northport, a 15-minute drive. The two homes listed below have a limited number of rooms, so you may want to contact the Northport Chamber of Commerce

▼

(516-754-3905) for any new establishments.

■ **The Moran House** (moderate). This charming late 19th-century Victorian sits on a quiet street with attractive homes next to the harbor. The house has stained-glass windows, a working fireplace, and a wraparound porch that's ideal for breakfast. Ask for the turret room with its five windows surrounding a queen-size bed. An inexpensively priced room with a shared bath and a water view is also available. Tolstoy supposedly stayed in the home when it was owned by a Russian count. *155 Bayview Ave., Northport, NY 11768; tel. 516-261-0091. About 12 mi. northeast of Walt Whitman Birthplace.*

■ **Sailor's Rest** (inexpensive). This three-floor 1850 colonial sits across from a small waterfront park and boatyard on a street with attractive homes. You can choose between two second-floor rooms: one with a water view, the other more spacious with a garden view. To always provide a private bath, the owners rent only one of the rooms at a time (unless a guest books both). A full breakfast is served on the front porch in the summer. *64 Bayview Ave., Northport, NY 11768; tel. 516-757-0216. About 12 mi. northeast of Walt Whitman Birthplace.*

FOR MORE INFORMATION
Tourist Office:

■ **Huntington Township Chamber of Commerce.** *151 W. Carver St., Huntington, NY 11743; tel. 516-423-6100; fax 516-351-8276. Open Mon.-Fri. 9-5. About 5 mi. north of Walt Whitman Birthplace.*

For Serious Walkers:

■ **Long Island Greenbelt Trail Conference, Inc.** You can explore several other trails in West Hills County Park (516-854-4423) by following a map available from this organization. The group also publishes other maps, including one of the Nassau-Suffolk Trail, which is located near West Hills. *23 Deer Path Rd., Central Islip, N.Y. 11722; tel. 516-360-0753.*

Shelter from the Storm

EXPERIENCE 14:
SHELTER ISLAND

Although only 90 miles away from Manhattan and near the city's summer playground, the Hamptons, it can feel quite remote on Shelter Island. Tourist-related development has been kept to a minimum, and the island—located

The Highlights: Pristine woodlands and tidal wetlands; sandy, undeveloped beaches where Native Americans and smugglers once roamed; excellent B&Bs.

Other Places Nearby: The Hamptons, historic Sag Harbor, award-winning vineyards.

between Long Island's North and South Forks—doesn't have even a single automated teller machine. For decades, local residents have resisted construction of an auto bridge to the Long Island mainland although such a bridge would allow them to go out for an evening in Manhattan or another locale without worrying about catching the last ferry home.

Shelter Island is surrounded by bays: Gardiners, the largest, to the east, and Noyack, Southold, and Little Peconic, all to the west. The remoteness has helped preserve Shelter Island's rolling country lands that reach to the edge of the sea. The most special part of those lands is Mashomack Preserve, a nearly 2,100-acre

▼

natural area that comprises nearly one-third of Shelter Island and is the site of this walking tour. The preserve, acquired by the Nature Conservancy in 1980, combines woodlands, fields, ten miles of coastline, tidal creeks, and numerous salt marshes.

No jogging, bicycling, or horseback riding is allowed, the Nature Conservancy says, because "Mashomack is a museum of life in process, a sanctuary where the natural cycles of flora, fauna, and ecosystems are allowed to complete themselves free from human interference." About 1,400 acres of beech and oak forest are being allowed to mature into an old-growth forest, a scarce phenomenon in the Northeast. On Mashomack's western side, a freshwater wetland—an eco-system that is rapidly disappearing throughout the nation—prospers, untouched by development.

The preserve also protects one of the densest populations of breeding ospreys on the East Coast. Ospreys are large birds that are quite a sight when they swoop down to snatch a fish out of the water. You'll be able to see them and their distinctive nests atop tree limbs from April through August. Some man-made platforms have also been built to assist breeding. This unique eco-system and the rest of Shelter Island was once the domain of the Manhanset tribe and their sachem Pogatticut. Every season except winter, the Manhansets camped at Sachems Neck (Mashomack Preserve), fishing in the creeks and hunting for bear, deer, wolves, and racoons. The Native Americans never built permanent lodging there, opting instead to paddle back and forth to the Long Island mainland by canoe.

British colonists arrived and claimed possession of Shelter Island in 1637. Fourteen years later, the deputy governor sold the entire island to four merchants for 1,600 pounds of sugar valued at $80. The Nicolls, a wealthy English family with close ties to the royal family, bought Sachems Neck in 1706, and their descendants owned the property until 1931.

▼

In between those years, many memorable events transpired. In 1776, during the Revolutionary War, the British won the Battle of Brooklyn and seized control of Long Island. Only one-third of Shelter Island's 27 families heeded George Washington's call to abandon their houses, travel across Long Island Sound, and relocate in Connecticut. After all the hard work establishing their homes, most residents couldn't simply sail away from beloved Shelter Island. They were forced to live under martial law for the next ten years and watch the British strip the island's fences for fuel. Food was scarce, the British pillaged their lands, and residents suspected of siding with the patriots were mistreated.

During the War of 1812, Shelter Island residents again feared a British invasion. The attacking British had burned nearby Sag Harbor and wrecked towns on the Connecticut coast, but this time they spared Shelter Island.

Throughout the rest of the 19th century and well into the 20th, Shelter Island remained an unknown rural spot on the map, home primarily to farmers and fishermen. Crops included potatoes, barley, and rye, and animals yielded meat, cheese, butter, and wool. Fishermen made their income largely through menhaden, an oily fish used for fertilizer and crushed into oil for varnish and paintbrushes. The processing of the fish released an awful smell into the island's air. The processing plants eventually shut down

In 1925, rich German banker Otto Kahn arrived on the island. Without seeing the Mashomack land, Kahn plunked down $250,000 for much of it, expecting that a bridge would be built to the mainland and real estate values would soar. During the next four years, Kahn pulled up only twice in his Rolls-Royce to see his property and apparently had no idea what was happening on his land when he wasn't around. Speedboats laden with all kinds of liquor were evading U.S. Coast Guard vessels and dropping their cargo at Mashomack in violation of Prohibition laws. The smugglers would pick up the

▼

booze from Caribbean and Canadian ships outside U.S. territori-
al waters and then head for Mashomack's tree-lined coast.
Buick roadsters—each able to handle 50 cases of liquor with
the rumble seat removed—picked up the booty and took off
for the ferries bound for New York City.

GETTING THERE
By car:

From New York City, take the Long Island Expwy. (I-495)
east until it ends at exit 73 in Riverhead. Follow Rte. 58, which
becomes Rte. 25, 28 mi. east to Greenport.

At the first traffic light in Greenport, turn right onto Second
St. Drive your car onto the ferry for a 7-minute trip to Shelter
Island. Follow Rte. 114 south for about 3 mi. as it zigzags down
the island past two traffic circles. Continue on Rte. 114 south
another 1/10 mi. past Heritage Rd. (on your right) and then
turn left into the front entrance of Mashomack Preserve.

Ferries leave every 15 to 20 minutes daily, from early
morning till late evening. No reservations accepted. Call the
Shelter Island Chamber of Commerce (*see* Tourist Information)
for a recorded message of ferry information; or you can call the
North Ferry Co. at 516-749-0139.

Walk Directions

TIME: 45 minutes to 3 hours
LEVEL: Easy or moderate
DISTANCE: 1 1/2, 3, or 6 miles
ACCESS: By car and auto ferry

The preserve is open
Wed.-Mon. 9-5 Apr.-Sep.
and Wed.-Mon. 9-4 Oct.-
Mar. The entire 6-mi.
walk has few uphill
stretches and is rated
moderate only because of
its length. It can be abbreviated to 1 1/2 mi. by following the
red trail in Point 2 below or to 3 mi. by following the yellow
trail in Point 3. You can pick up picnic provisions at the IGA

supermarket, north of the preserve on Rte. 114.

TO BEGIN

From the parking lot at Mashomack Preserve, proceed to the visitors center. Follow clearly marked signs to the trail entrance just outside the visitors center. Head uphill at a trail entrance sign. Go downhill and cross a wooden bridge. Wind through woods and, when you reach a clearing, bear right following a trail designated by a red arrow.

1. At a trail junction, turn right following the red arrow. You reach a gazebo on your right overlooking Miss Annie's Creek. *The Manhanset tribe set up fishing and hunting camps alongside this creek. The salt marsh is home to many species of fish and birds. Keep an eye out for an osprey darting down into the water for its prey.*

2. When you reach a trail marker a few steps ahead, go straight, ignoring the red-arrow trail on your left. *If you only want a 1 1/2-mi. walk, follow the red trail. You'll eventually reach a major junction, Point 10. Follow the red trail back to your car.* A minute or two after you ignore the red trail, you cross a wooden bridge. Cross the next road you come to and continue straight. Walk on the trail through a meadow. At a junction, turn left following a yellow arrow.

3. At the next junction of three trails, turn right following a green arrow (ignore a blue trail straight ahead and a yellow trail to the left). *If you wish to abbreviate the walk to 3 mi., follow the yellow trail and pick up these walking directions at the end of Point 8, below, as you pass the stone bench.* At the next junction, turn right. In a few minutes, you reach a road. Cross it and continue straight on the trail. Follow the trail as it winds down to the water (Smith Cove) and continue on with the water and a sandy beach to your right. Pass a stone bench on your left.

Proceed down some steps and turn left following the trail.

4. At the next junction, bear right following a green arrow. Ignore a narrow dirt path that leads to a wooden shelter on your right. Continue on as the trail winds to the left and passes a wooden bench on your right.

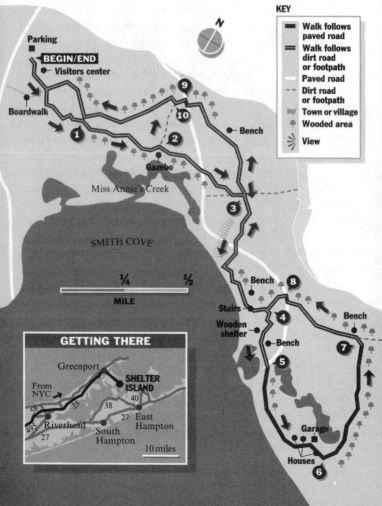

KEY

Walk follows paved road

Walk follows dirt road or footpath

Paved road

Dirt road or footpath

Town or village

Wooded area

View

Parking

BEGIN/END

Visitors center

Boardwalk

Bench

Gazebo

Miss Annie's Creek

SMITH COVE

¼   ½

MILE

Bench

Bench

Stairs

Wooden shelter

Bench

Garage

Houses

GETTING THERE

Greenport

From NYC

SHELTER ISLAND

Riverhead

South Hampton

East Hampton

10 miles

▼

5. About 10 yards farther, turn right onto a road following a green arrow. You emerge from the woods and pass houses on your left (Smith Cove is to your right). At a junction several steps past a garage on your left, continue straight, ignoring a road to the left. Pass alongside a house on your right and continue on into the woods.

6. At the next junction, turn left following a green arrow. At the next junction (the intersection of blue and green trails), continue straight, ignoring a trail to the right.

7. At the next junction, bear left following the green-and-blue arrow. Pass a stone bench on your right. When you reach a road, turn right onto it. Proceed about 25 steps.

8. Turn left onto a trail heading into the woods, following the green-and-blue arrow. In a minute, you reach a trail junction (Point 4); turn right following the green-and-blue arrow. Ascend steps. (You're retracing your earlier steps.) Cross a road and continue straight. At the next junction, turn left onto a grass path following the green-and-blue arrow. At the next junction of blue, yellow, and green trails (Point 3), continue straight, following a yellow arrow. Pass a stone bench on your right. At a road, turn right and proceed about 15 steps.

9. Turn left into the woods following a yellow arrow. In a minute, you reach a trail intersection.

10. Turn right following arrows for red, yellow, blue, and green trails. At the next junction, turn left onto a road, following the red and the yellow arrows. You're walking on pavement. At the next junction, bear right and continue on (ignoring a red-arrow trail to the left). At the next junction, continue straight (you're now following a red arrow), ignoring a trail to the right. You emerge from the woods at the visitors center.

▼

PLACES ALONG THE WALK

■ **Mashomack Preserve Visitors Center.** Informative displays and historical photographs provide an insightful look at the preserve. Pick up a trail map and browse in the interesting gift shop. *Mashomack Preserve, Shelter Island, NY 11964; tel. 516-749-1001. Open daily except Tue. 9-5 (till 4 Sat.-Sun. Oct.-Mar.). On Rte. 114, just north of the South Ferry.*

OTHER PLACES NEARBY

■ **Long Island Wine Country.** Most of Long Island's 17 wineries are on the North Fork, a short drive from the Shelter Island ferry dock in Greenport. Seven are located in Cutchogue, but the closest—Pindar Vineyards (516-734-6200) and The Lenz Winery (516-734-6010)—offer tours and tastings in Peconic, about eight miles west of the ferry dock. You can get a complete list from the Long Island Wine Council (516-369-5887).

■ **Sag Harbor.** This quaint, old whaling town has a nice waterfront and various 18th- and 19th-century buildings. You can visit the Sag Harbor Whaling and Historical Museum (516-725-0770) and the Custom House (516-941-9444), the 1790 Federal-style home of a customs master who was appointed by George Washington. *Located on Rte. 114 on Long Island's South Fork; south of the Shelter Island ferry terminal in North Haven.*

■ **The Hamptons.** New York City's vacation playground offers fabulous ocean and bay beaches, great fishing, and fine restaurants. From Westhampton to East Hampton, you'll also be hit with high prices, crowded public beaches on summer weekends, and limited short-term lodging choices (lodging in Hampton Bays is the least expensive). Try to visit during the week or after Labor Day, and check with each town about nonresident beach parking. Go to Southampton for fine shopping.

DINING

■ **Ram's Head Inn** (expensive). An elegant dining room in a large, well-maintained inn makes a perfect setting

▼

for the excellent New American dishes coming out of the kitchen. If the menu offers a black bean soup with a touch of cilantro cream, order it. For an entrée, try fettucine with lobster and asparagus, a succulent duck dish, or the fish of the day. There's also a spacious bar room. *108 Ram Island Dr., Shelter Island Heights, NY 11965; tel. 516-749-0811. Open daily for dinner. Call for off-season schedule which includes Sat. lunch and Sun. brunch. Follow Ram Island Dr. east over causeway to Big Ram Island. About 6 mi. north of Mashomack Preserve.*

■ **Island Grill** (moderate). Don't let the tired look of the restaurant's exterior fool you. Trained in France, chef Marcel Iattoni whips up creative country French and Italian dishes. His specialty is crispy duck in cherry sauce—the fowl is marinated for days and cooked slowly in its own fat. The chef also cooks a popular bouillabaisse and various pastas with seafood. For appetizers, try the cranberry-stuffed calamari and the eggplant terrine. *37 Shore Rd., Shelter Island Heights, NY 11965; tel. 516-749-1808. Open Fri.-Sun. for dinner, Sat.-Sun. for breakfast and lunch, first weekend in May-late Jun. and mid-Sep.-late Oct. Open daily for breakfast, lunch, and dinner late Jun.-mid Sep. About 4 mi. west of Mashomack Preserve.*

■ **The Dory** (moderate). The bar area in the front may look like a typical gin mill, but the food is fresh and creative. You'll find excellent appetizers like cornmeal-coated calamari with chipolte aioli and crab cakes with jicama-carrot slaw. Look for steamed mussels in ginger-lemon grass broth and such main courses as salmon filet with orange, sesame, and soy glaze on fried noodles. The best tables are on the back patio overlooking Chase Creek. *Bridge St., Shelter Island Heights, NY 11965; tel. 516-749-8871. Open daily for lunch and dinner mid-May-Oct. About 4 mi. northwest of Mashomack Preserve.*

LODGING

■ **Ram's Head Inn** (expensive). This attractive 14-room

▼

center-hall colonial offering fine dining sits on a hill above Coecles Harbor. The nicely furnished rooms, devoid of televisions, radios, and clocks, are small, so book a room or a suite with a private bath. Room 1 has views and its own bath, yet it still is small, with a full-size bed and a shared balcony. Rates include a buffet breakfast and use of boats, a beach, and a tennis court. Rooms with shared bath are moderately priced. *108 Ram Island Dr., Shelter Island Heights, NY 11965; tel. 516-749-0811. About 6 mi. north of Mashomack Preserve. Follow Ram Island Dr. east over a causeway to Big Ram Island.*

■ **Olde Country Inn** (expensive). Run by friendly hosts, this completely renovated farmhouse is the most attractive and comfortable place to stay on Shelter Island. The four well-appointed guest rooms are spacious and have private baths; ask for the Gold Room, which is so large it has two sitting chairs. There's an intimate bar area and a lovely common room with a piano. A full breakfast is served outdoors in summer. An expansion is expected to double the number of guest rooms. *11 Stearns Point Rd., Shelter Island Heights, NY 11965; tel. 516-749-1633. About 4 mi. northwest of Mashomack Preserve.*

■ **The Chequit Inn** (expensive). Owned by the proprietors of the Ram's Head Inn, this newly restored 27-guest-room Victorian with a covered veranda stands tall on a quiet main street in a tiny commercial district. You can walk to shops and are close to the North Ferry. All 27 rooms in the inn and an adjacent cottage have private baths. *23 Grand Ave., Shelter Island Heights, NY 11965; tel. 516-749-0018. Open mid-May-Oct. About 4 mi. northwest of Mashomack Preserve.*

■ **Beach House B&B** (moderate). This tasteful, modern house with gorgeous views of Shelter Island Sound sits on 200 feet of beachfront property. Three moderately priced rooms—including the largest guest room—have shared baths; an expensive room with private bath is also available. You can see in three directions from the room with two skylights. If you don't like dogs, be aware that the owner has three Bassett hounds.

▼

Box 648, Shelter Island Heights, NY 11965; tel. 516-749-0264. About 3 mi. west of Mashomack Preserve on South Silver Beach.

■ **House on Chase Creek** (moderate). Overlooking a wide creek, this country home near a handful of shops in a tiny commercial area has been handsomely restored. It's not as captivating as other B&Bs listed in this section, but it's a fine place to stay, with three antique-filled guest rooms, each with private bath. One room is tight, so try to book spacious Room 1, which has a king-size bed. An "extended" continental breakfast—often with French toast—is included. Rooms are moderately priced on weekdays, expensive on weekends. *3 Locust Ave., Shelter Island Heights, NY 11965; tel. 516-749-4379. Off Rte. 114 and Chase Ave., about 4 mi. northwest of Mashomack Preserve.*

■ **Stearns Point House B&B** (moderate). This attractive modern home lacks historic character but offers spacious rooms with king- or queen-size beds and private baths. The nicest is Room 2, a bit Spartan but bright. The beach is a short walk away. *7 Stearns Point Rd., Shelter Island Heights, NY 11965; tel. 516-749-4162. About 4 mi. west of Mashomack Preserve.*

FOR MORE INFORMATION
Tourist Offices:
■ **Shelter Island Chamber of Commerce.** Call or write for a brochure and a map of the island. A recorded message provides ferry information. *Box 598, Shelter Island, NY 11964; tel. 516-749-0399. No office hours.*

For Serious Walkers:
Follow the 11-mile blue trail for a five-hour walk through the Mashomack Preserve. You walk next to gigantic Gardiners Bay and through the Great Swamp.

Cowboys & Tribes, Poachers & Spies

EXPERIENCE 15: HITHER HILLS

Texans and even New Yorkers may find it hard to believe, but cowboys once drove huge herds of cattle on the panoramic seaside land you walk through in Hither Hills State Park. This narrow strip of rolling hills, sandy woodlands,

> **The Highlights:** Fabulous ocean and bay views, top beaches, "walking" sand dunes, great picnic spots.
>
> **Other Places Nearby:** A historic lighthouse, the beach resort areas of East Hampton and Montauk, gourmet dining.

and coastal beaches wedged between the Atlantic Ocean and Napeague Bay was the home of the country's first cattle ranch during the 17th century. For the next 200 years, Long Islanders flocked to the eastern end of the island's South Fork twice each year for the big event: watching the herd being driven to these grazing lands in May and then back in November or December.

The end-of-the-year drive was particularly significant because Long Islanders didn't celebrate Thanksgiving until the first Thursday after the herd was rounded up. Sometimes the weather remained warm late in the year, so the cattle were only rounded up in December. President George Washington declared in 1789 that Thanksgiving would be celebrated on the

▼

fourth Thursday of November, but Long Islanders ignored the edict until 1863, when President Abraham Lincoln implored them to join the fold.

Poachers in the late 1700s were attracted to the valuable livestock and, disguised as fishermen, raided the grazing cattle. Their crimes became a national issue, prompting President Washington to build the Montauk Lighthouse so that agents manning it could watch for rustlers as well as guide boats.

About 150 years later, in June 1942, other undesirables invaded. A German U-boat entered foggy Napeague Bay and dropped off four spies on the beach you stand on during this walking tour. The spies' mission was to blow up bridges and rail lines, cutting off supplies to Long Island's military-aircraft production plants.

A Coast Guard officer spotted them digging trenches to conceal their military uniforms and their supply of TNT. The spies bribed the officer to keep quiet, hiked to the Amagansett train station, and rode into New York City. The Coast Guard officer reported their arrival, and a manhunt ensued. Two of the Germans felt the heat and turned in their colleagues. They cut a deal with law enforcement officials, informing them that other spies had landed in Florida. FBI agents quickly apprehended the perpetrators. The two stool pigeons were sent back to Germany, and the others were executed.

Long before the escapades of the white man—more than 4,000 years ago—Native Americans roamed these lands. Little is known about their history, because they had no written language. When Dutch explorer Adrian Block became the first white man to visit Montauk in the early 17th century, the Meantauketts controlled the territory.

Wyandanch, the tribe's sachem, befriended another settler, Lion Gardiner, who bought a small island in Napeague Bay, becoming the first white man to buy land from the Native Americans on Long Island. Their friendship was genuine, and

Gardiner's family learned to speak the native tongue.

A peaceful band, the Meantauketts hunted for food in East Hampton, on what is now Gardiner's Island, and throughout Long Island's North Fork. They stalked deer and game and demonstrated their whaling expertise to the settlers. They were also skillful farmers, planting corn and beans.

Tribe member Stephen Pharaoh, also known as Stephen Talkhouse, became a local legend, acquiring the nickname The Great Walker by supposedly walking from Montauk to Brooklyn—a distance of about 125 miles—in one day. The site of Talkhouse's home is located in Hither Hills State Park.

Unlike so many other tribes, the Meantauketts' lifestyle was not ruined by the barrel of the white man's gun. Rather, it was another tribe, the Rhode Island-based Narragansetts, who stirred up trouble. The Narragansetts approached the Meantauketts and another Long Island tribe, the Shinnecocks, and tried to recruit them in a war against the European settlers. Wyandanch informed Gardiner about the Narragansetts' intentions, and the Meantauketts refused to join the plot.

The Narragansetts tried to incite conflict by murdering a white woman in Southampton and a Meantaukett tribesman and then by burning settlers' homes. The Meantauketts paddled to Block Island to kill the Narragansett chief but fell victim to an ambush and suffered great losses.

Montauk came under attack from the Narragansetts, who slaughtered numerous Meantauketts and kidnapped Wyandanch's daughter on her wedding day. The daughter's husband-to-be was killed. Lion Gardiner paid a ransom to free the daughter, and a thankful Wyandanch gave Gardiner a large parcel of land in what today is Smithtown.

Today, Hither Hills State Park's 1,755 acres straddle both sides of the two-lane Montauk Highway, the only access road to Montauk Point, the eastern tip of Long Island's South Fork. Gorgeous Atlantic Ocean beaches rim the park's southern edge, while the majestic beaches of Napeague Bay stretch along the

▼

park's northern border. As you look to the east up the shoreline of Napeague Bay, tall sandy cliffs topped by green shrubs and trees tower above the beach.

Between the bay and the ocean stands a dense forest filled with oak, pine, and Russian olive trees. Freshwater ponds dot the land, including Fresh Pond, whose massive size may make one conclude that it's a lake.

But the one geographic feature that really makes this land unique is the area of "walking dunes" to the west, sandwiched between Fresh Pond and Napeague Harbor. The parabolic walking dunes are covered with trees and shrubs, and some migrate in a southeasterly direction. Though wind currents constantly change their size and location, some dunes are 50 feet high, the tallest on Long Island.

GETTING THERE

By train:

The Long Island Railroad runs trains from Manhattan to many points on Long Island, including East Hampton, Amagansett, and Montauk. Hither Hills State Park is located between Amagansett and Montauk. For local cab service, call Bill's Taxi (516-329-5019), Holy Mackerel Taxi (516-668-1111, 800-840-TAXI), Pink Tuna (516-668-3838), Judas's Chariots (516-668-6900), or Amagansett Taxi (516-267-2006). Be forewarned: Rates to Hither Hills vary greatly from company to company.

By car:

From Manhattan, take the Long Island Expwy. (I-495) east to exit 70 (Manorville Rd.). At an intersection, turn right onto Rte. 111 south and continue on Rte. 111 until it ends. Turn left onto Rte. 27 (Sunrise Hwy.). Follow Rte. 27 past Hampton Bays and continue east as it merges with Rte. 39 and then becomes Montauk Hwy. Stay on Montauk Hwy. through East Hampton and then through Amagansett. A few miles east of Amagansett, pass a sign for Sea Crest-on-the-Ocean condominiums on your right and then a sign for "Hither Hills Western Boundary." Follow a sign bearing left to Montauk. Atop a hill, turn left into the overlook parking lot.

By bus:

The Hampton Jitney (516-283-4600, 800-936-0440) operates bus service from Manhattan to East Hampton, Amagansett, and Montauk. See above for connecting taxi service.

Walk Directions

TIME: 2 or 3 1/2 hours
LEVEL: Easy or moderate
DISTANCE: 3 or 6 miles
ACCESS: By car, train, or bus

This walk is primarily on flat sandy-bottomed land that is easy on the feet. If you want to see the walking dunes, follow the Optional Extension described below. Stop on the beach at Napeague Bay for an ideal picnic. Picnic provisions can be bought at the gourmet farm market on Montauk Hwy. in Amagansett. Ticks abound in Hither Hills State Park, so please take proper precautions, and don't stray from designated trails.

TO BEGIN

From the overlook parking lot, face west with the Atlantic Ocean to your left and Napeague Bay straight ahead and to your right. Head west on a grass patch next to Rte. 27.

1. After about 50 yards, at the beginning of a highway guardrail that's on your left, bear right and head downhill on a trail between the trees. You immediately reach a three-foot-wide sandy path that soon narrows. Continue on between two 1 1/2-foot-tall rocks. Follow the sandy trail to the left as it winds near Rte. 27 and proceeds through the trees. About 10 minutes after beginning the walk, you approach a six-foot-wide sandy road.

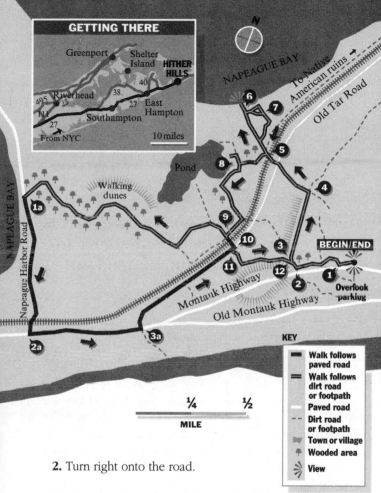

GETTING THERE

Greenport • Shelter Island • **HITHER HILLS**

NAPEAGUE BAY

495 • Riverhead 25 • 38 • 40 • 27 • East Hampton

111 • 27 • Southampton

From NYC

10 miles

N

NAPEAGUE BAY

To Native American ruins →

Old Tar Road

Pond

Walking dunes

NAPEAGUE BAY

Napeague Harbor Road

Montauk Highway

Old Montauk Highway

BEGIN/END

Overlook parking

KEY

- Walk follows paved road
- Walk follows dirt road or footpath
- Paved road
- Dirt road or footpath
- Town or village
- Wooded area
- View

¼   ½

MILE

2. Turn right onto the road.

3. At a junction of two dirt roads, follow the narrower dirt road on the right. Proceed sharply uphill on the road.

4. At a junction of two dirt roads, turn left. When you reach a wide paved road, cross it and continue on a sandy road to a stop sign and railroad tracks. **Beware of Long Island Railroad trains. Make sure to look in both directions**

179

▼

before crossing. Cross the railroad tracks.

5. At a junction several yards ahead, follow a sandy road that veers to the right. Ignore the road to the left leading to the pond and the narrow trail on your extreme right that goes through the woods to Native American ruins. **Beware of thorn bushes on both sides of the sandy road you're walking on.** Ignore a dirt road to the right and continue straight. You emerge from the woods near the shoreline of Napeague Bay. Proceed to the beach. *The beach with its tall dunes to the east makes a scenic picnic spot. Swimming, however, is prohibited.* With your back to the water, retrace your steps several yards.

6. Turn left, proceeding uphill on a sandy road. Go around either side of a loop.

7. At the top of the hill, turn right into the woods, proceeding away from the bay. *Take a last glimpse at the great bay views.* At the next junction, turn left onto the sandy road (this is the same road you walked on earlier that leads to the bay). At the next junction (Point 5) before the railroad tracks, turn right and head through the trees on a dirt road. Proceed forward on either side of a loop and follow the road as it turns to the right. Continue to the shoreline of the pond. *You can use the clearing just before the pond as a relaxing picnic spot.* With your back to the pond, retrace your steps and proceed several yards, ignoring a rocky path to the left.

8. Turn right into the woods and pass rocks that sit across the trail. Go up a small hill and follow the trail as it turns to the right and winds away from the pond. Ignore the next trail on your left and continue straight downhill through the trees, following white blazes. Follow the trail as it turns to the right just before a hill that ascends to the railroad tracks. Continue on, walking parallel to the railroad tracks that are on your left.

▼

9. At a trail junction *(see optional extension below if you'd like to add a few extra miles to this walk)*, turn left and cross the railroad tracks. **Beware of trains.**

10. At a paved road (Old Tar Rd.), turn right. Proceed only about ten yards.

11. Turn left and proceed past rocks uphill on a wide trail. *A small pine forest is on your left. On the trail, notice several nesting boxes designed to lure the Eastern bluebird back to its natural habitat.*

12. At the next junction, turn right and follow the sandy road (you're now walking between Points 2 and 3). Proceed about 30 yards and turn left a few steps past the brown Hither Hills sign that's on your left. (You're at Point 2.) Retrace your steps to the parking lot.

Optional Extension

TIME: An extra 1 1/2 hours
LEVEL: Moderate
DISTANCE: An extra 3 miles

This optional extension is also an easy walk that's primarily on flat ground. It's rated moderate, however, because of the total length of the walk.

TO BEGIN

Follow the above walk up to Point 9. At Point 9, ignore the trail on your left heading to the railroad tracks and turn right onto a dirt trail, following white blazes. *You're now walking through rolling terrain formed by the retreat of glaciers.*

Ignore a path to the right and stay on the trail as it winds to the left. After several minutes, you reach another trail junction. Turn right and follow white blazes. Wind your way through the

▼

woods on the white-blazed trail. You eventually walk next to tree-covered walking dunes on your right. *Some of the dunes in this area are migrating to the southeast. At 50 feet in height, they are the tallest dunes on Long Island.* Follow the path uphill atop the dunes and continue on as it winds through the woods. Continue on following white blazes for 15 to 20 minutes.

1A. When you emerge from the woods at paved Napeague Harbor Rd., turn left. Cross the railroad tracks.

2A. At a stop sign before Montauk Hwy. (Rte. 27), turn left and walk on grass alongside the highway (across the street are the Sea Crest-on-the-Ocean condominiums). **Be careful of vehicular traffic.** Pass a restaurant on your left and then a sign (across the street) for Hither Hills State Park.

3A. About 25 yards before a green sign for Montauk and Old Montauk Hwy., turn left onto a gravel road (Old Tar Rd.). The road becomes blacktop for a short stretch, then dirt and then paved. Proceed with the railroad tracks to your left. Turn right onto a dirt trail (Point 11) past rocks strewn across it. (The dirt trail is 10 yards before another road that heads off to the left across railroad tracks.) Continue on uphill and follow the directions in Point 12 back to your car in the parking lot.

PLACES ALONG THE WALK
■ **Hither Hills State Park.** Open daily sunrise-sunset. The park office (516-668-2554) is open daily 8-4:30 end of Apr.-mid-Nov. The off-site office (206 S. Fairview Ave., Montauk, N.Y. 11954; tel. 516-668-3781) is open daily 8-4. The campground (800-456-CAMP for reservations) is open end of Apr.-mid-Nov.

OTHER PLACES NEARBY
Besides the attractions listed below, there's an interesting nightlife scene in the Hamptons and its environs. Top rock,

▼

blues, and folk musicians, including such local residents as former *Saturday Night Live* bandleader G. E. Smith, perform at Stephen Talkhouse (516-267-3117), a bar/club in Amagansett. In East Hampton, Guild Hall's John Drew Theater (516-324-4050) presents such major theater productions as the worldwide premiers of plays by Robert Wilson and Joe Pintauro.

■ **Hamptons beaches.** The sandy beaches are the lure for most summer vacationers heading to West Hampton, Hampton Bays, East Hampton, and other Hamptons communities. Don't try to buck the trend: The bay and Atlantic Ocean beaches are some of the world's finest. *For beach and parking information in Montauk, Amagansett, and East Hampton, contact East Hampton Town Parks & Recreation, 159B Pantigo Rd., East Hampton, NY 11937; tel. 516-324-2417.*

■ **Charter fishing boat docks.** Montauk is one of the world's deep-sea fishing capitals. More than 50 charter boats head into the Atlantic Ocean in search of swordfish, mako shark, tuna, and other fish. *Charter boats include Blue Fin IV (516-668-9323), Sea Breeze (516-728-5444), and Mistress Too (516-668-2932). For a complete list, call the Montauk Chamber of Commerce (516-668-2428) and ask for a copy of the publication called On Montauk. Docks are 5 mi. east of Hither Hills.*

■ **Montauk Lighthouse.** At the tip of Long Island's South Fork, this landmark has fascinated visitors since it began operating in 1797. Its beam still shines, and now it's also a museum. *Box 943, Montauk, NY 11954; tel. 516-668-2544. Open daily late May-early Oct.; call for other days open during the rest of the year. At Montauk Point, about 7 mi. east of Hither Hills.*

■ **Okeanos Ocean Research Foundation.** This nonprofit organization offers whale-watching cruises out of Montauk. In winter and spring, Okeanos operates seal-watching cruises to four islands off Long Island's North Fork. *Riverhead, NY 11901; tel. 516-369-9840. Whale-watching cruises depart from Montauk Harbor's Viking Dock Sat.-Sun. at 10 mid-May-June 30; daily at 10:30 July 1-Labor Day, and daily at 10 the day*

▼

after Labor Day-mid-Sep. About 5 mi. east of Hither Hills.

DINING

■ **Caswells** (expensive). Montauk's finest restaurant, this fashionable establishment offers creative American cuisine featuring local seafood. Look for pan-roasted swordfish with red-lentil crust and Provençal relish, or the monstrous whole roasted Montauk sea bass. If seafood isn't your thing, try the filet mignon with three-pepper cognac sauce or the Australian rack of lamb. The salads and the wine list are excellent. *17 S. Edison St., Montauk, NY 11954, tel. 516-668-0303. Open daily for dinner Memorial Day-Labor Day and weekends for dinner the rest of the year. Off Montauk Hwy., about 4 mi. east of Hither Hills.*

■ **Nick & Toni's** (expensive). This establishment lures the rich and famous with its wood-burning oven specials such as braised rabbit with cipolline onions, roasted plum tomatoes, and thyme. You can also opt for such entrées as grilled tuna with white bean puree, wilted arugula, and crispy pancetta, or grilled pork tenderloin with stuffed polenta and balsamic mushrooms. Much of the Tuscan fare on the menu, including a variety of salad appetizers, is health-conscious. *136 North Main St., East Hampton, NY; tel. 516-324-3550. Open daily for dinner and Sun. for lunch Memorial Day-Labor Day. Closed Mon.-Tue. during the rest of the year. About 9 mi. west of Hither Hills.*

■ **The Maidstone Arms** (expensive). You can hear the floorboards creak in the elegant dining room of this historic old inn. Chef William Valentine, who formerly worked at top hotels in New Orleans and Los Angeles, uses local seafood to create such fascinating dishes as risotto with shellfish, tiger prawns, and goat cheese, and pan-seared cod accompanied by roasted potatoes, baby artichokes, and lima beans. Appetizers may include carpaccio of beef tenderloin with caponata and shaved Parmesan. *207 Main St., East Hampton, NY 11937; tel. 516-324-5006; fax 516-324-5037. Open daily for breakfast, lunch, and dinner. About 9 mi. west of Hither Hills.*

▼

■ **Dave's Grill** (moderate). This dockside restaurant with a smart New England nautical decor excels with such dishes as pan-seared mahi-mahi in ginger sauce and marinated, grilled pork chops with homemade apple chutney and potato scallion cakes. The grilled fish entrées are highly recommended. For dessert, try the homemade ice cream or the excellent tiramisu. Grab a table on the outdoor patio. *Box 1491, Flamingo Rd., Montauk Harbor, NY 11954; tel. 516-668-9190. Open daily for dinner late Jun.-Labor Day; Thu.-Tue. in Jun. and day after Labor Day-Sep. 30; Thu.-Sun. in May and Oct. Closed Nov.-Apr. About 5 mi. east of Hither Hills.*

■ **Clam Bar at Napeague** (moderate). At this outdoor clam bar, you'll find excellent informal grub: lobster rolls, fried clams, fried scallops, and such specials as grilled tuna salad and twin-culled lobsters. You can also count on high-quality desserts, including chocolate truffle pie and black-bottom key lime pie. Since there's no indoor seating, it's wise to head across the highway in inclement weather to the Lobster Roll restaurant. *Box 1107, Montauk Hwy., Amagansett, NY 11930; tel. 516-267-6348. Open daily for lunch and dinner mid-May-Columbus Day; open Sat.-Sun. mid-Apr.-mid-May and mid-Oct.-mid-Nov. East of Amagansett, on the north side of Montauk Hwy. About 4 mi. west of Hither Hills.*

LODGING

Few budget choices exist in East Hampton and Amagansett, two summer retreats preferred by celebrities. Some moderately priced rooms, however, can be booked in private homes by requesting a directory from the East Hampton Chamber of Commerce (516-324-0362). Montauk has some budget options (call the Montauk Chamber at 516-668-2428), but almost all lack character and charm. For many, the best bet may be Shelter Island's reasonably priced B&Bs (*see* Experience 14), only 30 to 45 minutes away.

■ **Bluff Cottage** (very expensive). A gorgeous turn-of-the-

▼

century beach cottage, this Dutch colonial near the ocean makes you want to move right in, with its French country antique furniture, four elegantly appointed guest rooms, and inviting porch. The Green Room is the nicest, though all are charming and have water views. The beach is a short walk away. *Box 428, 266 Bluff Rd., Amagansett, NY 11930; tel. 516-267-6172. About 6 mi. west of Hither Hills.*

■ **The Maidstone Arms** (very expensive). This upscale mid-18th-century Georgian inn and restaurant overlooks the village green and pond on East Hampton's busiest street. Like most inns of that era, the rooms are not large, but they have charm and are smartly decorated. Room 28 is one of the most spacious and has a pond view. All rooms have private bath, a phone, a TV, and air conditioning. *207 Main St., East Hampton, NY 11937; tel. 516-324-5006. About 9 mi. west of Hither Hills.*

■ **The Pink House** (very expensive). This house on the National Historic Register was built by a whaling captain in the mid-19th century and renovated in 1990 by friendly owner/architect Ron Steinhilber. Each of the five guest rooms (all with private bath) radiates warmth. The Blue Room has a queen-size bed, a large marble shower, and an inviting window seat where you look out at the village and its tiny historic cemetery. A small swimming pool sits in a quaint backyard. *26 James Ln., East Hampton, NY 11937; tel. 516-324-3400. About 9 mi. west of Hither Hills.*

■ **Montauk Manor** (expensive). Sitting atop a hill, this Tudor-style resort provides guests with a view of grasslands and the surrounding bay and ocean. Only half of the 140 modern, beach-motif rooms are rented to vacationers (the others are owner-occupied). Ask for a bay view room for the best views. The palatial lobby features dual fireplaces, white pillars, and a high, wood-beam ceiling. *236 Edgemere St., Montauk, NY 11954; tel. 516-668-4400. About 5 mi. east of Hither Hills.*

■ **Surfside Inn** (moderate). The shoe-box rooms lack closets and private baths, and you'll have a hard time finding a spot to open a suitcase. But the rooms are bright and clean, several have great ocean views, and the beach is across the street. Room 8 is the most spacious. Primarily a restaurant, the inn shows signs of wear and tear, but there's a nice L-shaped bar with a fireplace, and the dining area can be romantic by candlelight. *Box 2267, Old Montauk Hwy., Montauk, NY 11954; tel. 516-668-5958. About 2 mi. east of Hither Hills.*

FOR MORE INFORMATION
Tourist Offices:

■ **East Hampton Chamber of Commerce.** *37A Main St., East Hampton, NY 11937; tel. 516-324-0362; fax 516-329-1642. Office open Mon.-Sat. 10-4 Apr.-Jun.; Mon.-Fri. 10-4, Sat. 11-5 Jul.-Labor Day. Call for days and hours the rest of the year.*

■ **Montauk Chamber of Commerce.** *Box 5029, Montauk, NY 11954; tel. 516-668-2428. Open Mon.-Sat. 10-4, Sun. 10-3 Mother's Day-mid-Oct. Open Mon.-Fri. 10-4 and selected weekend days the rest of the year. On Main St. across from the village green; about 7 mi. east of Hither Hills.*

For Serious Walkers:

■ **East Hampton Village Clerk.** A map of Hither Hills' various walking trails can be obtained for $3. The office also sells walking-trail maps for Montauk State Park (516-668-3781) and an undeveloped area of East Hampton. *159 Pantigo Rd., East Hampton, NY 11937; tel. 516-324-4142. Open Mon.-Thu. 9-4, Fri. 9-6.*

Lost Tribes

EXPERIENCE 16:
PEOPLES FOREST

Today, quintessential New England remains alive in Connecticut's Litchfield Hills: white clapboard colonials and classic congregational churches, sun-dappled woodlands and stone-walled fields, rustic red barns, and tidy village greens shaded by fine old trees.

The Highlights: An unspoiled hardwood forest, an ancient soapstone quarry and other Native American sites on the National Register of Historic Places.

Other Places Nearby: A life-size replica of a 17th-century Algonquin village, historic New England inns.

But long before the arrival of European settlers, the Algonquin tribe made the Litchfield Hills its home, fishing in the crystalline lakes and stalking game in the forested hills. This walk takes you to those lands preserved as part of Peoples State Forest.

Connecticut has a rich Native American heritage that is even reflected in its name—a word meaning "Land on the Long Tidal River." As you explore the gentle landscape of the Litchfield Hills, it is not hard to imagine what the Algonquians saw: two mighty rivers, the Housatonic ("Place Beyond the Mountains") and the Farmington, and an abundance of lakes and woodlands. On this walk, you will explore lands lived on by these Native Americans and see the signs of a revolutionary invention that changed their way of life forever.

▼

Approximately 5,000 years ago, Native Americans began to modify their primarily nomadic lifestyle and to settle in seasonal villages of up to 100 people. Although hunting and fishing were the primary sources of food for the village, the men of the tribe began to cultivate plants such as corn, beans, pumpkin, squash, and herbs. Their nomadic lifestyle, however, was not completely abandoned, because they still moved with the seasons. At the onset of winter, the tribe sought protection inland amid the sheltering mountains and deep forests. As spring arrived, the tribe moved down to the fertile valleys to plant their crops and to fish along the coastline and rivers.

Villages were often situated by ponds, rivers, or along the coastline, and where game, seafood, fertile fields, water, and firewood were plentiful. Their houses, or wigwams, were 30 to 70 feet in diameter with cone-shaped roofs and large bark shingles. An opening was left in the roof for smoke, and entrances to the wigwam were covered with mats, deerskin, or bark. Bulrushes, hemp, and cords of bast (a type of reed) were collected and woven into mats that lined the interior of the wigwam, providing insulation against the cold. Inside the wigwam, a small hearth, often made of fieldstone, was used for cooking and to keep the one or two families living in the wigwam warm during the harsh New England winters. (You can see a fine example of a 17th-century pre-contact Native American village, complete with longhouses and wigwams, at the Institute for American Indian Studies in Washington, Connecticut. *See* Other Places Nearby.)

In the village, women took charge of the hearth and the preparation of cooking the meal while the men hunted for game and prepared the fields for planting. The squaw's only kitchen tools were a stone knife and two lumps of iron pyrites to start the cooking fire. There were no containers to cook in. A dramatic change in this domestic lifestyle was made possible by the discovery, roughly 4,000 years ago, of the malleable proper-

▼

ties of a local type of rock known today as "soapstone," mined in places like the one you'll visit on this walk. Experimenting with this rock, the Native Americans discovered that it was soft enough to work and fashion into various shapes with hard stone tools. Eventually, a clever craftsman designed a bowl, which revolutionized culinary life. Now the squaws could create mouth-watering herb-scented meat and fish stews that simmered for hours over hot wood-smoke fires. The craftsmen of the tribe proceeded to create an impressive assortment of soapstone bowls, pots, platters, cups, dishes, mortars, and pestles. In addition, the artisans crafted soapstone pipes, effigies, pendants, gorgets, as well as weights and plummets for fishing.

Work at the quarry was apparently a family affair. Young and old hiked to the quarry, raised a temporary lean-to, and divided the chores. Women and children pitched in to remove the quarry tailings or waste so that the men could access the deeper veins of steatite and chlorite. The squaws carried the rough soapstone blanks to the home site, where the craftsmen could shape and hollow out the rock into the proper kitchen or ritual items. As you walk to this ancient soapstone rock quarry, keep in mind that it was worked by the tribe for 4,000 years.

A revolutionary change to the tribal way of life came with the sudden and unexpected influx of European traders, explorers, and soon-to-be settlers that marked the beginning of the 17th century and the end of a lifestyle that had remained unchanged for centuries. The creative genius of the Native Americans was wasted on warfare and further weakened by plagues and diseases brought by the settlers. Within 200 years of the white man's arrival, most Native Americans were gone, leaving little trace of their culture but the remnants of the soapstone quarry you'll see along this walk.

GETTING THERE
By car:

All trails are in Peoples State Forest in Pleasant Valley, CT. From I-84, exit at Waterbury and go north on Rte. 8 to Winsted.

▼

From the junction of Rtes. 8 and 44 in Winsted, follow Rte. 44 east for slightly more than 3 mi. Take a left onto Rte. 318 north and follow for 1 mi. Cross the Farmington River on the metal bridge and continue on Rte. 318 east and Rte. 181 north (they merge for less than 1 mi.). When they split, take Rte. 181 north for 1/2 mi., then turn left onto Park Rd. Parking and the entrance to the Elliot Bronson Trail are on your left.

If you wish to take the shorter version of this walk, visit the Native American sites on the first part of the walk and retrace your steps to your car. Drive south on Rte. 318; take a right onto East River Rd. (just before crossing a metal bridge), and follow for 1 mi. Turn right onto Greenwoods Rd. (a sign says: Ullmann Picnic Grove, Nature Museum & Forest Office, and James Stocking Big Spring and Beaver Brook Recreation Area), which is the main entrance to Peoples State Forest. Follow Greenwoods Rd. for 1 4/10 mi. to the entrance of the Charles Pack Trail (on your right), identified by a blue blaze with a yellow center. Park along the road.

Walk Directions

TIME: Up to 4 hours
LEVEL: Easy to moderate
DISTANCE: Up to 7 1/2 mi.
ACCESS: By car

The trails have a peculiar blaze system consisting of two colors: an outer blue circle and an inner circle painted the color of the particular trail you're on. All trail heads are marked by brown signs. Peoples State Forest is open daily from 8 a.m. to sunset. Picnic groves and pit toilets are located at various points on this walk. You can pick up picnic supplies at the Old Riverton General Store in Riverton, about 2 mi. north of the state forest entrance.

If you want to shorten the walk to one hour, follow the instructions below to the soapstone quarry and then retrace your steps to your car. To shorten the walk to three hours, go to the quarry, retrace your steps to your car, and drive to the parking area where the Charles Pack Trail begins at Greenwoods Rd. (*see* Getting There). Then walk into the forest a short distance to Point 5, where you follow the directions below. Continue on until you return back to Point 5, where you go right and retrace your steps to your car.

TO BEGIN

At a brown sign for the Elliott Bronson Trail, follow the blue/red trail into the forest. In two minutes, the trail joins an old woods trail. Bear right onto it. *From the Revolutionary War through the Civil War, this road was used to haul charcoal produced in the forest.*

1. After walking less than ten minutes, take a left onto the blue-blazed side trail toward the soapstone quarry. Along the way, you pass the ruins of a charcoal hearth and a coal miner's shelter, with its collapsed chimney. Just beyond these ruins, the trail bears to the right and begins a sharp but short ascent. In a few minutes, you arrive at an impressive ledge, whose rocks are in an upright position. Continue on for three minutes to the face of the ancient Native American quarry. When you are done exploring the area, retrace your steps to Point 1.

If you want to shorten the walk, go right and head back to your car. Otherwise, go left on the blue/red trail over Ragged Mountain.

2. At a fork, bear left and continue on the blue/red trail. Follow the trail upward through a pine and hardwood forest. When you reach the crest of Ragged Mountain, there are limited views. On your descent through hardwoods and mountain laurel, you pass the ruins of more charcoal hearths and an outcrop of ledges that afford beautiful views of the forest to the north. About 10 minutes from the ledges, you come to a picnic area nestled in a pine grove. Follow the trail as it descends.

KEY

Walk follows
paved road

Walk follows
dirt road
or footpath

Paved road

Dirt road
or footpath

Town or village

Wooded area

View

Park Road

Beaver Swamp

Beaver Brook

Parking

Bridge

Greenwoods Road

Nature
center

East
River
Road

Indian
caves

Parking

BEGIN/END

Park Road

¼   ½
MILE

GETTING THERE

181
318 8   PEOPLES
STATE
FOREST

44   7   Winsted
44   4
44   202
Torrington   202
8   New
Britain

22   7
84   691

84
Waterbury   84

684   8
7   Danbury   15
91
10 miles

▼

3. Turn right onto the paved Greenwoods Rd. *If you have enough time, stop at the Nature Museum on your left.* Otherwise, proceed a short distance past the museum on Greenwoods Rd.

4. Make a right onto the blue/orange trail (the Agnes Bowen Trail), which parallels Greenwoods Rd.

5. When you reach an intersection with the blue/yellow-blazed Charles Pack Trail, turn right. *You are following an old wagon path.* Within about 10 minutes, you reach Beaver Brook Bridge, which goes over a stream rumored to be a favorite of bears that live in the area. *Thousands of years ago, when the Native Americans camped here, a glacial deposit of rocks created a dam that transformed the brook you are crossing into a lake teeming with wildlife. Looking upstream to your left from the bridge, you can still see some of the rocks that formed the dam.*

Just past the bridge, follow the trail as it begins a short climb up the face of a kame terrace, whose flat top and steep sides provided a well-drained area for Native Americans to camp. *For the next 20 minutes or so, you will walk in the footsteps of the woodland tribes who made this area their home from 2000 B.C. to 600 A.D. Recently, archeaologists found 18 ancient village sites and a rich concentration of artifacts. As a result, the entire terrace has been added to the National Register of Historic Places.*

Beginning your descent, you pass the ruins of a colonial house foundation on the right side of the trail. *Note the remains of a meat-smoking chamber in the base of a large hollow chimney. The original house was built in the early 1800s, and the last house on this site was torn down in 1880. You will see many stone walls in this area making their serpentine way through the overgrown woodlands that were once some of Litchfield County's richest cultivated fields and cow pastures.*

6. About 25 minutes from the colonial ruins, you cross a dirt road. Continue straight ahead on the blue/yellow-blazed trail.

▼

7. In another 25 minutes, you again cross the dirt road. Continue following the blue/yellow trail. You shortly come to another lovely picnic area in a cluster of hemlocks next to a clear, rushing brook.

8. When you reach the paved Beaverbrook Rd., go left. Follow this old road for a half hour through a forest of hemlocks edged with mountain laurel.

9. When you reach the blue/orange-blazed Agnes Bowen Trail, turn left and head back into the forest. Follow the trail all the way back to Point 4, where you go left. Turn left again at Point 3, and then retrace your steps over Ragged Mountain to your car.

PLACES ALONG THE WALK

■ **Peoples State Forest.** *E. River Rd., Pleasant Valley, CT; tel. 860-379-2469. Forest open daily; campground (860-379-0922) open mid-Apr.-Nov.*

■ **Nature Museum.** Housed in a small fieldstone building, this museum exhibits Native American artifacts and examples of the park's flora and fauna. A diorama of the stone quarry is on display. *Greenwoods Rd., Peoples State Forest. Open Sat. 10-4 Jul.-Aug., Sun. 12:30-4:30 Jun.-Columbus Day weekend.*

OTHER PLACES NEARBY

■ **Dennis Hill State Park.** A unique summit pavilion is located at an elevation of 1,627 feet. From the summit, you can see Haystack Mountain, Mount Greylock, the Green Mountains, and a portion of New Hampshire. *Rte. 272, Norfolk, CT; tel. 860-482-1817. Park open daily. Regional headquarters office open daily 8-3:30 Memorial Day-Labor Day; open Mon.-Fri. 8-3:30 the rest of the year. About 16 mi. west of Pleasant Valley.*

■ **Haystack Mountain State Park.** To reach the 34-foot-high stone tower, drive halfway up the mountain to the parking

▼

area. It is a half-mile hike on rugged terrain to the 1,716-foot summit of Haystack Mountain, from which you can see Long Island Sound and peaks in Massachusetts and New York on a clear day. *Rte. 272, Norfolk, CT; tel. 860-482-1817. Park open daily. Regional headquarters office open daily 8-3:30. Memorial Day-Labor Day; open Mon.-Fri. the rest of the year. About 14 mi. northwest of Pleasant Valley.*

■ **Hitchcock Museum.** Riverton was originally called Hitchcocksville, after the famous chair maker who operated here. This museum, located in a church built in 1829, offers visitors the opportunity to view the stenciling and hand-striping of old Hitchcock chairs, as well as a collection of hand-painted early American furniture. *1 Robertsville Rd., Riverton, CT 06085; tel. 860-738-4950. Open Thu.-Sun. 12-4 Apr.-Dec. Admission. About 4 mi. north of Pleasant Valley.*

■ **Institute for American Indian Studies.** Tour a life-size replica of a 17th-century pre-contact Algonquin village, and view displays of tribal artifacts. *38 Curtis Rd., Washington, CT 06793; tel. 860-868-0518. Open Mon.-Sat. 10-5, Sun. 12-5. Closed Mon.-Tue. Jan.-Mar. Admission. Just off Rte. 199, about 26 mi. southwest of Pleasant Valley.*

■ **Loon Meadow Farm.** Enjoy a ride in a horse-drawn carriage through the village and countryside of Norfolk. Hayrides and sleigh rides are also offered in season. *41 Loon Meadow Dr., Norfolk, CT 06058; tel. 860-542-6085. Open daily by appointment. About 13 mi. from Pleasant Valley.*

DINING

■ **West Street Grill** (expensive). Although it's a bit far from the walk, we've included this restaurant because it has been named one of the country's top restaurants by several leading critics. In the stylish modern dining room, celebrity-spotting is the order of the day. Chef-owner James O'Shea serves contemporary American cuisine, including popular grilled Parmesan aioli bread, house-smoked salmon with corn-

▼

cakes and creme fraiche, and grilled sashimi tuna. *43 West St., Litchfield, CT 06759; tel. 860-567-3885. Open daily for lunch and dinner. On the green in Litchfield, about 18 mi. southwest of Pleasant Valley.*

■ **Old Riverton Inn** (moderate). In this historic inn, expect menu items such as stuffed pork chops with homemade apple sauce and broiled Boston scrod. The dining room retains its Early American ambience, with its heavy beams and original paneling. Before dinner, check out the inn's Hobby Horse bar, painted with murals by Bobby Walsh, who created murals for the 1930 New York World's Fair. *Rte. 20, Riverton, CT 06065; tel. 860-379-8678. Open Wed.-Sat. for lunch and dinner, Sun. for dinner (starting at noon). About 4 mi. north of Pleasant Valley.*

■ **The Pub** (moderate). Located in the historic Royal Arcanum Building, this relaxed English-style pub offers more than 150 kinds of beer from around the world. The restaurant's menu includes a full range of American foods, enhanced with touches of current culinary trends. The dinner menu changes daily but might include dishes such as chicken satay with cucumber relish, roast duckling with green peppercorns, and sautéed trout seasoned with rosemary. *Rte. 44, Station Pl., Norfolk, CT 06058; tel. 860-542-5716. Open Tue.-Sun. for lunch and dinner. About 13 mi. northwest of Pleasant Valley.*

■ **The Tributary Restaurant** (moderate). In this cozy, renovated barn on the banks of the Mad River, the simple decor features old photographs of family, friends, and Winsted's history. You can enjoy traditional fare such as prime rib or lower-cholesterol offerings such as ginger-orange sole or chicken sautéed in peach brandy. Breads and desserts are made in the restaurant's own bakery. *19 Rowley St., Winsted, CT 06098; tel. 860-379-7679. Open Tue.-Sun. for lunch and dinner. Off Rte. 44, about 4 mi. west of Pleasant Valley.*

■ **Jessie's Restaurant** (inexpensive). Located in a spacious colonial house, Jessie's serves Italian fare in two intimate

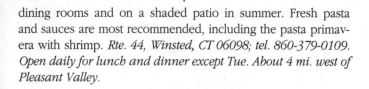

dining rooms and on a shaded patio in summer. Fresh pasta and sauces are most recommended, including the pasta primavera with shrimp. *Rte. 44, Winsted, CT 06098; tel. 860-379-0109. Open daily for lunch and dinner except Tue. About 4 mi. west of Pleasant Valley.*

LODGING

■ **Greenwoods Gate Bed & Breakfast** (very expensive). This 1797 colonial is a Connecticut gem. Four deluxe suites are delightfully decorated and chock full of luxurious amenities. A favorite of guests is the E. J. Trescott Suite, with its soothing blue-and-white wallpaper, antique brass-and-iron double bed, and separate sitting room. The two-level Levi Thompson Suite is separated from the rest of the house and is enhanced by an ultramodern bathroom with Jacuzzi. *105 Greenwoods Rd. East, Norfolk, CT 06058; tel. 860-542-5439. On Rte. 44, about 13 mi. northwest of Pleasant Valley.*

■ **Angel Hill Bed & Breakfast** (expensive). A special feature of this gracious 1880 Victorian is its wide wrap-around screened porch, perfect for breakfast or an afternoon nap. Ask for the bright and airy Garden View Suite, with its king-size bed, whirlpool tub and shower, and seven windows overlooking gardens and woodlands. Another favorite is the lavish Victorian Cottage Suite, with queen-size canopy bed, sitting room, and large bath with double Jacuzzi. *54 Greenwoods Rd., Norfolk, CT 06058; tel. 860-542-5920. On Rte. 44, about 13 mi. northwest of Pleasant Valley.*

■ **The Manor House** (expensive). This large and sumptuous Victorian Tudor mansion elegantly integrates antique decor (including 20 Tiffany stained-glass windows) and modern conveniences. The Spofford Room features lovely views, a private balcony, canopy king-size bed, and fireplace. The Lincoln Room contains a romantic sleigh bed; the English Room has a two-person Jacuzzi. *69 Maple Ave., Norfolk, CT 06058; tel. 860-542-5690. About 13 mi. northwest of Pleasant Valley.*

▼

■ **Mountain View Inn** (moderate). This lovingly restored 1875 Victorian inn in the heart of Norfolk has seven cozy rooms, six with private bath. Different in shape and decor, the rooms are furnished with antiques, including four-poster and brass beds. Ask for Room 4, which has a screened porch overlooking the grounds. *Rte. 272, Norfolk, CT 06058; tel. 860-542-5595. About 13 mi. northwest of Pleasant Valley.*

■ **Old Riverton Inn** (moderate). There's plenty of charm, comfort, and value at this inn that has been serving weary travelers since 1796. All 12 rooms are decorated with Hitchcock furniture, and all have private baths and cable TV. Book the deluxe suite with its fireplace, or one of the front rooms with a view of the Farmington River. The inn is located just minutes from a network of hiking trails. *Rte. 20, Riverton, CT 06065; tel. 860-379-8678. About 4 mi. north of Pleasant Valley.*

FOR MORE INFORMATION
Tourist Office:
■ **Litchfield Hills Travel Council.** Offers a free 40-page brochure. *Box 968, Litchfield, CT 06059; tel. 860-567-4506; fax 860-567-5214. Open Mon.-Fri. 10-6.*

For Serious Walkers:
■ **Connecticut Forest & Park Association.** This private association maintains and documents 700 miles of trails—a number of which are in Litchfield County, including a portion of the Appalachian Trail. Many of the trails are on private land. You can order the association's book, *The Connecticut Walk Book*, for $17 including postage. *16 Meriden Rd., Rockfall, CT 06481; tel. 860-346-2372.*

A Blast From the Past

EXPERIENCE 17:
MINE HILL PRESERVE

The Highlights: An elevated trail through a hardwood forest that's on the National Register of Historic Places, old mine shafts, tunnels, and granite quarries.

Other Places Nearby: Award-winning country inns, beautiful nature trails.

The Litchfield Hills are known for their unspoiled natural beauty, colonial architecture, and urbane country lifestyle. Today, it is hard to imagine that during the Revolutionary War, the peaceful area you will walk through was a major iron ore region, smoky with blast and puddling furnaces, crowded with hundreds of workers, and congested with a constant flow of ox carts hauling ore. As a major supplier of armaments to the Continental army, the area's lush woodlands were almost completely eradicated to make the thousands of bushels of charcoal needed to produce iron. Long after the Revolution, the production of iron continued to be a major industry in the area.

On this walking tour in the nearby somnolent village of Roxbury, you can explore Mine Hill Preserve, where you will find Connecticut's most extensive ruins of blast furnaces, tunnels, and roasting ovens.

▼

The first commercial mining operations began in the middle of the 18th century, inspired by the hope of finding silver. Operations were implemented in 1751 and again in 1764. Little silver was found, and the two efforts were business failures. Among the pre-Revolutionary investors in the early operations was Ethan Allen, the hero of the battle of Fort Ticonderoga and a Roxbury native.

Early in the 1800s, commercial interest in this site was revived by the possibility of mining the abundant iron ore. Under a succession of owners, there was some construction and mining activity, culminating in 1865 with the purchase of the property by the Shepaug Spathic Iron & Steel Company. Between 1865 and 1868, the firm greatly expanded the mine tunnels and constructed a rail bed to convey the ore down the hill. Workmen built two ore roasters, and from the mine's own granite quarries, they built a blast furnace, a steel puddling furnace, and a rolling mill. Long wooden buildings enclosed the working area around these structures. Halfway between the mine and the furnace area, Mineral Spring Brook was dammed to create a reservoir with a reliable water supply. Underground pipes connected the pond to at least three hydrants placed at strategic points in the ironworks. As you walk through Mine Hill Preserve, you can see many of these structures still standing.

In the spring of 1867, the plant was ready to process the ore into cast iron. By the late 1870s, however, the mine ceased to operate because of internal financial problems and the increased competition from the large pit furnaces newly opened in Minnesota and Pittsburgh.

Mine Hill's large supply of granite was commercially tapped in 1850. The opening of the Shepaug Valley Railroad, with a station in Chalybes, made it possible to transport the granite to New York. The railroad ran along the foot of Mine Hill, where the old railroad grade is still discernible today. Eight

▼

granite quarries operated at various times in Mine Hill Preserve. Unfortunately, historic records of the quarrying activity are scant. The upper quarry closed in 1905, and the Shepaug Valley Railroad stopped operating in 1935, with the closing of Rockside Quarry.

Mine Hill was later purchased by the Roxbury Land Trust, with funds from Roxbury residents and the Knapp Foundation. Its iron mine and furnace complex were included in the National Register of Historic Places in August 1979.

In present-day Litchfield Hills, pristine villages have replaced the smoky settlements, and there are few physical remains of the once-thriving mining industry. The sylvan beauty of the hills has returned, making the area a haven for many celebrities, including Meryl Streep, Michael J. Fox, Whoopi Goldberg, Dustin Hoffman, and many more.

GETTING THERE

By car:

From I-84, take Rte. 67 north to Roxbury. Mine Hill Preserve is located off Rte. 67, 2 3/10 mi. north of Roxbury Town Hall. After crossing the Shepaug River, turn right onto Mine Hill Rd. Proceed past the lumberyard and the houses, and follow the dirt road to the signs for the parking area located on the right side.

Walk Directions

TIME: 2 1/2 to 3 hours
LEVEL: Easy to moderate
DISTANCE: 3 1/2 miles
ACCESS: By car

The main loop of this trail is marked with a blue blaze. There also is a 3/4-mile nature loop blazed in yellow that is linked to the main trail. Pick up picnic supplies in nearby Roxbury. The area closes at sunset; **do not enter the area near nightfall because shafts are dangerous.**

▼

TO BEGIN

Walk from the parking lot into the woods, following the blue blazes. Walk over a footbridge to an information board.

1. Just beyond the information board, turn left and head up the blue-blazed Donkey Trail. In a few minutes, you pass the back side of two enormous fieldstone roasting ovens on your right. *The trail got its name because donkeys hauled carts filled with ore from the mines to the furnaces along iron rails. The rails were removed for scrap during World War II, but the slightly elevated railbed through the forest provides a good view of the ruins.*

2. You reach an intersection with a 3/4-mile yellow-blazed nature loop walk on the right. Continue straight (unless you want to follow the nature loop, which reconnects to the blue-blazed Donkey Trail further on). You next arrive at the first of two tunnels you will see along the way. *On a hot summer day, you can feel the cool air rising from the mouth of the shaft. Mine Hill is honeycombed with tunnels, **all too unstable to enter.*** Just beyond the first tunnel, follow the trail as it ascends steeply. At the top of the trail, you come to the entrance of a second tunnel. Continue on the trail as it bears to the right and evens out. In about 10 minutes, you come to the end of the elevated portion of the Donkey Trail and to a series of four mine shafts. In a few more minutes, you pass a series of old foundations, as well as additional shafts used for mine ventilation.

3. You reach a trail intersection, where you go left, continuing to follow the blue blazes. Walk for about 45 minutes along a boulder-strewn path that makes its serpentine way through the hardwood forest dominated by hemlocks and mountain laurels. You pass an additional shaft and an abandoned granite quarry. *Stones from these quarries were used in the construction of the Brooklyn Bridge and Manhattan's Grand Central Terminal and East River Dr.*

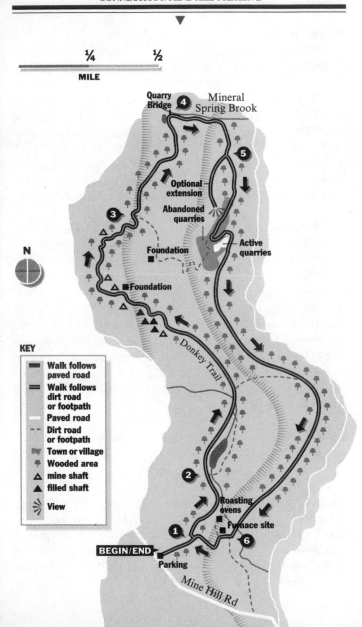

¼ ½
MILE

Quarry Bridge 4 Mineral Spring Brook

5

Optional extension

Abandoned quarries

3

Foundation

Active quarries

N

Foundation

Donkey Trail

KEY

Walk follows paved road
Walk follows dirt road or footpath
Paved road
Dirt road or footpath
Town or village
Wooded area
△ mine shaft
▲ filled shaft
View

2

Roasting ovens

Furnace site

1

6

BEGIN/END

Parking

Mine Hill Rd

▼

4. When you reach Quarry Bridge, turn right on the blue-blazed trail, which follows Mineral Spring Brook. This trail is littered with granite blocks and ledges.

5. About 10 minutes after departing from Point 4, you reach an intersection. Turn left on the blue-blazed trail. For a view of the largest quarry face, with hundreds of granite blocks piled at its base, continue straight (don't go left) a short distance to an overlook. Retrace your steps to Point 5, and go right to resume the walk. The blue-blazed trail now proceeds along a dirt road with corn fields on your left and gray granite ledges on your right.

6. When the trail veers sharply right, notice the ruins of the furnace site, which you should take time to explore. Walk around the blast furnace and climb the four terraces to the roasting ovens, which provide a commanding view of the site. After exploring the site, continue on, following the blue-blazed trail back into the woods to the parking lot. *In the 19th century, this furnace site hustled with activity. Donkey carts were unloaded and the ore was heated to remove unwanted byproducts. The ore was mixed with charcoal and marble and loaded into the blast furnace for smelting. The molten ore was removed by letting it run into channels dug into the sand in front of the furnace. Here it cooled to form iron bars known as pigs.*

OTHER PLACES NEARBY

■ **Flanders Nature Center.** Hike on an award-winning botany trail. Wild flowers peak in May, and 25 varieties of ferns can be seen in June. Flanders also operates the Whittemore Sanctuary on Route 64. *Flanders Rd. and Church Hill Rd., Woodbury, CT 06798; tel. 203-263-2711. Trails open daily dawn to dusk. Off Rte. 6, about 10 mi. east of Mine Hill.*

■ **The Glebe House and Gertrude Jekyll Garden.** This minister's farm, or "glebe," dating from the 1770s, was where the first American bishop of the Episcopal Church was elect-

▼

ed in 1783. The house has fine period furnishings from the area, as well as original paneling. Surrounding the house is the only garden in the U.S. designed by Britain's most famous 20th-century gardener, Gertrude Jekyll. *Hollow Rd., Woodbury, CT 06798; tel. 203-263-2855. Open Wed.-Sun. 1-4 Apr.-Nov. Open Dec.-Mar. by appointment only. Admission. About 10 mi. east of Mine Hill.*

DINING

■ **The Mayflower Inn** (very expensive). This distinguished English-style country hotel offers luxurious dining in a series of elegant, softly illuminated dining rooms or, in summer, on a wide porch overlooking the Shakespeare garden. The regional American menu with lots of creative twists changes daily. Menu items have included Jonah crab cakes with lobster caviar mayonnaise, cream of lobster soup with Armagnac, and grilled Atlantic salmon on crushed chive potatoes. *118 Woodbury Rd., Washington, CT 06793; tel. 860-868-9466; fax 860-868-1497. Open daily for lunch and dinner. On Rte. 47, about 10 mi. north of Mine Hill.*

■ **The Bistro** (expensive). One of New Milford's historic buildings has been artfully converted into a two-level restaurant. The elegant dining room combines original red-brick walls with nine stylized windows under a high ceiling. The menu features specialties such as an appetizer of crispy goat cheese and potato tart. Try the sesame seared talapia (a farm-raised Caribbean fish) presented on a bed of jasmine-scented rice and stir-fried vegetables. *31 Bank St., New Milford, CT 06776; tel. 860-355-3266. Open daily for lunch and dinner. Off Rte. 202 in the town center; about 10 mi. west of Mine Hill.*

■ **The Boulders Inn** (expensive). You get full advantage of this country inn's site overlooking Lake Waramaug, whether in the main dining room, with its three-sided view of the lake, or on one of the three terraced outdoor decks. While savoring the view, try the young mesclun salad with Stilton cheese,

▼

apples, and roasted walnuts, or, as an entree, grilled sirloin with roasted shallot and bacon bordelaise and dauphine potatoes. *Rte. 45, New Preston, CT 06777; tel. 860-868-0541. Open daily except Tue. for dinner Memorial Day-Oct.; Wed.-Sun. Nov.-Dec.; and Thu.-Sun. Jan.-May. In Oct., dinner begins at noon on Sun.; otherwise at 4. About 15 mi. north of Mine Hill.*

■ **The Curtis House Restaurant** (inexpensive to moderate). Good Yankee fare served in the ambience of a historic colonial dining room. The menu features chowders and bisques, flaky-crust pot pies, roast beef, and, of course, Yankee pot roast. All dinners include potato, vegetable, salad, dessert, and coffee. *506 Main St. South, Woodbury, CT 06798; tel. 203-263-2101. Open daily for dinner and Tue.-Sat. for lunch. On Rte. 6, about 10 mi. east of Mine Hill.*

LODGING

■ **Mayflower Inn** (very expensive). Situated on 28 manicured acres, this recently refurbished 100-year-old country inn features three American shingle-style buildings with 25 rooms and suites, all decorated with 18th- and 19th-century antiques, imported tapestries, and linens. Wood-burning fireplaces, balconies, verandas, formal gardens, and woodlands complete the setting at this refined retreat, a member of the distinguished Relais & Chateaux lodging association. *118 Woodbury Rd., Washington, CT 06793; tel. 860-868-9466. On Rte. 47, about 10 mi. north of Mine Hill.*

■ **The Boulders Inn** (expensive). Located at the foot of Pinnacle Mountain overlooking beautiful Lake Waramaug, this award-winning inn has 17 luxuriously appointed rooms and suites that are tastefully decorated with antiques and have many amenities. Some rooms have lake views. If you want extra privacy, ask for a room in one of the inn's several hillside cottages set in the woods overlooking the lake. The cottages have decks and fireplaces; some have whirlpools. *Rte. 45, New Preston, CT 06777; tel. 860-868-0541. About 15 mi. north of Mine Hill.*

▼

■ **Homestead Inn** (moderate). A tastefully restored 1853 Victorian house overlooking the New Milford green. The main house has eight guest rooms, all recently redecorated with floral drapes and spreads and furnished with country antiques. All rooms have private baths, cable TV, air conditioning, and phones. Rooms 24 and 25 have beautiful views of the green. *5 Elm St., New Milford, CT 06776; tel. 860-354-4080. Off Rte. 202 in the town center; about 7 mi. west of Mine Hill Preserve.*

■ **The Curtis House** (inexpensive). Connecticut's oldest continuously operating inn, it first opened its doors in 1754. The main house has 14 guest rooms, simply furnished in early American colonial style. Eight have private baths, and many include canopied beds. There are four rooms in the former carriage house. *506 Main St. South, Woodbury, CT 06798; tel. 860-263-2101. On Rte. 6, about 10 mi. east of Mine Hill.*

FOR MORE INFORMATION
Tourist Office:

■ **Litchfield Hills Travel Council.** Leave a message on the answering machine if you'd like a brochure. *Box 968, Litchfield, CT 06059; tel. 860-567-4506; fax 860-567-5214. Open Mon.-Fri. 10-6. The council also operates a booth daily 10-4 mid-Jun. to mid-Oct. on the Litchfield green.*

For Serious Walkers:

■ **Connecticut Forest & Park Association.** This private association maintains and documents 700 miles of trails—a number of which are in Litchfield County, including a portion of the Appalachian Trail. You can order the association's book, *The Connecticut Walk Book*, for $17 including postage. *16 Meriden Rd., Rockfall, CT 06481; tel. 860-346-2372.*

A Utopian Dream

EXPERIENCE 18: GUILFORD

Most Americans know the story of the pilgrims, who came to the New World to find religious freedom and escape persecution in their native land of England. But few have heard of the voyages of men such as Henry

> **The Highlights:** A wild, rugged forest, centuries-old roads, abandoned quarries.
>
> **Other Places Nearby:** A beautiful New England village, well-preserved colonial homes, pretty seascapes and countryside.

Whitfield, who abandoned a well-to-do life and set out during the 17th century in search of freedom in a land unsettled by the white man. In this southern Connecticut walking tour, you'll discover the wooded lands near Guilford, a village that Whitfield and like-minded friends and followers founded in their attempt to establish a utopian community.

Born in England in 1597, Whitfield had all the privileges and advantages of a young wealthy Englishman. He attended the finest schools, but instead of following in the footsteps of his father, a well-respected attorney in London, he entered the ministry and quickly obtained a position in a rich diocese, where he worked for two decades. He and his wife, also of a distinguished family, lived in great comfort.

▼

Whitfield, however, was a man of conscience, according to a local history book written in the late 1800s by Bernard Christian Steiner, a Guilford resident who based his accounts on original documents in the town's possession. Although Whitfield was a minister in the established church, he sympathized with and sheltered some of the well-known nonconformists of his time—men who sought a purer interpretation of the Bible and eschewed what they felt to be the lax principles of the time. England's leadership did not take kindly to these nonconformists and tried to make life difficult for them. Whitfield began to feel the heat. Sometime in the 1630s, he and his friends began to think of escaping to the New World and enlisted the help of an agent named George Fenwick to scout out the possibilities there.

Early reviews were mixed. Reports of disease, cold weather, and wars with Native Americans gave people cold feet, and it took some time for Whitfield and his group to make up their minds. Finally, in the spring of 1639, Whitfield and about 25 young men, and an unknown number of women, children, servants, and workers, set out from London for the long sail across the Atlantic. With them came livestock, a bevy of supplies useful for starting a new community, and skilled workers under contract for several years.

Whitfield or one of his group apparently knew the people who had settled in what later became New Haven, so that's where they headed. However, according to the local historian Steiner, they had no intention of settling with their brethren there but rather wanted to stake out a new community. It would be a utopian community, where they would join "together in one entire plantation and be helpful each to the other in any common work, according to every man's ability and as need shall require, and we promise not to desert or leave each other or the plantation, but with the consent of the rest, or the

▼

greater part of the company who have entered into this engagement." That was the covenant they signed on their six-week voyage to the New World.

Whitfield didn't waste any time after his arrival in New Haven in July 1639. He headed east along the shoreline to explore some land of which he had heard favorable reports. He bypassed the forest covered by this walk because it was too rugged, but he liked the nearby land, which would later become Guilford. With the help of a settler with some knowledge of the local tribal language, he negotiated the purchase of this land from a sadly weakened Native American tribe that was decimated by the white man's diseases and the warfare their presence had sparked. The sachem queen of the Menuncatucks signed with her mark a contract drawn up in classic English legalese, giving the settlers ownership of the land for the price of 12 coats, 12 fathom of wampum (beads made of shell), 12 glasses, 12 pairs of shoes, 12 hatchets, 12 pairs of stockings, 12 hoes, four kettles, 12 knives, 12 hats, and 12 spoons.

The Native Americans didn't leave right away and apparently helped with some of the early construction of the settlers' plantation. Development was not helter-skelter. The new government designed their plantation around a public green—just like back home in England. Whitfield's home, located a short distance from the green, was the most opulent and still stands, built of stone taken from nearby quarries like the one you'll see along the walk. If you decide to also stroll through downtown Guilford, you'll see the homes of other early settlers. Their meeting house was built on the middle of the north end of the public green but no longer stands.

The settlers divided up the land and paid according to the size of the lots. These funds went to the public treasury that helped pay for the construction of roads (merely clearings through the forests in the early days) and a few public buildings. This new government improvised, borrowing a lot of common law from England but adapting it to their principles.

▼

The settlers made their living the same way as their descendants for generations to come: farming, fishing, shell fishing, and related local businesses.

The great passion that brought these young settlers to the New World dissipated in some, and there was somewhat of a reverse migration led by Whitfield in the 1650s, when conditions in England improved. Those who remained lost some of their utopian independence, in part due to fears of conflict with Native Americans or Dutch settlers, and the settlement eventually recognized the authority of the state of Connecticut. But the quiet simple life they sought has endured for centuries.

GETTING THERE:
By car:

Heading north from New York on I-95 (the Connecticut Tpke.), take exit 58 for Guilford. Turn right at the end of the ramp and follow Church St. (Rte. 77) to the town green. Make a right at the green and then a quick left, following the road alongside the green. At the end of the green, turn right onto Rte. 146 (Water St.) and drive just over 1 mi. Before the road veers left under railroad tracks, bear right into a parking area at the entrance to the West Woods trail complex, which is located at the corner of Rte. 146 and Sam Hill Rd.

Walk Directions

TIME: Up to 2 hours
LEVEL: Easy to moderate
DISTANCE: Up to 4 miles
ACCESS: By car

This park has so many trail options that there is an itinerary for every level of walker. The trails are well-blazed, but there are so many blazes it can become confusing. In fact, the walk directions do not indicate every intersection for fear of confusing the issue. Make sure you follow the blaze indicated in the directions. For

▼

about half this itinerary, you will mostly follow the white trail, blazed by a round white circle. For the return, you will mostly follow the orange trail, blazed by a round orange circle. Along the way, numerous trails enable you to cut across to others, and are marked with colored squares that correspond to the trail colors they connect. The best picnic spot is at the Lost Lake overview just before Point 3, but there are many open rock ledges that provide a good place to relax and take in the dense forest, with its tidal inlets, swamps, and steep granite ridges. Pick up picnic foods in the many shops on Rte. 1, between Church St. and Soundview Rd.

TO BEGIN

From the parking area, walk up a broad, well-marked footpath. It leads through the forest, with railroad tracks on your left.

1. At an intersection with the orange trail (where you will come out on your return), continue straight. On your left, you soon see a jumble of boulders. *This marks one of the old quarries in the park. Some of the stone in this area ended up in New York City's Grand Central Station and brownstones.* Continue on and you soon reach a viewpoint of Lost Lake to your left. *Before this became a lake, settlers came here to harvest salt hay, for which they had many uses on their farms.*

2. When you arrive at an orange-blazed trail, ignore it and continue on. Ignore a second orange-blazed trail. Continue on as the trail winds up to a granite ledge offering great views of Lost Lake. *Native Americans and later an occasional settler probably sat at this spot to enjoy a similar view, although the lake was probably more like a swamp in earlier times. If you're feeling lazy or just want a short walk, retrace your steps to your car.*

3. In a rocky area just beyond the overlook, you reach an intersection with a yellow-blazed trail. Follow the round white

▼

blazes, which bear right up through a line of rocks. Proceed on the white-blazed trail on a spine of granite rising above swampy areas. If you find yourself descending too far to the right or left along this stretch, you've probably veered off the white-blazed trail.

4. After passing a small set of power lines, you reach a large intersection with the blue trail. Continue straight, ignoring the blue-blazed trail. *An old route between Guilford and Stony Creek, the blue trail probably once offered access to the salt marshes, where hay was harvested.*

5. In a short distance, you arrive at another large intersection with a green trail. Go right. You soon cross an intersection with the orange trail. *If you want to return to your car, turn right and follow the orange blazes.* Otherwise, continue straight and pass two more green-blazed trails that go to the right. *In this area, you will see stone walls that possibly date from colonial times.*

6. At the next four-way intersection, turn right and follow the green trail uphill. In a short distance, you come to an intersection and a sign that says "Nature Trail, Walking Only." Continue straight on the green trail, whose blazes are in the shape of a triangle. Ignore several trails that intersect the green trail. Follow the green trail as it proceeds on a ridge that's parallel to the ridge you walked on earlier on the white trail. *Notice that a swampy valley divides the two ridges.*

7. Go right at an intersection with the blue trail, which follows an old road through the woods. Ignore a couple of trails that go off to your right.

8. At an intersection with the orange trail, go left and follow the orange blazes. Pass Indian Cave, whose appearance certainly suggests a suitable shelter for this forest's earlier

▼

inhabitants. Follow the orange trail back toward Point 1, making sure you follow the orange blazes through the various intersections along the way. When you arrive at a large, three-

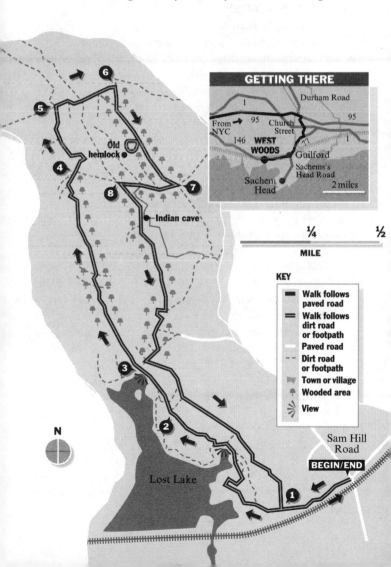

GETTING THERE

Durham Road
1
95
Church Street
From NYC
146 **WEST WOODS**
95
1
Guilford
Sachems's Head Road
Sachem Head
2 miles

¼ ½
MILE

KEY

Walk follows paved road

Walk follows dirt road or footpath

Paved road

Dirt road or footpath

Town or village

Wooded area

View

N

Old hemlock

Indian cave

Lost Lake

Sam Hill Road

BEGIN/END

way intersection with the white-circle trail, turn left and walk a short distance back to your car.

OTHER PLACES NEARBY

■ **Village of Guilford.** Considered one of New England's best-preserved colonial villages, it offers a charming walking tour and interesting old homes you can visit. Pick up the excellent walking tour map in the Guilford tourist office or buy a copy of Sarah Brown McCulloch's *A Walking Guide* in the village book store on Church Street by the village green. Be sure to include Fair Street and the green on your walk.

■ **Hammonasset State Park.** One of Connecticut's best beaches, located adjacent to a nature preserve. *Boston Post Rd., Madison, CT 06443; tel. 203-245-2785. Open daily. Admission. About 10 mi. east of Guilford, off I-95 exit 62.*

■ **Henry Whitfield State Museum.** The impressive 1639 stone home of Guilford's founder, Reverend Henry Whitfield. The museum has furnishings from the 17th to 19th centuries, weaving and textile equipment, and exhibits on local and state history. *Whitfield St., Box 210, Guilford, CT 06437; tel. 203-453-2457. Open Wed.-Sun. 10-4:30 Feb. 1-Dec. 14. Admission. South of the village green.*

■ **Hyland House.** Built in 1660 by one of Guilford's earliest residents, the house displays furnishings and household utensils in use during colonial times. *84 Boston St., Guilford, CT 06437; tel. 203-453-9477. Open Tue.-Sun. 10-4:30 Jun.-Sep. Admission. Located a few hundred feet east of the village green.*

■ **Thomas Griswold House.** Furniture and china from the 18th and 19th centuries are displayed in a house built in 1774 and occupied by the original family for five generations. There's also a blacksmith shop, a barn, and a museum store. *171 Boston St., Guilford, CT 06437, tel. 203-453-3176. Open Tue.-Sun. 11-4 Jun. 15-Sep. 5 and weekends only through Columbus Day weekend. Admission. Located a few hundred feet east of the village green.*

DINING

■ **Le Petit Cafe** (expensive). Very small, and a favorite with locals for its excellent French cuisine. Call ahead well in advance for a weekend reservation. *2251 Montowese St., Branford, CT 06405; tel. 203-483-9791. Open Wed.-Sun. for dinner. On Rte. 146, about 9 mi. west of Guilford.*

■ **Cafe Lafayette** (expensive). The ambience is very special in this former Congregational church built in 1839 and listed on the National Register of Historic Places. Hand-painted textured walls and murals surround you. The American/international menu with regional influences features specials such as salmon filet with spinach and Portobello mushroom ravioli, and the restaurant's famous veal, pork, and spinach meatloaf. You can get a less expensive meal in the adjacent tavern room. *725 Boston Rd., Madison, CT, 06443; tel. 203-245-7773, 800-660-8984. Open Mon.-Sat. for lunch and dinner, Sun. for brunch and dinner. On Rte. 1 in the center of town; 5 mi. east of Guilford.*

■ **Restaurant du Village** (expensive). When you pass through the iron-gated brick courtyard and enter this tiny restaurant with its charming decor of whitewashed walls and Provencal prints, you feel you're in the French countryside. The outstanding country French cuisine includes specialties such as crispy roast duckling with sun-dried cherries and ginger in red wine sauce. All food, including the pastries and bread, is prepared on the premises using local ingredients. *59 Main St., Chester, CT 06412; tel. 860-526-5301. Open Tue.-Sun. for dinner Memorial Day-Columbus Day; Wed.-Sun. the rest of the year. Off Rte. 154, about 28 mi. northeast of Guilford.*

■ **Bistro on the Green** (moderate). Located in a Victorian building, this restaurant has a relaxed, informal atmosphere whose linoleum floors and ceiling fans contrast with the formality of table-clothed place settings. Beef bourguignon, homemade pastas such as lobster-stuffed ravioli, and gourmet pizzas make for an eclectic menu. *25 Whitfield St., Guilford, CT*

▼

06437; tel. 203-458-9059. Open daily for lunch; Tue.-Sat. for dinner; and Sat.-Sun. for breakfast. Next to the village green.

■ **Friends & Co.** (moderate). Some of the more original specialties at this casual family restaurant include a grilled goat cheese sandwich as well as "southwest pasta": penne with barbecued chicken, sweet peppers, and broccoli, with a sauce of tequila, cream, and smoked mozzarella. The decor features an eclectic combination of seafaring art and objects. *11 Boston Post Rd., Madison, CT 06443, tel. 203-245-0462. Open daily for dinner, Mon.-Fri. for lunch, and Sun. for brunch. Closed Mon. for lunch May-Aug. About 2 mi. east of Guilford on Rte. 1.*

■ **Lenny's Indian Head Inn** (inexpensive). Come prepared to roll up your sleeves and dig into what some say is better seafood than you'd get in Cape Cod. A favorite with boaters, this cafe is best known for its lobster-and-steamers dinner, as well as for its whole fried clams and fried oysters. The ambience is extremely casual. No reservations or credit cards accepted. *205 S. Montowese St., Branford, CT 06405, tel. 203-488-1500. Open daily for lunch and dinner. On Rte. 146, about 8 mi. west of Guilford.*

LODGING

You'll have to drive up to a half hour to take advantage of the best offerings in the area. During summer, check with hotels regarding their minimum-stay requirements on weekends.

■ **Saybrook Inn & Spa** (very expensive). Although the hotel was built only recently, the interior decor provides a luxurious, traditional, and very quiet environment. There are 62 rooms, including 7 suites, all with private baths (the suites have whirlpool baths). The luxury Soundview rooms have views of Long Island Sound. The deluxe rooms have the same decor and amenities but no views. There's a fitness center, a pool, and a la carte spa services. *2 Bridge St., Old Saybrook, CT 06475, tel. 860-395-2000, 800-243-0212. On Rte. 154, about 20 mi. east of Guilford.*

▼

■ **The Inn at Cafe Lafayette** (very expensive). Luxurious rooms and suites, furnished with antiques from the 17th, 18th, and 19th centuries and handwoven rugs. All have private marble baths and are insulated for noise. Located in a historic former Congregational Church, with rooms above the restaurant. All linens are 400-count Egyptian cotton. Unfortunately, there are no views, because the inn is in the center of town. *725 Boston Post Rd., Madison, CT 06443, tel. 203-245-7773, 800-660-8984. Open year-round, but rates are less expensive Nov. 15-May 15. On Rte. 1, 5 mi. east of Guilford.*

■ **Madison Beach Hotel** (expensive). This waterfront building has been a hotel since the 1920s. It has 34 rooms, all facing the water; the rooms on the second through fourth floors have balconies. Guests may use the hotel's private beach (the hotel supplies beach towels and chairs). Continental breakfast included. Rooms are long and narrow with colonial-style decor. There is live music on weekends, so you may want to ask for quiet room away from the action. *94 W. Wharf Rd., Madison, CT 06443, tel. 203-245-1404. Closed Jan.-Feb. Off Rte. 1, about 6 mi. east of Guilford. Make a right on W. Wharf Rd. and proceed to the end.*

■ **Riverwind Inn** (expensive). This colonial house, built at the beginning of the 19th century, has eight guest rooms, all with period furnishings and baths. One popular room is the huge, romantic Champagne & Roses Room, which has a private balcony and walls hand-stenciled with roses. Some rooms are moderately priced. If you like B&Bs, you'll find few better. *209 Main St., Deep River, CT 06417, tel. 860-526-2014. On Rte. 154, about 25 mi. northeast of Guilford.*

■ **Tidewater Inn** (expensive). Ten rooms with antique furnishings in a former stagecoach stop along the old Boston Post Road (now Route 1). Some rooms have a fireplace, others have canopy beds, all have antique charm. The inn is located on attractive grounds adjacent to a forest, but the calm is marred during the day by busy Route 1. *949 Boston Post Rd.,*

▼

Box 1190, Madison, CT 06443, tel. 203-245-8457. On Rte. 1, about 6 mi. east of Guilford.

■ **The Cottage on Church Street** (moderate). This separate cheerful cottage on the property of an 1850 house has been newly renovated in traditional style. It includes one bedroom with king-size bed, a sitting room, a dining area, and a bath. There is a microwave, a refrigerator, and a coffee-maker (but no stove). The cottage is on a road that's busy during the day, but the bedroom faces a back garden. *190 Church St., Guilford, CT 06437, tel. 203-458-2598; fax 203-458-0109. A short distance south of I-95 exit 58.*

FOR MORE INFORMATION
Tourist Office:
Guilford Visitors Information Bureau. The bureau, which has a table at the Nathaniel Green Community Center, offers pamphlets of information and provides a recorded announcement of upcoming events. *Nathaniel Green Community Center, 32 Church St., Guilford, CT 06437; tel. 203-458-0408. You can pick up pamphlets at the community center Mon.-Fri. 8:30-4:30. On Sat. 10-4 and Sun. 12-4, a volunteer is there to answer questions.*

The Soldiers' Camp

EXPERIENCE 19: JOCKEY HOLLOW

Few forests in the region compare in grandeur with Jockey Hollow, a part of the Morristown National Historical Park. Huge old trees have gradually shaded the underbrush to create a wide open forest floor, giving visitors

The Highlights: A Revolutionary War encampment, a stunning old forest, an 18th-century farmhouse.

Other Places Nearby: Washington's Headquarters, numerous museums, the home of a famous furniture designer, a historical farm.

a glimpse of what the virgin forest must have looked like to the Revolutionary War soldiers who set up camp here more than 200 years ago. If you want to experience this beautiful land as they did during this walking tour in north-central New Jersey, don't come during spring or summer when the soaring tree boughs throw a dappled light over the bright green carpet of ground cover. Come in the dead of winter, when it's icy cold and hues of brown, gray, and white better tell the story of the men who suffered here for the cause of revolution.

To appreciate the heroism of the soldiers who camped here, it's important to know that these men did not have to fight. The shivering, often starving men who passed their win-

▼

ters in Valley Forge and Jockey Hollow could have left at almost any time by simply walking out of the camps and heading home, and many did. Conditions couldn't have been much worse on the way home than in the crowded, poorly equipped and fed encampments, and the chances of getting caught for desertion were small, although the penalty severe.

T he soldiers of the Revolutionary War fought a far different kind of war than anything familiar to people of this century. At General George Washington's insistence, the revolutionaries waged a modified version of classic 18th-century warfare, which included lengthy lulls in fighting, an entourage of hangers-on and women, and a general unwillingness of generals to fight during the cold of winter. After the major campaigns of the war during spring, summer, and fall, the troops in the north retreated to winter encampments, notably Valley Forge, Pennsylvania, in the early part of the war and Jockey Hollow, near Morristown, New Jersey, later on. Washington wintered in Jockey Hollow with his wife and family in the Ford family's home, which still stands and is open to the public.

Today, we may revel at the glory of the cause, but the issues surrounding the Revolutionary War were not so clear-cut to Americans back then. Loyalties were divided, especially in areas around New York City and to the south, and Washington may, in part, have picked Morristown as a winter encampment because there was more sympathy for the cause there. It was not like the Civil War or World Wars, when Americans lined up to join the army. One of Washington's greatest challenges was to find enough men to fight the war; the other was to feed the men and find the money to pay for their food.

The few hundred residents of Morris Town, as it was known then, got their first taste of this army when several thousand soldiers set up camp in the winter of 1777. During the winters of 1779 and 1780, up to 10,000 men and an

▼

unknown number of women invaded the quiet valley village. Most camped on the farm of the Wick family in a 2,000-acre area known as Jockey Hollow, while the high-ranking officers lodged in the homes of townspeople. There are few accounts of what the common soldiers thought of their stay, but military records and officers' correspondence tell some of the story, both good and bad.

Soldiers at Jockey Hollow did not encounter the devastating diseases that killed more than 3,000 people at Valley Forge but instead confronted historically harsh weather without the benefit of adequate clothing, food, or shelter. The first snows came in November when the soldiers began to arrive, followed by a string of bad storms in December and January. The arriving army immediately built log huts, but many had to endure the snowstorms in canvas tents until the huts were completed. Organized into nine major encampments, each representing a different brigade, the soldiers usually built the huts on small terraces hollowed out of hillsides, following a uniform size and design that slept a dozen men. The officers' huts were built last, generally above the soldiers' huts, and accommodated four men.

The soldiers often received few rations for weeks because of poor weather and the Continental army's pitiable supply system. More than 1,000 deserted, and there were numerous arrests for consorting with the enemy, assaulting officers, and attempted mutiny. Local residents frequently had to contend with drunken soldiers, robberies, and finally the foraging parties designed by General Washington to obtain food for the men while controlling the amount taken from any single local resident. Unfortunately, several years of war had robbed the fledgling U.S. dollar of any appreciable value, making it difficult to appease farmers with promises of payment. Despite the difficulties, the officers, at least, managed to have some fun, based on some of their letters describing elaborate dinners and parties in the homes of Morristown residents.

▼

Of all Washington's fears, the greatest was the perpetual risk of mutiny. In May 1780, Washington had to subdue a rebellion by the Connecticut Brigade. The following New Year's Day, in the Pennsylvania Line encampment (between Points 2 and 19 on this walking tour), the soldiers had had enough. A number of them killed an officer, rallied additional troops, and stormed off down the Elizabeth-Mendham Road, which you will follow on this walk. General Anthony Wayne and others were able to resolve the situation before any more harm was done.

During their encampment, the soldiers knocked down thousands of trees, virtually overrunning the farm and woodlands of the Wick family, which owned much of the land. After the war, the huts fell gradually into decay and were swallowed by forest. Locals farmed the land, hunted, or gathered wood, and tried to erect some waterworks in the 19th century to improve the water supply in Morristown. Based in part on efforts by powerful local residents, the land of Jockey Hollow became a national park in 1933. Many of the soldiers' sites were excavated as part of a public works program during the Depression. Otherwise, you will find their encampments much as nature has left them after 200 years— barely visible but for the subtle rows of terraces you see along the hillsides beneath the underbrush and the scattered piles of stones left over from their hearths and foundations.

GETTING THERE
By train:

From New York City, take the PATH train to Hoboken, where you connect to New Jersey Transit's Gladstone Line (201-762-5100) to Bernardsville. From there, call a taxi to take you to Jockey Hollow, a trip of about 5 mi. You can call for the return trip from a phone booth at the park. Phone Mendham Village Taxi (201-543-9550 or 800-789-8294).

▼

By car:

At the junction of I-287 and I-80 in New Jersey, head south on I-287 to exit 36. Go straight to Lafayette Ave., where you go right. Proceed a short distance to Morris Ave., where you go right. When you hit the Morristown green, go around it, bearing right on Morris Ave., and then left on Speedwell Ave., to Washington St. (Rtes. 24/510). Turn right and drive three blocks to Western Ave., where you go left following the National Park Service signs to Jockey Hollow. It's about 3 1/2 mi. to the visitors center. Follow signs to parking.

Walk Directions

TIME: 2 1/2 hours
LEVEL: Easy to moderate
DISTANCE: Up to 5 mi.
ACCESS: By car or train

This park has a remarkable number of trails for all levels of walkers and signs placed at almost every trail intersection. This walk was designed by Eric Olsen, park historian and ranger, to connect the various encampments. To add color, he collected quotes from soldiers or officers in the various camps, some of which have been included in the walk directions. You can shorten this walk by taking one of several shortcuts mentioned in the instructions, or pick up a detailed walk map in the visitors center and fashion your own itinerary. For picnic foods, you can find shops in Morristown or at a delicatessen on Western Ave.

TO BEGIN

Walk to the visitors center, which also serves as the main entrance to the park. On the other side of the center, continue straight up a trail leading to a picket fence.

1. At a three-way intersection, go right on a broad grassy path that's mowed in summer. *This is Elizabeth-Mendham Rd., a road no longer used that's one of the oldest in the region. The*

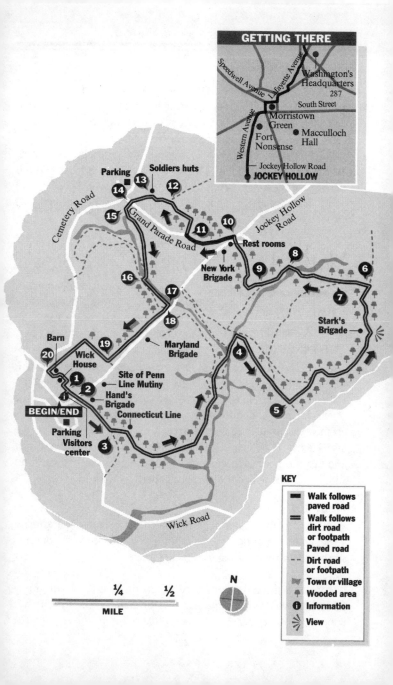

GETTING THERE

Speedwell Avenue
Lafayette Avenue
Washington's Headquarters
287
South Street
Morristown Green
Western Avenue
Fort Nonsense
Macculloch Hall
Jockey Hollow Road
JOCKEY HOLLOW

Parking
Soldiers huts
Cemetery Road
13
14
12
15
Grand Parade Road
11
10
Jockey Hollow Road
Rest rooms
New York Brigade
9
8
6
16
7
17
Stark's Brigade
18
Maryland Brigade
4
Barn
19
5
20
Wick House
1
Site of Penn Line Mutiny
2
Hand's Brigade
BEGIN/END
Connecticut Line
3
Parking
Visitors center

Wick Road

¼   ½
MILE

N

KEY

▬ Walk follows paved road
═ Walk follows dirt road or footpath
 Paved road
--- Dirt road or footpath
🌲 Town or village
🌲 Wooded area
ⓘ Information
🔆 View

▼

setting hasn't changed much since colonial times, when the Wicks farmed this land. You may want to visit the tiny Wick House before proceeding, or stop in on your way back.

2. Cross Jockey Hollow Rd. and continue following the old road into the forest. *To the left is the site of the encampment of Hand's Brigade. Down this old road, the men of the Pennsylvania Line mutiny stormed out of camp.*

3. At the next trail junction, go left. You are now on the Grand Loop Trail, also known as Patriot's Path, marked by an odd-shaped black blaze on a white disk. You shortly come to the Connecticut Line on your left. Continue on the trail for some time, passing two well-marked intersections and a stream. *On Jan. 22, 1780, three men of the Connecticut Line were sentenced to be whipped for "breaking into a store in Morristown and assisting another soldier to get a ladder and steal a bucket of rum while on sentry duty."*

4. At a three-way intersection, go right onto Old Camp Rd. Trail, one of the roads built by soldiers connecting the camp to a tavern on what is now Rte. 202. Go past one trail intersection, pass by a barrier, and follow the trail to the right of a house.

5. Just past the house, go left onto a trail into the woods leading to the Mt. Kemble Loop Trail. When you reach the loop trail, bear right onto it. In a short distance, you arrive at a small break in the forest to the right. *There's a stunning view of a meadow, forests, and hills beyond, marred only by the traffic noise that comes from Rte. 202 and I-287, out of sight in the valley below. On a clear day, the towers of Manhattan's World Trade Center reach above the rolling hills before you. On the hill behind you lie the remains of the Stark's Brigade, whose soldiers fought in almost every major battle of the war. If you explore the thickly wooded hillside, you'll see remains of terraces where the*

▼

soldiers built their huts. When you're done, continue on the Mt. Kemble Loop Trail in the direction you were going. After a short while, you will come to a driveway, where you'll see a house on your right. Continue straight a short distance.

"The soldiers are destitute of both tents and blankets. Our only defense against the inclemency of the weather consists of brush wood thrown together. Our lodging the last night was on the frozen ground. Those officers who have the privilege of a horse can always have a blanket at hand. Having removed the snow, we wrapped ourselves in great coats, spread our blankets on the ground, and lay down by the side of each other, five or six together with large fires at our feet, leaving orders with the waiters to keep it well supplied with fuel during the night. Notwithstanding large fires, we can scarcely keep from freezing."

6. At a fork, bear left downhill, continuing on Mt. Kemble Loop Trail.

7. At the next fork, bear right following the sign to the Grand Loop Trail. Bear left at the next intersection, heading downhill.

8 At a fork, go left. You pass a small pond on your left and see signs of the waterworks Morristown constructed in the last century in its effort to bring more water into town.

9. At the next fork, bear right onto the New York Brigade trail and follow it toward a parking area with rest rooms, which is the site of the New York Brigade encampment.

"The colonel, observing that the open and abominable practice of drunkeness prevails in his regiment without the least shame or restraint to the prejudice of good order and discipline, hereby strictly forbids any liquor to be sold in the huts belonging to the regiment by anybody whatsoever and orders the offenders to be confined and punished for disobedience of orders. The offi-

▼

cers are requested to pay strict attention that the increasing disorder be prevented."

10. When you get to the parking lot, go to the front of the rest rooms and cross the road. Proceed down a paved road marked "Do Not Enter." This is a one-way road.

11. When you arrive at a plaque marking the "Grand Parade," go right across the open field toward its far left corner. (Do not proceed on the trail that enters the forest along the road.) At the edge of the woods, follow the trail to the soldiers' huts that veers left into the woods and goes uphill.

At the place of execution set up on the Grand Parade, "two soldiers were brought to the gallows for the crime of robbery. One of them was pardoned under the gallows and the other executed. The poor criminal was so dreadfully tortured by the horror of an untimely death that he was scarcely able to sustain himself, and the scene excited the compassion of every spectator. It is hoped that this example will make such an impression as to deter others from committing similar crimes." (It did not, but General Washington's habit of pardoning men on the scaffold seems to have helped increase his stature in the soldiers' eyes.)

12. At the top of the hill, go left following the sign to the soldiers' huts. Just before you reach them, you come to a trail junction, where you can go left to see the remains of an open hearth used by soldiers. Either trail takes you to the huts, reconstructed to show the huts of officers (on the upper part of the hill) and those of soldiers.

13. After visiting the huts, walk on the path across the field toward a parking area in the distance.

14. At the road, you see plaques explaining the soldiers' huts. Cross the road and walk onto a small meadow to the right

▼

of the forest. *Under a grove of nearby cedar trees, locals set up a plaque in the 1930s marking the spot of a soldier cemetery at which no remains have ever been found.*

15. A short distance from the road, go left into the forest, following signs to the Soldier Hut Trail. You shortly will see more signs of waterworks built in the last century by locals.

16. Immediately after crossing a stream, go left on the small trail that parallels it. *You can also go a little further and take a larger trail: Both lead to the same place.*

17. At the parking area, go right, following a dirt trail that parallels the paved road. This is the Grand Parade Trail.

18. After crossing a stream again, go left, following the sign to the Grand Parade Trail. Do not go straight ahead onto the Aqueduct Loop Trail. Go right on the Grand Parade Trail just before it hits Jockey Hollow Rd., and follow it back through the woods parallel to the road. *You can cut through the woods on your left to see the Maryland Brigade encampment.*

19. At a Y, go right following a sign to the Wick House. *You can cross the street here to see the site of the Pennsylvania Line mutiny.* Follow the trail along the back of the Wick property, which offers splendid pastoral scenes in spring, summer, and fall. The trail bears left around the property and heads toward the entrance to the Wick House.

20. When you reach an old shed and the park road, go left toward a parking lot, which you cross to reach a footpath that takes you to the Wick House. Visit the house and then proceed around it past the old garden to the Elizabeth-Mendham Rd., where you go left and walk a short distance to Point 1. Go right and retrace your steps through the visitors center to your car.

▼

PLACES ALONG THE WALK

■ **Wick House.** This furnished 18th-century farmhouse is worth a quick visit when you pass it on the walk. *Open daily 9:30-4:30. Closed Mon.-Tue. Dec.-Mar.*

OTHER PLACES NEARBY

■ **Craftsman Farms.** The former home of Gustav Stickley, designer of "mission" furniture and a leader in the Arts and Crafts movement, dates from 1911 and is undergoing restoration. Visitors may walk on the 26 acres of grounds. *2352 Rte. 10 and Manor Ln., Parsippany, NJ 07054; tel. 201-540-1165; fax 201-540-1167. House open Thu. 12-3 and Sat.-Sun. 1-4, Apr.-Oct., and by appointment year-round. Grounds open daily during daylight hours. Admission. About 8 mi. northeast of Jockey Hollow by way of I-287 and I-80.*

■ **Fosterfields Living Historical Farm.** On this farm you can see demonstrations of various agricultural activities as they were performed from 1880 to 1910. You can also visit The Willows, a 19th-century Gothic Revival house built by Paul Revere's grandson and since restored, that features exhibits, tours, and demonstrations interpreting domestic life of yesteryear. *73 Kahdena Rd., Morristown, NJ 07960; tel. 201-326-7645. Farm open Wed.-Sat. 10-5, Sun. 12-5, Apr.-Oct. Call for off-season hours. Admission (free on Wed.). Willows open Thu.-Sun. 1-4:30, Apr.-Oct. Admission. From Morristown, take Rte. 510 (Washington St.) west 1.1 mi. About 4 mi. northwest of Jockey Hollow.*

■ **Historic Speedwell.** Once the country estate of ironmaster Stephen Vail, the eight museum buildings feature exhibits interpreting 19th-century domestic and industrial life. The seven acres of grounds include picnic facilities. *333 Speedwell Ave. (Rte. 202), Morristown, NJ 07960; tel. 201-540-0211. Open Thu.-Fri. 12-4, Sat.-Sun. 1-5, May-Oct. Special events in Dec. Admission. 1 mi. north of Morristown town square. About 3 mi. north of Jockey Hollow.*

▼

■ **Macculloch Hall Historical Museum.** The restored brick Federal-style mansion houses an impressive display of furniture and decorative arts. The gardens include an exceptional collection of old-fashioned roses. *45 Macculloch Ave., Morristown, NJ 07960; tel. 201-538-2404; fax 201-538-9248. Museum open Thu. and Sun. 1-4. Admission. Gardens open daily dawn-dusk, free of charge. 2 blocks south of Morristown green. About 3 mi. north of Jockey Hollow.*

■ **Washington's Headquarters.** This is another unit, in addition to Jockey Hollow, of the Morristown National Historical Park. The ten acres at this location include the Ford Mansion, which General Washington used as his headquarters from December 1779 to June 1780, and a museum. The mansion, furnished in period style, is shown only by guided tour. The museum features self-guiding exhibits and a movie depicting life of the period. *10 Washington Pl., Morristown, NJ 07960; tel. 201-539-2085. Open daily 9-5. Mansion tours hourly 10-4. Admission. Just east of I-287 exit 36. About 5 mi. northeast of Jockey Hollow*

DINING

■ **Bernard's Inn** (expensive). Popular and highly rated, this restored turn-of-the-century inn offers fine dining in an elegant setting with high ceilings, mahogany woodwork, and chandeliers. The "progressive American" menu features only fresh ingredients; even the desserts are homemade. The extensive wine list won an award from *The Wine Spectator*. Live entertainment is offered every evening. Jacket required for dinner. *27 Mine Brook Rd., Bernardsville, NJ 07924; tel. 908-766-0002. Open Mon.-Sat. for lunch and dinner. Across from Bernardsville train station on Rte. 202. About 5 mi. south of Jockey Hollow.*

■ **Dennis Foy's Townsquare Restaurant** (expensive). Chef-owner Dennis Foy's contemporary American cuisine receives high ratings from locals and reviewers. The menu, which is changed every few months to feature seasonal foods,

▼

includes delicacies such as tian of crab, an appetizer, and medallions of venison. *6 Roosevelt Ave., Chatham, NJ 07928; tel. 201-701-0303. Open Mon.-Fri. for lunch and dinner, Sat. for dinner. 1/2 block from Main St. (Rte. 24). About 10 mi. east of Jockey Hollow.*

■ **Grand Cafe** (expensive). This restaurant has an elegant ambience, with its high ceilings and antique furnishings. Specialties include an appetizer of warm lobster salad with angel hair pasta and shiitake mushrooms, and a main course of smoked striped bass, grilled and served on a bed of baby greens with ragout of wild mushrooms and salsify. *42 Washington St., Morristown, NJ 07960; tel. 201-540-9444. Open Mon.-Fri. for lunch and dinner, Sat. for dinner. Just off Morristown town square. About 4 mi. north of Jockey Hollow.*

■ **Black Horse Inn** (moderate). Two restaurants in one: the upscale inn, housed in a building on the Historic Registry that became a stagecoach stop in 1742, and the more informal, inexpensive pub, in the former barn. Both serve fairly standard continental food, including steaks and seafood. *1 W. Main St., Mendham, NJ 07945; tel. 201-543-7300. Inn open Tue.-Sun. for dinner. Pub open daily for lunch and dinner. On Rte. 24 at corner of Mountain Ave. About 5 mi. west of Jockey Hollow.*

■ **Fresh Fields Cafe** (moderate). Chef-owner Kevin Collins serves "creative American" cuisine. For an appetizer, try the hickory-smoked tuna with scallion corn waffles and a rosemary caper sauce; follow it with filet mignon with blue-cheese mashed potatoes, fried leeks, and fried sage. *641 Shunpike Rd., Chatham, NY 07928; tel. 201-377-4072. Open Tue.-Fri. for lunch and dinner, Sat.-Sun. for dinner. In the Hickory Square shopping mall, near the intersection of Green Village Rd. and Shunpike Rd. About 10 mi. east of Jockey Hollow.*

LODGING

■ **Bernard's Inn** (expensive). This inn has 21 elegant rooms. Unfortunately, none have good views, and those in the

▼

front face a small downtown area that's busy during rush hour. Room 5 is one of the best but faces the main road. Some suites are very expensive. *27 Mine Brook Rd. (Rte. 202), Bernardsville, NJ 07924; tel. 908-766-0002. On Rte. 202, about 5 mi. south of Jockey Hollow.*

■ **Publick House** (inexpensive). The rooms in this 1810 inn are pleasantly furnished in country style with antiques from different periods. Rooms 303 and 304 are the most spacious but face the main road. Rooms 203 and 204 have the same decor and dimensions but are close to the downstairs bar. Though the hotel is in the center of town, it's quiet at night. *111 Main St., Chester, NJ 07903; tel. 908-879-6878. About 10 mi. west of Jockey Hollow by way of Rtes. 24/510.*

FOR MORE INFORMATION
Tourist Offices:

The Jockey Hollow Visitor Center. *Tempe Wick Rd., Morristown National Historic Park, Morristown, NJ; tel. 201-543-4030. Open daily 9-5 May-Oct.*

Morristown National Historical Park. *10 Washington Pl., Morristown, NJ 07960; tel. 201-539-2085; fax 201-539-8361. Open daily 9-5.*

Historic Morris Visitors Center. *14 Elm St., Morristown, NJ 07960; tel. 201-993-1194. Open Mon.-Fri. 10-3. About 3 1/2 mi. north of Jockey Hollow.*

For Serious Walkers:

The Jockey Hollow visitors center sells copies of a trail map that can be used to significantly extend the above walk.

A Hideaway for Nature's Friends

EXPERIENCE 20:
NORVIN GREEN

There is hardly any written history about New Jersey's Norvin Green State Forest, and few New York area residents have even heard of it. It's not an easy place to find, it has no state-run facilities, and

> **The Highlights:** Spectacular views of a reservoir, mountains, and the Manhattan skyline in an undeveloped forest; old mines, an ecology center.
>
> **Other Places Nearby:** Wawayanda State Park (*see* Experience 21), historic B&Bs, good restaurants.

there's no tourist infrastructure outside its front gate. But after you walk through this undeveloped forest and see its awesome beauty, you'll be quite glad that it may be the New York metropolitan area's best-kept secret.

You stand atop one of the forest's highest points and gape at a 360-degree panorama of the Ramapo Mountains, the Wanaque Reservoir, and New York's Harriman State Park and Sterling Forest, with the majestic Empire State Building, World Trade Center towers, and the rest of the Manhattan skyline in the background. Norvin Green is never crowded, so you can often enjoy its spectacular viewpoints without another person around.

▼

You also pass by a small waterfall, cross a wooden bridge over a rushing brook, and visit two abandoned mines. Imposing Blue Mine is filled with water, just as it was in 1858 after its decline as a working iron-ore mine. Nearly 30 years later the water was pumped out, and the mine produced 300 tons of iron ore each month. But the water kept refilling and had to be pumped out, and the mine, whose iron-ore vein was 16-feet thick, was finally abandoned in 1905.

About three-quarters of a mile northeast of Blue Mine stands Roomy Mine, which opened in the early 1840s. Miners used a nearly horizontal passageway on the hillside to enter, and you can still walk in about 50 feet.

But there's more to Norvin Green State Forest than the beauty of its land. It's the setting for a fascinating 20th-century story of European immigrants who came here to enjoy nature and outdoor recreation, but who repeatedly had to fight off suspicious government law enforcement officials attempting to monitor their activities.

Prior to World War I, working-class German and Austrian immigrants in the New York City area formed a group called the Nature Friends. The group was modeled after like-named groups in Europe that loved nature and had become disenchanted with their governments' pro-war policies. In Austria, the group tried to get countrymen out of the beer halls and face-to-face with nature, while members in Germany were known to carry lumber on their backs long distances into the woods to build shelters.

In this country, the Nature Friends had a rocky start. Immigrants from Germany, one of the countries America was at war against, were eyed with suspicion by U.S. government authorities during World War I, and some of the Nature Friends were briefly held in prison in White Plains, N.Y. Their nature camp in New York's Westchester County was destroyed by a fire of unknown origin. They searched for a new area and, in north-cen-

▼

tral New Jersey, established 40-acre Camp Midvale, now the site of the Weis Ecology Center where you begin this walking tour.

Group members came on weekends to hike, swim, and play a German game called fistball which resembled volleyball but used a string instead of a net. They maintained the nearby trails, even walking at night to see the stars from High Point, the fabulous viewpoint you visit on your walking tour. From High Point, they looked down at the Ramapo Mountains, a name that derived from an Indian word meaning "place of the slanting rock."

The Nature Friends bought more land, built a clubhouse, a pool, and 60 bungalows. Everyone pitched in to help their friends settle in, and they welcomed people of any race to join their group. Exhibits were set up on a shelf for children: an old bird's nest and bones of a wolf and other animals. The kids could also feed sheep, rabbits, a goat, ducklings, and turtles.

Besides enjoying the outdoors, many of the Nature Friends enjoyed debating world politics, including radical politics. They believed that the older generation in Europe had abused the land and led them to war, and that it was time to build a new society based on the best of socialist ideology. They were anti-fascist, and some were avowed communists.

The good times turned rough, however, when the Cold War began soon after World War II. Senator Joseph McCarthy went on a rampage, fingering suspected communists everywhere in the country. Camp Midvale became a target and in 1947 was listed on the U.S. Attorney General's subversive list. The Ku Klux Klan was suspected of burning a cross there, and FBI agents constantly had their eyes on the camp. In September 1951, the FBI's Newark office began a round-the-clock surveillance while on the lookout for eight communist leaders.

They had no luck at the camp, whose members continued to maintain a good relationship with townspeople nearby. A local newspaper editor visited the camp and saw 12 old men playing cards. "Look what's going to overthrow the govern-

▼

ment," joked one of the Nature Friends.

But it wasn't a jovial time for many. FBI Director J. Edgar Hoover declared that Camp Midvale was a center for indoctrinating youth in communist front tactics, and agents compiled 12,000 pages of documents about the Nature Friends. FBI agents waited at the bottom of the hill outside the camp and jotted down license plate numbers, and they interviewed people on the street outside their homes. Decent people became frightened, wondering what might happen to them and their jobs.

Various actors, musicians, and others in the creative arts, including several who were on the government's subversive list, joined hands with the Nature Friends. Actor Herschel Bernardi was on the cultural staff one summer and organized various skits. Another actor, John Randolph, and his wife Sarah Cunningham, staged excerpts from Chekhov plays. Ruby Dee and Ossie Davis performed, and folk singer Pete Seeger played a concert in front of an audience of 1,200. John Wilson, an artist in residence, was commissioned years later to create the bust of Martin Luther King in the U.S. Capitol Building.

Trying to shake the government's subversive tag, the Nature Friends changed their name to the Metropolitan Recreational Association. Some of the older members began dropping out of the group, and the group became beset with financial problems. They continued to uphold their ideals, participating in the struggle for civil rights for black Americans.

In October 1966, a suspicious fire burned the Nature Friends' old clubhouse to the ground. No one was charged. Later that month, police arrested 19 people with weapons who reportedly were plotting a raid on Camp Midvale.

Without their clubhouse, it was never the same for members. Visiting one another in their homes couldn't replace the camaraderie of the clubhouse. Seventy families held a meeting and decided to sell the land for $1 in return for guarantees that the land wouldn't be commercially used and that the seventy families would have access to the land for the rest of their lives.

▼

The families rejected a half-million-dollar offer from a commercial developer.

Camp Midvale is now the site of the Weis Ecology Center, a study center that is carrying on the outdoor traditions of the Nature Friends. As you visit the center at the beginning or the end of your walking tour, you can imagine the many memories shared by the Nature Friends. "We had an estate," recalls one of the Friends. "We felt like millionaires during the Depression."

GETTING THERE
By car:

From Manhattan, go west over the George Washington Bridge into New Jersey. Follow Rte. 4 west through Hackensack and Teaneck. Rte. 4 turns into Rte. 208. Take Rte. 208 north to Skyline Dr. (exit 57). Turn right onto Skyline Dr. and follow it over a mountain. At a stop sign, stay left (you're still on Skyline). At a second stop sign, turn left onto Rte. 511 south. Go 1 7/10 mi. Turn right onto West Brook Rd. Cross Wanaque Reservoir. At a fork in the road, bear left on West Brook. Pass Wanaque Reservoir sign on your left. Pass Townsend Rd. and make the next left turn onto Snake Den Rd. Pass Ellen St. and then turn right into the Weis Ecology Center parking lot.

Walk Directions

TIME: 1 to 3 hours
LEVEL: Easy to difficult
DISTANCE: Up to 4 miles
ACCESS: By car

The walk ascends steeply to great mountaintop vantage points but should be no trouble for most walkers. You'll be out of breath during one 15-minute uphill stretch and for a minute or two near the end of the walk on the approach to Roomy Mine. If you want to abbreviate this walk while still getting great mountaintop views, you can proceed to Point 4 or Point 5—the far better view—and

▼

retrace your steps back to the parking lot. Such an abbreviated walk will still include a steep uphill ascent. If you're looking for an easy walk, simply reverse the directions below starting at Point 10 and visit the mines. From the parking lot, for example, you would turn left onto Snake Den Rd. and turn right at Point 10 into the woods just before Ellen St. Then you'd follow the trail with the white house on your left and walk between a wooden fence on your left and a trail post on your right.

TO BEGIN

From the parking lot next to the Weis Ecology Center, walk to the paved Snake Den Rd. and turn right. Ignore a road on your right going into the ecology center. Follow the paved road uphill as it winds to the left and then to the right. Ignore a road on your left and continue uphill about 50 yards following red blazes.

1. Turn right and proceed between two tall trees into woods following red blazes. Follow the trail as it bears to the left over rocks alongside a waterfall. Proceed uphill with the waterfall and a gushing stream on your right.

2. At the rocks next to the top of the waterfall, turn left and follow blue blazes back to the paved road (ignore the red-blazed trail crossing the stream to the right). Turn right and proceed on the paved road until it ends. Continue straight on a wide, rocky dirt path, ignoring a private road to the left. Follow blue blazes uphill for a minute until you reach a tree on your right with two blue blazes. Proceed about a dozen steps.

3. Turn left in front of a big rock with blue and yellow blazes. Proceed through the woods uphill to the right. Follow a path as it turns sharply to the right.

4. At a trail junction (two trees display blue and yellow

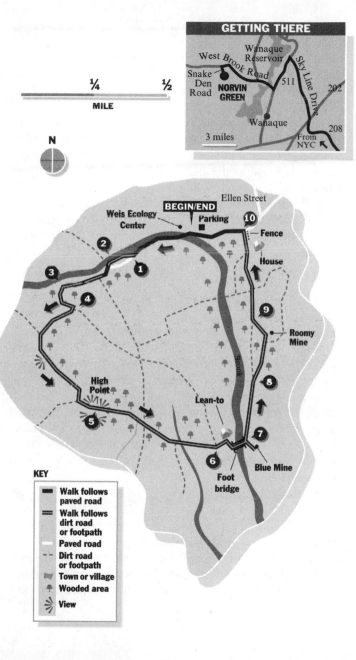

GETTING THERE

Wanaque Reservoir
West Brook Road
Snake Den Road
NORVIN GREEN
Sky Line Drive
511
202
208
Wanaque
From NYC
3 miles

¼ ½
MILE

N

Ellen Street
Weis Ecology Center
BEGIN/END
Parking
10
Fence
House
2
3
1
9
Roomy Mine
4
Brook
High Point
8
Lean-to
5
7
6
Foot bridge
Blue Mine

KEY

- Walk follows paved road
- Walk follows dirt road or footpath
- Paved road
- Dirt road or footpath
- Town or village
- Wooded area
- View

▼

blazes) turn right following blue blazes, ignoring a yellow-blazed trail heading uphill to the left. The blue-blazed trail gets progressively steeper. After 15 to 20 minutes on this trail, you walk over some huge rocks and have a great vantage point. *This is a good picnic spot. There's also an excellent view on the flat rocks several yards before this vantage point.* Continue on the blue-blazed trail downhill. Ignore a narrow white-blazed trail to the right and head uphill on the blue-blazed trail. You reach a blue-blazed boulder atop the hill. Proceed on the blue-blazed trail. After several minutes, you meet a red trail on your right. Ignore the red trail that proceeds to the left downhill and continue on to the right of a boulder. You are now following red blazes uphill. Continue up a rock face.

5. At the top of the hill, High Point, relax and enjoy the unbelievable scenery. *This is an ideal picnic spot with views in all directions of the mountains and Wanaque Reservoir. Looking southeast you have a view of Manhattan's Empire State Building and the World Trade Center towers.* Continue on toward the reservoir following red blazes downhill. Stay on the red-blazed trail as it turns sharply to the left and proceeds over rocks downhill. Go downhill through the woods and follow the red-blazed trail as it turns sharply to the right, ignoring an unmarked trail to the left. In a minute, turn left at a skinny tree with red blazes that's on your right and follow the red-blazed trail on its steep downward descent.

In about 20 minutes, you cross a tiny spring, which may not be visible in summer. Continue following the red blazes and stay on the trail as it turns sharply to the right downhill. Step on rocks and cross a wide brook (ignoring a white-blazed trail that goes off to the right before you cross the stream). Head uphill. Descend the hill and you reach a junction of yellow and red trails (yellow and red blazes are on trees on both sides of the trail).

▼

6. Turn right onto the red-blazed trail, ignoring a yellow trail to the left. In about a minute, two fallen trees block the trail. Turn left on the rocky trail that has both red and yellow blazes and proceeds away from the brook. Continue past the lean-to on your left and through the clearing. Head downhill to the bank of the brook. *Across the brook is Blue Mine.* Cross the wooden bridge.

7. Turn right. Blue Mine is several steps ahead on your left. After visiting the mine, retrace several steps to the wooden bridge (don't cross it) and continue on the red- and yellow-blazed trail uphill to your right. Walk up the rocky trail with the brook to your left. Cross a small stream. In a few minutes, you reach a junction of yellow and red trails.

8. Bear right on the yellow trail, ignoring a red trail to the left. Proceed on as the trail ascends. *To the right on the side of the rocky hill is Roomy Mine.*

9. At a trail intersection, turn right and follow the red-blazed trail. Proceed uphill. In several minutes, the terrain levels off. Continue on and walk underneath a tree that has fallen across the trail. Head straight past the yellow trail junction (yellow blazes on trees on both sides of trail). You are following both red and yellow blazes through the woods. You emerge at a clearing and it seems as though you are walking through someone's backyard. Stay to the right and walk between a trail post (with yellow and red blazes) on your left and a wooden fence on your right. A white house is also on your right.

10. Turn left onto a paved road. The parking lot is ahead on your right.

PLACES ALONG THE WALK
■ **Weis Ecology Center.** This private, nonprofit environmental education center is geared mainly for families, offering a

▼

wide variety of nature programs. Walkers are welcome on the center's 160-acre grounds and may use the picnic facilities and bathrooms free of charge. *150 Snake Den Rd., Ringwood, N.J. 07456; tel. 201-835-2160. Office open Wed.-Sun. 8:30-4:30. Grounds open daily 9-dusk.*

OTHER PLACES NEARBY

Wawayanda State Park (*see* Experience 21) is less than 13 miles northwest of Norvin Green State Forest.

■ **New Jersey State Botanical Gardens.** Located within Ringwood State Park, the 96-acre botanical gardens surround Skylands Manor, a reproduction of a 400-year-old English Jacobean mansion. The manor is closed to the public, but you can enjoy its many gardens. *Morris Rd., Ringwood Manor, NJ 07456; tel. 201-962-7031, 201-962-9534. Open daily 8-8. Admission (no admission charged on weekdays or any day after Labor Day and before Memorial Day). Off Rte. 511 or Rte. 287, about 10 mi. northeast of Norvin Green State Forest.*

■ **Ringwood State Park.** This 4,054-acre park is a favorite of outdoors enthusiasts and contains a National Historic Landmark, the Ringwood Manor House, which features Hudson River School paintings and a fine collection of furnishings. The park's Shepherd Lake has a bathing beach and lures anglers. *1304 Sloatsburg Rd., Ringwood, NJ 07456; tel. 201-962-7031. Park open daily 8-8. Manor open Wed.-Sat. 10-4, Sun. 12-4; last tours start at 3:30. Admission. Off Rte. 511, about 10 mi. northeast of Norvin Green State Forest.*

DINING

There are a limited number of recommended restaurants near Norvin Green State Forest. Besides the two restaurants below, use those listed in Experience 21, Wawayanda.

■ **Cafe Panache** (expensive). Excellent modern French-Italian dishes come out of the kitchen of this restaurant which formerly was a pancake house. If an appetizer of lobster bisque

▼

with lobster ravioli is on the menu, order it. Crispy farmhouse duckling with citrus ginger sauce—seared and then pan-fried by the chef—is spectacular. The menu offerings aren't revolutionary but the kitchen's execution is. You must bring your own liquor. *130 E. Main St., Ramsey, NJ 07446; tel. 201-934-0030. Open Mon.-Fri. and Sun. for lunch and dinner; Sat. for dinner. About 15 mi. east of Norvin Green State Forest.*

■ **Ruga** (expensive). Don't let the exterior and the ugly parking lot of this restaurant deter you. Inside, the decor is simple, yet elegant and modern, with the works of Estonian painter Eduard Ruga hanging on the walls. The chef delivers excellent contemporary American dishes. Expect such appetizers as mesquite-grilled shrimp and such entrées as rack of lamb and horseradish-crusted salmon. *4 Barbara Ln., Oakland, NJ 07436; tel. 201-337-0813. Open Mon.-Fri. for lunch and dinner and Sat. dinner. About 11 mi. east of Norvin Green State Forest.*

LODGING

There are no quality accommodations in the area. (*See* Experience 21, Wawayanda.)

FOR MORE INFORMATION
Tourist Office:

■ **Norvin Green State Forest.** There are no state information centers in Norvin Green State Forest. For information about the forest, call or write Ringwood State Park. *1304 Sloatsburg Rd., Ringwood, NJ 07456; tel. 201-962-7031. Open daily 8-8.*

For Serious Walkers:

The blue-blazed trail at Norvin Green proceeds north to the Long Pond Ironworks. Northwest of Norvin Green are various Bearfort Mountain trails, including those in Abraham S. Hewitt State Forest. For a map of surrounding trails, pick up the New York-New Jersey Trail Conference's Trail Map 21.

After the Fiery Furnace

EXPERIENCE 21: WAWAYANDA

As you wander through the oak forest of the 13,000-acre Wawayanda State Park, it's hard to believe you're less than an hour's drive away from the hustle and bustle of Manhattan. The only sounds you hear are wildlife scurrying about, and don't be surprised if you see a black bear ambling in the distance.

An estimated 40 to 60

The Highlights: Unique woodlands that are home to black bear, a rain forestlike swamp trail, remains of an iron manufacturing community, a scenic lake for boating and swimming.

Other Places Nearby: Spectacular mountain and skyline views in Norvin Green State Park (*see* Experience 20); historic homes, excellent dining and lodging.

black bears—up to 20 percent of the entire population in New Jersey—live here. Don't let that statistic worry you, because black bears are vegetarians and have never caused a serious injury to a human in the state's history, according to a ranger at the park. Instead, relax and enjoy the wonders of this 13,000-acre park which straddles Sussex and Passaic counties and has 40 miles of trails, including a section of the Appalachian Trail.

The park's centerpiece is Lake Wawayanda, a picturesque

▼

lake surrounded by pine trees that offers visitors swimming, boating, and bass fishing. Four islands dot the 255-acre lake, and water lilies float near the shore.

But the most remarkable geographic feature of the park is its rare inland Atlantic white cedar swamp. As you walk through the more than 2,000 acres of swamp land and its glacial lake, it feels like you're walking through Costa Rica instead of New Jersey. The swamp is the home of various endangered plant and wildlife species.

Consider yourself lucky that you're walking through this land today rather than during the 19th and late 18th centuries. Years ago, noisy iron furnaces shot plumes of smoke into the air, and the sound of saws, axes, and trees toppling to the ground was everywhere. Every day the land was scarred by companies that exploited its timber and mineral resources. It was called the Double Pond area at that time because there were two separate ponds on the site of today's Wawayanda Lake. As you walk today along the lake's north shore, you'll see a huge charcoal blast furnace and the remains of the iron-smelting town of Double Pond.

In 1785, David Alyea bought property at Double Pond and became one of the first to try to exploit the land. Alyea built sawmills, including one next to a brook that emptied into Double Pond.

In 1845, William Ames and John Rutherfurd acquired Double Pond. They immediately dammed the two ponds, raising the water level and creating today's Wawayanda Lake with its various isolated coves. The partners manufactured iron, cut wood, and ran a flour mill and a country store. They built a giant furnace—42 feet tall and 11 feet wide—that you'll pass by on this walking tour. Workers built homes near the furnace, and an active community with its own post office developed.

When running smoothly, the furnace produced about eight tons of pig iron daily. Much of it was shaped into wheels for

▼

railroad cars. To yield a ton of iron, the Wawayanda furnace had to be fed with two tons of iron ore, a quarter ton of limestone, and 180 bushels of charcoal. Nearly all of the ore was extracted from Wawayanda Mine, about 2 1/2 miles northeast of the lake near the New York border. The furnace was shut down in 1856 but reopened to fill government orders for swords and shovels during the Civil War. In 1867, it made its last blast.

Two years later, Pennsylvania-based Thomas Iron Company bought the land with an eye toward extracting iron from Wawayanda's mines. Mining began in 1880 at the Green Mine, located on Wawayanda Road. A wagon carried the iron ore down a mountain to a freight train where it was transported to smelting plants in Pennsylvania.

Despite the mining activity, the YMCA moved the country's first summer camp—which began in Monroe, NY, in 1885—to Lake Wawayanda a year later. The camping programs lasted until 1891, when coal baron Victor Wilder of nearby Warwick, NY, purchased the land.

Wilder, a former Civil War officer who owned mines in West Virginia and Kentucky, avoided labor problems by hiring only black laborers from the South. Wilder may have had plans to turn the lake into a private park, but the park had no rail access, and Wilder sold the land back in 1902 to the Thomas Iron Company, which had 10 years earlier sold the property's mineral lease to a company run by famous inventor Thomas Edison.

As the mining heyday wound down, the YMCA again established a summer camp at Lake Wawayanda. The camp, run by the organization's Newark chapter, was located at the beach and boat launching area where you begin your walking tour. The founder, Charles Scott, later had one of the lake's islands, Scott Island, named after him. Scott's camp continued each summer until 1919, when it move to Andover and stayed there under the name Camp Wawayanda until the mid-1950s.

A year before the YMCA's departure, the New Jersey Zinc Company bought the Lake Wawayanda property despite the

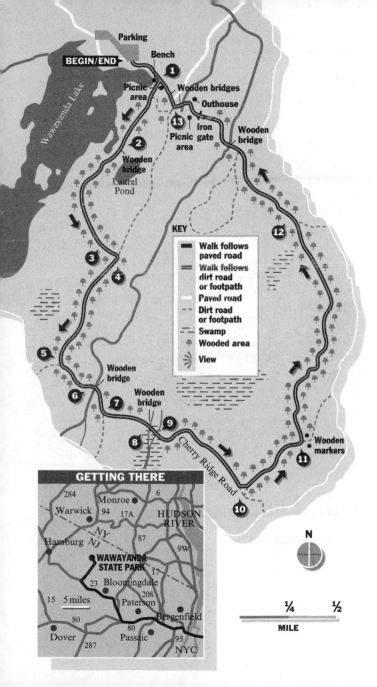

Parking

Bench

BEGIN/END ➤ ❶

Picnic area

Wooden bridges

Outhouse

Wawayanda Lake

❷

❸

Picnic area

Iron gate

Wooden bridge

Laurel Pond

Wooden bridge

❹

KEY

▬▬	Walk follows paved road
══	Walk follows dirt road or footpath
──	Paved road
- - -	Dirt road or footpath
╌ ╌	Swamp
🌲	Wooded area
))))	View

❺

❻

Wooden bridge

❼

Wooden bridge

❾

❽

Cherry Ridge Road

Wooden markers

❿

⓫

⓬

⓭

GETTING THERE

284 Monroe 6

Warwick 94 17A HUDSON RIVER

NY / NJ 87

Hamburg 9W

WAWAYANDA STATE PARK 17

23 Bloomingdale

15 5 miles 208

Paterson

80

Dover 287 80 Passaic 95 NYC Bergenfield

N

¼ ½

MILE

▼

protests of the city of Newark. The city said it needed the lake as a source of drinking water—a more important use than the zinc company's plan to log the surrounding forest. The city was overruled by the Public Utilities Commission, which noted that Newark had had plenty of chances to buy the property.

The zinc company cut down trees for decades while allowing the general public to use the lake for recreation. In 1963 the company relinquished the land to the state of New Jersey which designated it as a state park and opened a bathing beach 15 years later.

Today, about 150 years after the Wawayanda furnace began operating, the park has rebounded from its environmental battering. As you walk around its lake and through its forests, you're looking at a park that hasn't looked this good in many years.

GETTING THERE

By car:

From New York City, go west on Rte. 80 or Rte. 46 to Rte. 23 north. Exit Rte. 23 north at Union Valley Rd. Follow Union Valley Rd. for 4 mi. until you reach a stop sign. Continue straight about 3/4 mi. and turn left before the Shop-Rite shopping center. (You are still on Union Valley Rd.) Proceed 2 mi. and then bear left at the Y junction (West Milford Florist is on your left) onto White Rd. Continue 4/10 mi. until you reach a stop sign. Proceed straight up the mountain road, Warwick Tpke. Follow the road 4 mi. and turn left into Wawayanda State Park.

Walk Directions

TIME: 3 1/2 hours
LEVEL: Moderate
DISTANCE: 6 mi.
ACCESS: By car

There is one steep hill near the beginning of the walk, but the footing is not very difficult. You may have to step carefully around mud at a few points on the Cedar Swamp Trail. Wood planks (watch for the loose ones) provide assistance over a particularly swampy

▼

stretch of the trail. The best place to picnic is alongside the lake before or after the walk. Several huge boulders make great tables, or use the park's picnic tables and grills by the boathouse. You can also picnic on the mountaintop at Point 2 or at the picnic tables at Point 12. Some picnic provisions—particularly fresh fruits and vegetables—can be picked up at nearby L&L Farms, which also operates a food concession. As you exit the park's main entrance, turn left and you'll see L&L Farms on your right. If you are looking for more substantial picnic provisions, visit the Backyard Grill or Lovey's (*see* Dining) in Warwick, a short drive away.

TO BEGIN

From the parking lot, walk to the left of the boathouse and follow the wide gravel path. The lake is to the right and the woods are to the left.

1. At the fork in the path (there's a park bench to your right), turn right and proceed with the lake to your right. *The stone ruins to your left are the remains of the 19th-century iron smelting town of Double Pond. Eight tons of pig iron were produced daily when the furnace ran smoothly.* Pass the boulders in the middle of the trail and follow the loop trail uphill to the right (ignore the part of the loop going to the left). Follow the blue blazes uphill and continue through the woods.

2. In about 10 minutes, you reach a bridge. Pass over it, with a dam to your right and a waterfall to your left. Continue on the blue-blazed trail as it ascends through the woods. Follow the trail as it winds back and forth and makes a steep ascent up a small mountain. You reach the mountaintop about 20 minutes after leaving the bridge.

3. Veer to the left down the mountain following the blue-blazed trail.

▼

4. When you reach a wide, rocky trail (with three blue blazes on the rock in front of you), turn right and follow the yellow blazes. *If you want to shorten the walk, turn left at Point 4 and follow a trail that leads back to the parking lot.* Otherwise, walk about 20 minutes on the yellow-blazed trail.

5. At the trail head (three yellow blazes on rocks), turn left onto a dirt road called Cherry Ridge. Continue on for about 10 minutes.

6. Pass over a wooden bridge. Follow the road as it curves uphill to the right. Continue on for five minutes.

7. At the trail head (three red blazes), turn left. You're still on Cherry Ridge Rd. (some rocks to your right are painted with the letters "CRR"). Proceed for a few minutes.

8. Walk over a wooden bridge, with a stream to your left and your right. Pass a large swamp on your right.

9. When you reach a sign saying "Bridge Out", step carefully over the rocks across another stream. Follow the road as it curves to the right uphill.

10. At the rotary, turn left and take 15 to 20 steps. Turn left again and follow the yellow-blazed trail between the trees and through the woods. Pass by swamp land to your left.

11. Just before the wooden marker saying "Banker TR" (yellow blazes), turn left into the woods and follow the blue-blazed trail. A marker saying "Cedar Swamp TR" is to your right. *Savor the feeling of walking through what feels like a tropical rain forest in northern New Jersey.* After about 30 minutes, you walk across numerous planks, with the swamp to your left. Continue through the woods on the blue-blazed trail for 10 minutes.

▼

12. At the end of the blue trail (three blue blazes on a tree), proceed straight onto a yellow-blazed trail and follow it as it curves to the left. **Be careful on the muddy stretches of the trail.** Continue straight (past a red trail to your left). Pass over a wooden bridge and follow the trail, which now is blazed both yellow and blue.

After about 15 minutes from the start of the yellow trail in Point 12, you reach an iron gate. Walk around the gate and continue on the trail into the picnic area (outhouses are on the right). Proceed on the trail as it circles through the picnic area (ignore turnoff to the left leading to picnic tables) and follow the yellow blazes. Bear right and follow the trail over a wooden bridge spanning a stream.

13. At the trail junction about 20 yards past the bridge, turn right and take the uphill trail that passes between the furnace on your right and the stone wall on your left. *This is Wawayanda furnace, where iron was produced in the mid-19th century.* Cross over a small wooden bridge. On your left are the stone ruins that you saw in Point 1. Continue straight and retrace your steps back to the parking lot.

PLACES ALONG THE WALK

■ **Wawayanda State Park.** A lifeguard-protected beach with a food concession and changing facilities is open during the summer. Canoes, rowboats (with or without small motors), and paddle boats can be rented (201-764-1030), and there is a launching area for private boats. Three campsites for groups of seven or more individuals are available Apr. 1-Oct. 31. *Box 198, Highland Lakes, NJ 07422; tel. 201-853-4462; fax 201-853-1383. Open daily sunrise to sunset. Admission. Park headquarters located near the main Warwick Tpke. entrance.*

OTHER PLACES NEARBY

■ **Action Park.** Billing itself as the world's largest water

▼

park, this popular attraction offers such activities as white-water rafting, swimming in a tidal-wave pool, and bungee jumping. The park is inside a 2,000-acre resort that transforms into 52-slope Vernon Valley Great Gorge ski area in the winter. If a water park isn't your thing, guests at the resort can tee off at one of four golf courses, play indoor sports at a spa and fitness center, or go fishing, boating, hiking, or biking. *Box 848, McAfee, NJ 07428; tel. 201-827-2000; fax 201-209-3322. Action Park open daily 10-8 Memorial Day-Labor Day. Vernon Valley Great Gorge ski area open mid-Dec.-mid-Mar. Admission. On Rte. 94 in Vernon, NJ, about 8 mi. west of Wawayanda*

■ **Warwick, N.Y.** Homes and buildings in this little-known village date back to the 18th and 19th centuries. Tour the oldest structure, the Shingle House, built in 1764, and the 1810 House, with its antique furniture and enticing herb garden. The village has a variety of quality shops and fine eateries. A farmers market is held on Sunday from 9 to 2 in the South Street parking lot. *The Shingle House and the 1810 House are only open. Tue. and Sat. 2-4:30 Jun.-Sep. About 6 mi. north of Wawayanda.*

DINING

■ **Chateau Hathorn** (expensive). Look for venison, pheasant, or rabbit on the seasonally changing Swiss-with-a-touch-of-French menu, or order the roast rack of lamb or flambéd chateaubriand. Recommended appetizers include smoked trout with apple-horseradish cream sauce and frog legs sautéed with herbs, garlic, shallots, tomatoes, and mushrooms. Leave room for cinnamon apple fritters with vanilla sauce. *33 Hathorn Rd., Warwick, NY 10990; tel. 914-986-6099; fax 914-987-1534. Open for dinner daily except Tue. About 6 mi. north of Wawayanda.*

■ **Sugar Loaf Inn** (expensive). The "nouveau-rustic" decor works surprisingly well at this cozy restaurant with wood-beamed ceilings, ceiling fans, and the best food in the area. Expect such unique dinner entrees as roast veal filled with

▼

spinach, mushrooms, and brie with pink peppercorn and basil sauce. For an appetizer, try the goat cheese layered with fresh pesto, sun-dried tomatoes, roast garlic, and eggplant. Intoxicating desserts may include toffee pecan pie. *Kings Hwy., Sugar Loaf, NY 10981; tel. 914-469-2552. Open Tue.-Sat. for lunch and dinner; Sun. for brunch and dinner. On Rte. 13, about 14 mi. northeast of Wawayanda*

■ **Ten Railroad Ave.** (expensive). Situated across the street from an old stone railroad station, this handsome restaurant in a former 19th-century hotel serves Spanish-Italian cuisine with good results. The soups are wonderful, particularly garlic, shrimp bisque, and cream of mushroom. For an entree, try the veal chop, the paella marinera, or the mussels in green sauce. At lunchtime look for the more moderately priced gourmet sandwiches such as prosciutto, cheese, and roasted peppers. *10 Railroad Ave., Warwick, NY 10990; tel. 914-986-1509. Open Mon.-Fri. for lunch and dinner, Sat. for dinner. About 6 mi. north of Wawayanda in the heart of Warwick.*

■ **Amity Bakery Cafe** (moderate). Old blues tunes sizzle out of the speakers and the creative kitchen delivers only the freshest ingredients at this funky country cafe and bakery. The dainty cinnamon swirls delivered to the table in the bread basket as well as other baked goods are perfect picnic provisions for the walk. Breakfast and lunch is inexpensive, dinner prices moderate. Look for such creative entrees as roasted Cornish game hen in an apple-calvados glaze with walnut stuffing or an appetizer of scallop flan. *110 Newport Bridge Rd., Amity, NY 10990; tel. 914-258-3500. Open Thurs.-Sun. for breakfast, lunch, and dinner. About 9 mi. northwest of Wawayanda.*

■ **Lovey's** (inexpensive). This gourmet shop specializes in good sandwiches and flavorful soups, including potato leek, tortilla, cabbage, and chicken. Don't miss the muffins, scones, and pies coming out of the bakery oven. *6 High St., Warwick, NY 10990; tel. 914-986-5552; fax 914-986-3214. Open daily for breakfast and lunch. About 6 mi. north of Wawayanda.*

▼

■ **Backyard Grill** (inexpensive). Locals love this tiny, eight-table restaurant specializing in grilled chicken, ribs, and steak. It's an eat-in or takeout place that provides quality food and fast service. The grilled chicken breast on foccacia bread (with olive oil, sea salt, and rosemary) makes a special treat to take along on your walking tour. Other favorites are the chicken and ribs combo and the steak, chicken, or vegetable fajitas. *31 Forester Ave., Warwick, NY 10990; tel. 914-987-1822. Open daily for lunch and dinner. About 6 mi. north of Wawayanda.*

LODGING

■ **Chateau Hathorn** (moderate). A restored turreted mansion, this establishment is primarily a restaurant but offers four modern rooms. Room 4, equipped with a lavender Jacuzzi, is spacious and provides a view of the hillside. *33 Hathorn Rd., Warwick, NY 10990; tel. 914-986-6099; fax 914-987-1534. About 6 mi. north of Wawayanda.*

■ **Inn at 40 Oakland** (moderate). Designed by the architect who created Teddy Roosevelt's Sagamore Hill home, this 1890 Victorian features a wraparound porch and a distinctive turret suite. All six rooms have private baths, comfortable chairs, air conditioning, telephones, and televisions. The guest room at the front of the house has its own porch and is the largest. *40 Oakland Ave., Warwick, NY 10990; tel. 914-987-8269; fax 914-987-9513. About 6 mi. north of Wawayanda.*

■ **Peach Grove Inn** (moderate). Elegance abounds in this 1850 Greek Revival farmhouse with high ceilings, faux marble walls, large antique-filled rooms, and gold-plated bathroom sinks. The most expensive of the four rooms (all with private bath) features a queen-size four-poster bed and a working fireplace. If you'd like to be away from the road, ask for the $95 room with the iron-and-brass bed overlooking the farm. A full breakfast—with such dishes as cheese strata, corn pancakes, or French toast—is included. *205 Rte. 17A, Warwick, NY 10990; tel. 914-986-7411. About 6 mi. north of Wawayanda.*

▼

■ **Warwick Valley Bed & Breakfast** (moderate). Built in 1902, this Federal-style home was recently renovated and offers four rooms—each with a private bath and central air conditioning. Room 1 has the largest double bed. A full breakfast is served, and there's a comfortable, small living room for all guests. Located in Warwick's historic district, it's a short walk to the center of town. *24B Maple Ave., Warwick, NY 10990; tel. 914-987-7255. About 6 mi. north of Wawayanda.*

■ **Apple Valley Inn** (inexpensive). It's easy to relax under the wood-beam ceilings of this rustic six-bedroom country inn built in 1831. The Jonathan Room sports a canopied antique bed and a lovely meadow view. Only the Red Delicious Room offers a private bath. Spend some time in the cozy second-floor sitting room and notice the original Hudson Valley art on the fireplace screen. Outside the inn, take a walk in the apple orchard, fish for trout in the brook, or swim in the pool. *Box 302, Glenwood, NJ 07418; tel. 201-764-3735. At the junction of Rtes. 517 and 565, about 13 mi. northwest of Wawayanda.*

FOR MORE INFORMATION
Tourist Offices:
For information about Wawayanda, contact the park at Box 198, Highland Lakes, NJ 07422, 201-853-4462. The park office is open daily 8-4:30. For information about the nearby Warwick area, contact the Warwick Valley Chamber of Commerce, Box 202, Warwick, NY, 10990, 914-986-2720, fax 914-986-6982. The chamber office, located in a red caboose on South St., is open Mon.-Fri. 9:30-4:30.

For Serious Walkers:
The above walk can be found in the North Jersey Trails map (trail map 21) published by the New York-New Jersey Trail Conference. About 24 different trails weave through Wawayanda State Park. Norvin Green State Forest (*see* Experience 20) is only a short drive away.

High Atop the Endless Mountain

EXPERIENCE 22: HIGH POINT

Most mountaintop viewpoints in the New York City area require much effort before you can cherish their sight lines. That's not the case on this walking tour in New Jersey's northwestern corner. You drive to the top of the state's highest peak, 1,803-foot High Point, and walk only a few minutes to

The Highlights: Panoramic views of the upper Delaware River valley and three states from New Jersey's highest point; a rare Atlantic white cedar bog, superb dining at a restored turn-of-the-century hotel.

Other Places Nearby: A bustling Pennsylvania resort village, the beautifully landscaped gardens of Grey Towers National Historic Landmark, a spectacular drive along cliffs overlooking the Delaware River.

one of the finest views in the Northeast: a panorama of the upper Delaware River valley where you overlook wide expanses of New Jersey, New York, and Pennsylvania.

The view is best from High Point Monument, a stately, trim pinnacle of stone resembling the Washington Monument that rises 220 feet into the air. A classic obelisk faced with cream-colored New Hampshire granite and surrounded by spotlights, the monument dominates the skyline in all directions by day and

▼

night. It was built in 1930 to honor New Jersey's war veterans.

Today, the unobstructed view stretches to the ramparts of the Catskills in the north and to the Delaware Water Gap in the south. The views west look out over the bends and curves of the Delaware River to the towns of Port Jervis, New York, and Milford, Pennsylvania. To the east are the rolling meadows of the Wallkill River valley and, beyond, the New Jersey Highlands where the rocky heights of the Wawayanda escarpment rise.

The monument is surrounded by many miles of secluded woodland trails in 14,000-acre High Point State Park, a destination that has become increasingly popular with walkers, hikers, and bird watchers. The park tops a section of an almost continuous mountain wall which stretches from the Delaware Water Gap along the northwestern edge of New Jersey into New York state.

The Lenape tribe called this high ridge the Kittatinny, or "Endless Mountain," and so it must have seemed to them. As you proceed on your walking tour, it will become apparent why the steep, forested ridge has been a blockade to travel, commerce, and development for centuries and has served as a secluded haven to diverse upland wildlife.

Composed of tough sandstone and coarse "Shawangunk" conglomerate, the Kittatinny Ridge is extremely resistant to weathering, standing high above the silted river valleys lying on either flank. Atop the ridge, spring-fed glacial ponds such as Lake Marcia are evidence of the massive glaciers that flowed across this landscape just 12,000 years ago, scraping out deep hollows, exposing polished bedrock, and leaving behind immense glacial erratics (geologically out-of-place boulders carried from hundreds of miles away by the glaciers and dropped like so many loose marbles).

Over the centuries, as the climate warmed and mellowed, life changed. The conifers were replaced by deciduous trees, the maples and oaks we see today. In a few places, groves of ancient Atlantic white cedars continued to survive and thrive. The Dutch were the first Europeans to "own" High Point, but they did so as absentee landlords. The English who followed turned narrow Native American footpaths over the ridgetops into wider roads. The Lenape tribe was driven out, and the Delaware and Wallkill River valleys were cleared for farm fields and pastures. But the mountain at High Point, overlooking these agricultural efforts, was seen as having little value by the settlers.

From the 1820s on, three generations of the wealthy Rutherfurd family, which made its fortune in iron manufacturing, consolidated land holdings on the mountain. As late as 1828, panthers could still be seen in these hills, but heavy deforestation slowly took a toll on wildlife. By the late 1800s, much of the mountain's old-growth forest had been clear-cut, with the valuable wood being sold as fuel and for building material. The once-clean mountain air was now smudged with numerous charcoal fires.

In 1890, the High Point Inn, an Adirondack-style Victorian hotel accommodating up to 200 people, was constructed atop the mountain. The resort, which hosted such notables as Thomas Edison, was praised for the "beauty of its scenery, and healthfulness of its climate."

In 1908, hard financial times closed the High Point Inn, and the mountain tract was purchased by Anthony Kuser. The Kuser family remodeled the old High Point Inn as their mansion and developed a vast mountaintop estate with carriage roads and trails. They even temporarily introduced elk and reindeer to the upland woods, and for several years shoppers at local department stores were entertained by staged visits from "Santa's reindeer."

In 1923, the Kuser family generously donated their entire 10,600-acre estate to New Jersey as High Point State Park. Seven years later the High Point Monument was unveiled, financed by the philanthropic Kusers.

In the 1930s, the Appalachian Trail (running 2,100 miles from Maine to Georgia) was routed through High Point State Park. President Franklin Roosevelt's Civilian Conservation Corps constructed a marvelous loop trail here in 1934: the Monument

▼

Trail with its crushed stone treadway, massive stone steps, and views of three states. Bear, coyote, deer, and bobcat inhabit the park and occasionally can be seen from the trail.

GETTING THERE
By car:

From New York City, take I-80 west to Rte. 23 north. Go through the town of Sussex and, 5 mi. further, through the hamlet of Colesville. Exactly 1 mi. north of the intersection with Rte. 519, drive up Kittatinny Ridge and turn right into High Point State Park. Go about 1 1/2 mi. to the High Point Monument parking area.

When traveling from the north, exit I-84 at the Rte. 23 exit in Port Jervis, and drive 4 1/2 mi. south on Rte. 23 to the High Point State Park entrance. Turn left into the park, and proceed 1 1/2 mi. to the parking area.

Walk Directions

TIME: 2 1/2 or 4 hours
LEVEL: Moderate
DISTANCE: 3 1/2 or 5 miles
ACCESS: By car

This walk makes a 3 1/2-mi. loop along the Kittatinny Ridge to glacial Lake Marcia. There are several great viewpoints that can double as picnic spots, or you can picnic beside the placid waters of Lake Marcia. You can add an extra 1 1/2 mi. of easy, flat walking by following the woods road at Point 5. The woods road leads to an Atlantic white cedar bog with stately stands of white cedar and rare carnivorous sun-dew and pitcher plants. Follow a self-guided nature trail (brochure available at High Point State Park office on Rte. 23) .

TO BEGIN

Begin your walk at the edge of the High Point Monument

▼

parking area just behind the stone comfort station. Here you'll find round metal markers painted with red and green semicircles. These blazes, placed on posts and trees, are the symbol for the Monument Trail which you will follow throughout your walk. Head toward the monument, following the crushed-stone walkway past a park bench. *Note the beautiful views of the Delaware River Valley.* Go right, around the front of the monument. Stop at the monument and enjoy the 360-degree views. Return to the crushed stone trail and follow the blazes steeply downhill, away from the monument and toward Lake Marcia, visible below through the trees. Pass a small state park water

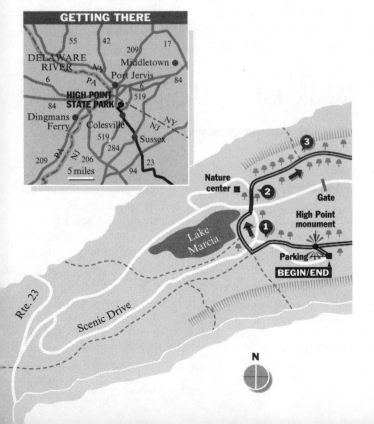

▼

access building on your left. Cross a paved road.

1. Following the blazes, turn left into the woods and walk through a small field of boulders deposited by the glaciers 12,000 years ago. Ignore the white-blazed Appalachian Trail on your left. Staying on the red-and-green blazed Monument Trail, leave the woods, cross another paved road, and descend gently to the shore of Lake Marcia. Swerve right around the side of the lake on an old carriage path. At the end of the lake, go straight ahead on a paved road between two small stone pillars. Pass the High Point nature center on your left, a rustic building of fieldstone that was constructed in the 1930s.

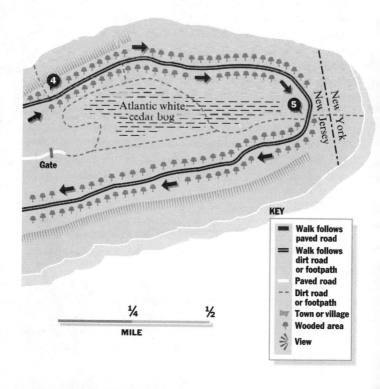

KEY

▬	**Walk follows paved road**
═	**Walk follows dirt road or footpath**
	Paved road
- - -	**Dirt road or footpath**
⬂	**Town or village**
♠	**Wooded area**
⬀	**View**

¼   ½

MILE

▼

fieldstone that was constructed in the 1930s.

2. Turn sharply right off the paved road onto a grassy path, going gently uphill. *Notice the views of High Point Monument to your right through a forest of pitch pine and oak.* Descend gradually, then more steeply. *Steenykill Lake can be seen below and off to the left through the trees.* Descend on a pathway of crushed shale, then go down large natural stone steps built in the 1930s by the Civilian Conservation Corps.

3. Ignore a major blue-blazed trail leading left down to Steenykill Lake. Stay on the red-and-green blazed Monument Trail. Cross a pretty little bridge over a small brook. Climb steadily to a ridge and enjoy views down into the Delaware Valley. *Note how the trees are stunted here (naturally "bonsai-ed") due to their northern exposure to brutal winter winds and ice storms.* Level out along the ridge and then descend slightly. *Enjoy more good views.* Descend more steeply, then ascend slightly to another good view of the Delaware Valley, the town of Port Jervis, and the Pocono Plateau.

4. Ignore the turquoise-blazed Shawangunk Ridge Trail on the left. Continue straight, following red-and-green Monument Trail blazes downhill into a small valley sheltered between two ridges. Ignore the turquoise-blazed trail on the right. Slowly begin climbing. Reach a small stream and cross a bridge.

5. Ignore the little woods road to your right leading into the Atlantic white cedar bog. *If you want to extend the walk to the bog, turn right onto the woods road and follow the loop around the bog. Retrace your steps to the Monument Trail, turn right onto it, and follow directions below.*
Climb steeply uphill on the Monument Trail, and turn right when you reach the top of the Kittatinny Ridge. Ascend gradually but steadily along the ridge. *Note the views to the left over the Wallkill River valley (once filled with a vast 200-foot-deep lake created by melting glacier water). Also look right through*

the trees to the Delaware River and Port Jervis. Come out of the forest into High Point Monument parking area.

OTHER PLACES NEARBY

■ **Grey Towers National Historic Landmark.** A meticulously landscaped French manor house that was once the home of conservationist Gifford Pinchot, who led the U.S. Forest Service under President Theodore Roosevelt. *Box 188, Milford, PA 18337; tel. 717-296-6401. Open daily 10-4 Memorial Day-Labor Day. Call for off-season schedule. On Oldowego Tpke., about 15 mi. northwest of High Point State Park.*

■ **Hawk's Nest.** Do you love those car commercials with next year's stylish models cruising a winding, stonewall-edged mountain road that drops away to a roaring river far below? Well, here's your chance to drive such a road. The stretch of New York Highway 97 on the east side of the Delaware River from Port Jervis north to Hancock has been popular with the car-company advertisers for years. Dubbed the Hawk's Nest, the stretch of road provides breathtaking views and a chance to see hawks, eagles, and falcons. *About 9 mi. from High Point State Park. Take Rte. 23 north into Port Jervis and connect to Rte. 6 west; follow Rte. 97 north along the river.*

■ **Town of Milford.** This Pennsylvania town is a place to hunt antiques and enjoy fine dining and lodging. Local galleries display modern art and contemporary crafts. Don't miss the shops in the Upper Mill Complex at Water and Mill streets. *On Rte. 6, about 15 mi. northwest of High Point State Park.*

DINING

■ **Santini's Ristorante** (expensive). A favorite with locals for 18 years, Santini's features cuisine from the Abruzzi region of Italy (with family recipes passed down from generation to generation). Dominick "Tar" Santini, a three-time Golden Gloves champ, does all the cooking, and his wife, Flo, is your hostess. Everything is made on site: the pastas, cream and tomato sauces,

▼

sausage, and meatballs. Try Flo's favorites: the veal bolognese or the scungilli and calamari combination. *103 Rte. 6, Port Jervis, NY 12771; tel. 914-856-4447. Open daily except Tue. for lunch and dinner. About 5 mi. northeast of High Point State Park.*

■ **Erie Hotel Restaurant** (expensive). This restaurant in a restored turn-of-the-century hotel has quickly developed a reputation as one of the finest in the Port Jervis area. Located next to a restored railroad depot, it features a railroad motif with imitation gas light, private booths, and walls decorated with 19th-century local street scenes. A beautifully carved and mirrored 1890s bar rounds out the period decor. Try the salmon broiled in sherry and butter or the crab and filet mignon. *9 Jersey Ave., Port Jervis, NY 12771; tel. 914-858-4100. Open daily for lunch and dinner. Off Rte. 6, 4 1/2 miles north of High Point.*

■ **Bernhard's Red Mill** (moderate). The etched wooden sign at the entrance welcomes "hunters, skiers, and friends of the mountains." Though located within the walls of a restored Civil War-period mill, the decor is akin to a rustic Alpine hunting lodge. Chef Bernhard Oesen attended a culinary institute in Salzburg, and his continental cuisine and extraordinary desserts reflect that training. Wienerschnitzel, sauerbraten and the rum walnut Black Forest cake are highly recommended. *Box 401, Sussex, NJ 07461; tel. 201-875-4929. Open Tue.-Sun. for lunch and dinner. On Rte. 23, 7 mi. south of High Point State Park.*

■ **Peppercorn** (moderate). Though it has a plain exterior with an interior decor done simply in dark wood and seascapes, Peppercorn features fine Italian food, prepared with loving care. The linguine amatriciana—sautéed with pancetta, onion, plum tomato, basil, and pecorino romano—and the veal champagne are extraordinary. *1 Libertyville Rd., Wantage, NJ 07461; tel. 201-702-1011. Open daily except Tue. for lunch and dinner (Sat. dinner only). Sun. dinner begins in the afternoon. On Rte. 23, about 9 mi. south of High Point.*

■ **The Dimmick Inn Steakhouse** (moderate). A Revival-style Connecticut colonial structure built in 1854, the inn is

▼

flanked on two sides by an open porch (where meals are served in nice weather). A spacious dining room is decorated with tasteful flower prints and features piano jazz. The menu is heavily oriented toward steaks, fish, and other grilled foods. *101 East Harford St., Milford, PA 18337; tel. 717-296-9363. Open daily for lunch and dinner and Sun. brunch. About 15 mi. northwest of High Point State Park.*

■ **Hawk's Nest Restaurant** (inexpensive). This little restaurant with a plain exterior provides informal dining with a spectacular picture-window view. It is perched on stilts atop a cliff hundreds of feet above the swirling waters of the upper Delaware River. Enjoy the chicken in a basket, great burgers and steaks, or stuffed shrimp while watching kayakers shoot the rapids. *600 Rte. 97, Sparrowbush, NY 12780; tel. 914-856-9909. Open daily for lunch and dinner and Sat.-Sun. breakfast Apr.-Nov. About 9 mi. northwest of High Point State Park.*

LODGING

■ **Cliff Park Inn** (expensive). Located atop the high palisades overlooking the Delaware River Valley, this 10-room inn has been in the Buchanan family since it was built as a farmhouse in 1820. This resort's focus is its nine-hole golf course and its restaurant. The large main house has an open porch where guests can relax on wicker rockers and watch golfers go by. The seven rooms and cottages all have private baths. *Cliff Park Rd., Milford, PA 18337; tel. 717-296-6491. Inn open daily. Heading east on Rte. 6, turn right at Milford Rd.*

■ **Black Walnut Country Inn** (moderate). When you drive through the wrought-iron gate of this 160-acre meticulously manicured estate and pull up at the Tudor-style country inn, you know no expense has been spared to make you feel like a special guest. An elegant working marble fireplace graces the living room, and an outdoor hot tub overlooks a lake. There are ponds for boating and walking trails. *509 Fire Tower Rd., Milford, PA 18337; tel. 717-296-6322, 800-866-9870. Off Rte. 6,* *about 14 mi. northwest of High Point State Park.*

■ **Pine Hill Farm Bed and Breakfast** (moderate). Atop the Pocono Plateau, this farm offers a spectacular vista looking down into the Delaware Valley and back at High Point Monument. This grand country home has been lovingly decorated with antiques. The main house has three beautifully furnished rooms, each with private bath. The caretaker's cottage has a screened-in porch and two private suites. *Box 1001, Cummins Hill Rd., Milford, PA 18337; tel. 717-296-7395. Off Rte. 209 south, about 15 mi. northwest of High Point State Park.*

■ **Tom Quick Inn** (moderate). All 14 rooms at this 1882 dual-turreted Victorian hotel were recently refurbished. Rooms are furnished with an eclectic collection of antiques and four-poster beds. Downstairs there's a good restaurant known for its roast turkey with homemade gravy. *Broad St., Milford, PA 18337; tel. 717-296-6514. Off Rte. 6, about 15 mi. northwest of High Point State Park.*

FOR MORE INFORMATION
Tourist Offices:
■ **High Point State Park.** *Open daily 8-8 Apr.-Oct., 8-4:30 Nov.-Mar. Office open daily 9-4:30 (later closing hour Apr.-Oct.). Monument open daily 9-4:30 Jul.-Aug. and weekends May, Sep., and Oct. 1480 Rte. 23, Sussex, NJ 07461; tel. 201-875-4800.*

■ **Pocono Mountains Vacation Bureau, Inc.** *1004 Main St., Stroudsburg, PA 18360; tel. 717-424-6050, 800-762-6667. Office open Mon.-Fri. 9-5.*

For Serious Walkers:
High Point State Park has many miles of trails, including several miles of the Appalachian Trail. The park office provides a map, but the best one is published by the New York-New Jersey Trail Conference.

The Lessons of Time

EXPERIENCE 23: DELAWARE CANALS

To the people who lived in the Delaware River valley north of Philadelphia in the 1830s, the Delaware River canal system must have seemed like an astounding achievement that would endure for a millenium. Instead, these colossal

> **The Highlights:**
> Picturesque old canals, sweeping river views, historic towns, an old mill.
>
> **Other Places Nearby:**
> Interesting museums, waters for canoeing and rafting, good restaurants and historic inns.

undertakings turned a profit for no more than a generation or two and fell into total disuse within 100 years. Today, these beautiful canals on which you walk exist only because of the efforts of preservationists who view them as an invaluable historic monument and a focal point for tourism, one of the region's main industries.

This walk takes you on two separate canal systems. The one on the east bank of the Delaware River in New Jersey, known as the Delaware and Raritan Canal, was built in the 1830s to feed water from the Delaware north to the Raritan River and eventually New York harbor. The feeder canal along which you walk extends 20 miles northwest of Trenton,

▼

while the main canal reaches 40 miles northeast to New Brunswick.

The canal's ingenious design, dug by hand tools without mechanical equipment, enabled barge traffic to go between New York and Philadelphia with a relatively small number of locks. Later, barges used the feeder canal northwest of Trenton to bring coal down from mines in the upper Delaware River valley. A railroad, supposedly New Jersey's first, was built along the bank of the canal three years after it opened. On this walking tour, you follow the abandoned rail bed on the stretch north of Stockton.

O n the west side of the river, between 1817 and 1845, Pennsylvania built a canal system known both as the Pennsylvania Canal and the Delaware Canal. It allowed barges to travel downstream to Philadelphia from the coal mines up north. Much of it today has filled with silt, but it's a picturesque site: The old towpath and what remains of the canal arc gracefully along the Delaware.

These gargantuan undertakings took years to get off the ground. Dozens of people labored to convince authorities of the value of these enterprises and to raise the necessary capital, and the developers fought many difficult battles with other business people with conflicting plans and interests. When the work actually began, the construction crew—comprised mainly of European immigrants—paid a dear price. Thousands lived in filthy shanty towns, and hundreds died in cholera epidemics. Most were unceremoniously buried in mass graves with no markers. One of the graves supposedly is on Bull's Island, where you begin the walk. Other unfortunate workers who died were simply dumped into the ground along the construction route—the route you follow.

The immigrants made little in wages but enough to

▼

attract an abundant supply of workers necessary to build the huge undertaking in a relatively short time. For much of the Delaware and Raritan Canal's 60-mile length, the canal measures 75 feet wide and 8 feet deep. It has more than 100 locks and bridges and extensive masonry you can still admire today as you proceed along the walk.

After a somewhat slow start, the canals eventually made money for their investors. For several decades, the waterways contributed to the growth of the towns along the way, such as New Hope, Lambertville, and Stockton. A special culture developed around the canals, which were peopled by mule drivers, lock operators, and barge drivers. Their diverse roles in maneuvering barges and mules through narrow canals gave rise to many local customs and legends that are now all but forgotten.

The canals prospered for a while, but they constantly struggled to compete with the railroad. By the end of the 19th century, they no longer turned a profit and were used only intermittently until the Depression. Today, instead of coal barges, the canals serve joggers, walkers, bicyclists, and canoers and are part of a series of state and national parks charged with their preservation and their development for tourists. The ambitious enterprises that opened with such great promise in the last century are no more than a monument now.

GETTING THERE:
By car:
From Manhattan, take the most convenient Hudson River crossing and go to I-78 westbound in New Jersey. Take I-78 to the exit for I-287 southbound, which you follow to exit 13, Rtes. 202/206. Follow the signs to Rte. 202 southbound and take it to the last exit before the toll bridge over the Delaware River. Get off at the exit for Rte. 29, Stockton, Lambertville, and go left at the end of the ramp.

▼

Make the next right on Rte. 29 and follow it about 5 mi. north through Stockton to the Bull's Island Recreation Area. Go left into the park entrance, cross over the old railroad, and proceed into a parking lot just beyond the park office.

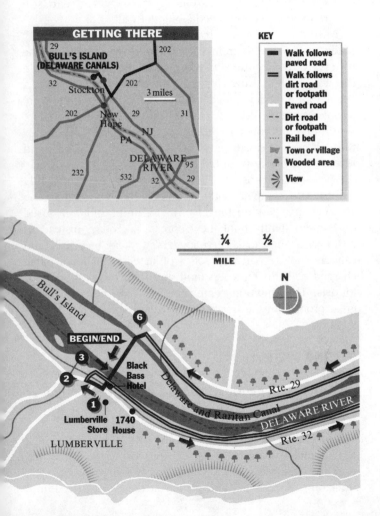

▼

Walk Directions

TIME: Up to 3 1/2 hours
LEVEL: Easy to difficult
DISTANCE: Up to 7 miles
ACCESS: By car

You walk along two canals on a towpath and an abandoned railroad and stroll through two old towns. The walk starts in New Jersey, takes you over the river into Pennsylvania, and then back over the river into New Jersey. The paths parallel small country roads for a good portion of the way, so you will encounter some traffic noise. You can shorten the walk any time you like simply by turning around and retracing your steps. Mountain bikes can also be rented at the Lumberville Store (215-297-5388), just 100 feet to the left of Point 1 on the map. Pick up picnic supplies at Meil's in Stockton (*see* Dining) or at the Lumberville Store.

TO BEGIN

With your back to the park entrance, walk to a pedestrian bridge and cross over the Delaware River. *Enjoy the beautiful views up and down the broad river.*

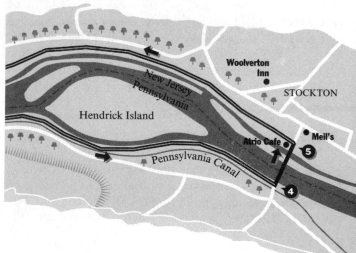

▼

1. On the other side, go right. Proceed along the paved road through Lumberville for about 100 yards.

2. Make a right turn across the small bridge that takes you to the towpath of the Delaware Canal.

3. Turn right onto the towpath. *If you'd like to see an aqueduct that carried the canal over a small creek, go left at Point 3 and walk a short distance. Then rejoin the walk at Point 3.* Follow the towpath for about two hours or so, until you approach a bridge over the Delaware River that goes back to Stockton. *The towpath lies between the canal and the river, so there are wonderful views of both. At one point, you pass through a well-kept quarry operation where rock is both mined and cut.*

4. Walk under the bridge over the Delaware River. Take the stairs that lead up to a walkway. Follow the walkway across to Stockton, and walk a short way into the village.

5. About 100 yards after the bridge, you reach an old railroad right-of-way marked by a wooden gate to your left. Go left and follow the railroad bed for about 1 1/2 hours back toward Bull's Island Recreation Area. *You might want to stop at Prallsville Mills along the way* (see *Places Along the Walk*).

6. When you reach a small paved road, a phone booth, and a park bench, you know you're back at Bull's Island. Make a left and retrace your steps to your car.

PLACES ALONG THE WALK

■ **Bull's Island Recreation Area.** Part of the Delaware and Raritan Canal State Park, this recreation area includes a campground, a 24-acre natural area, and places for boating and fishing. *2185 Daniel Bray Hwy., Stockton, NJ 08559; tel. 609-397-2949. Open daily year-round; campground open Apr.-Oct.*

▼

■ **Prallsville Mills.** This complex of mills—a gristmill, a linseed oil mill, a sawmill, and associated buildings—is currently under restoration. Listed on the National Register of Historic Places, the complex is part of the Delaware and Raritan Canal State Park but is maintained by volunteers. *Tel. 609-397-3586. Grounds open daily year-round; buildings open only for special events (call for schedule).*

OTHER PLACES NEARBY

■ **Doylestown.** The county seat of Bucks County, it features a number of interesting museums, including the Mercer Museum (215-345-0210), the Fonthill Museum (215-348-9461), the Moravian Pottery & Tile Works (215-345-6722), and the James A. Michener Art Museum (215-340-9800). Call the Tourist Commission (*see* For More Information) for detailed brochures. *About 8 mi. west of Stockton.*

■ **Point Pleasant Canoe & Tube, Inc.** You can canoe, raft, or tube down the Delaware River. *Box 6, Byram Rd., Point Pleasant, PA 18950; tel. 215-297-8181. Open daily Apr.-Oct. Admission. Just off Rte. 32, about 5 mi. northwest of Stockton.*

DINING

For additional options nearby, *see* Experience 24. Because liquor licenses are difficult to obtain in this area, many fine restaurants have a "BYOB" policy. You can pick up alcoholic beverages at Phillips' Fine Wines and Liquors (609-397-0587) on Bridge Street in Stockton.

■ **Evermay on the Delaware** (very expensive). Only on weekends does this classy inn open its top-rated restaurant's doors to the public. Warning: Don't come here to eat and run; be prepared to savor the elaborate, three-hour, six-course prix-fixe dinner, preceded by hors d'oeuvres and aperitifs. *River Rd., Box 60, Erwinna, PA 18920; tel. 610-294-9100; fax 610-294-8249. Open Fri.-Sun. (and holidays) for dinner. On Rte. 32, about 10 mi. northwest of Stockton.*

▼

■ **Black Bass Hotel** (expensive). The food at this 1745 inn has had an excellent reputation for years. The seasonal Continental cuisine includes specialties such as Charleston Meeting Street crab and roast lamb chops served with phyllo pastry, stuffed with red onion and shiitake mushrooms. There are five dining rooms, some with river views. At peak hours, such as lunchtime on the weekend, the service can be slow. (The inn also has inexpensive river-view guest rooms that are very small and share hall baths.) *3774 River Rd., Lumberville, PA 18933; tel. 215-297-5770; fax 215-297-0262. Open Mon.-Sat. for lunch and dinner, Sun. for brunch and dinner. Along the walk on Rte. 32, about 3 1/2 mi. northwest of Stockton.*

■ **Atrio Cafe** (moderate). The three young owners of this new restaurant have already attracted a following. The menu changes four times a year, accenting the fresh ingredients of the season. Look for the fresh seafood specials and the rack of lamb. *515 Bridge St., Stockton, NJ 08559; tel. 609-397-0042. Open Tue.-Sun. for lunch and dinner.*

■ **The Carversville Inn** (moderate). Chef-owner Will Mathis, who hails from Virginia, has established one of the area's best restaurants, serving a cuisine that's "American with a southern accent." Popular entrees include roast boneless duck with dried tart cherry-port wine sauce, and fresh pasta (a different type is offered each night). The ambience in this 1813 stone inn, a former stagecoach stop in a quaint hamlet, is cozy, especially in front of the rear dining room's walk-in fireplace. *6205 Fleecydale Rd., Carversville, PA 18913; tel. 215-297-0900. Open Wed.-Sun. for lunch, Tue.-Sun. for dinner. About 5 mi. northwest of Stockton.*

■ **The Stockton Inn** (moderate). You come to this one-time stagecoach stop for the ambience and the history, more than for the food. This is the "small hotel with a wishing well" of the Rodgers and Hart song. The inn, part of which dates to 1710, offers several charming dining environments: three dining rooms lined with murals of colonial scenes, another with a huge stone fireplace, and an outdoor area next to a waterfall. *1 Main St., Stockton, NJ*

▼

08559; tel. 609-397-1250. Open daily for lunch and dinner.

■ **Meil's Restaurant & Bakery** (inexpensive). If you want simple but tasty home-style fare, this extremely popular cafe is your best bet. Decor, ambience, and attitude are casual. House favorites are the meatloaf, potato pancakes, and corn fritters. Almost everything is made in-house with fresh ingredients, including the pastries, which are also available for takeout. No credit cards or reservations accepted. *Corner of Bridge and Main Sts., Box 397, Stockton, NJ 08559; tel. 609-397-8033. Open Mon.-Sat. for breakfast, lunch, and dinner; Sun. for brunch and dinner.*

LODGING

■ **1740 House** (expensive). Most of the rooms in this quiet hotel near the walk have views of the Delaware River. Rooms are adequately sized and nicely decorated. Try to get the suite, if possible. It's cozy and has a living room with many windows and a view of the river. *River Rd., Lumberville, PA 18933; tel. 215-297-5661. Along the walk, about 3 mi. northwest of Stockton.*

■ **Evermay on the Delaware** (expensive). This inn's main building was renovated in Victorian style in 1871. Set on 25 acres, its front rooms offer river views. If traffic noise is a concern, ask for a garden-view room. A cottage and a carriage house contain additional rooms. A few small rooms are moderately priced. *River Rd., Box 60, Erwinna, PA 18920; tel. 610-294-9100; fax 610-294-8249. On Rte. 32, about 10 mi. northwest of Stockton.*

■ **Isaac Stover House** (expensive). Owned by TV personality Sally Jessy Raphael, this inn underwent total renovation and redecoration in 1995 from elegant to drop-dead elegant (yet comfortable and inviting). Each room has a unique style and ambience. The romantic Yellow Room, for example, has a steel queen-size canopy bed and lovely yellow-gold wallpaper. Rooms on the river side enjoy the sound of the rapids, but there may be some traffic noise. *845 River Rd., Erwinna, PA 18920; tel. 610-294-8044. On Rte. 32, about 10 mi. northwest of Stockton.*

■ **The Woolverton Inn** (expensive). If a classy rural

▼

retreat is what you seek, you couldn't do much better than this elegant B&B. A 1790 stone manor house set on 10 acres next to a farm, its location is serene and only a five-minute walk downhill to Stockton and the towpath. There are eight guest rooms and two suites, with upscale yet comfortable traditional furnishings and recently renovated private baths (one with Jacuzzi). The spacious common living room opens to an inviting veranda. *6 Woolverton Rd., Stockton, NJ 08559; tel. 609-397-0802.*

■ **Tattersall Inn** (moderate). There are six guest rooms in this B&B, a plastered fieldstone house set back from the road, about a four-minute walk from the canal. All rooms have queen-size beds, private baths, and air conditioning. Most popular is the Royal Lavender room, with canopy bed, large bath, and lavender fabric on the walls. Included are breakfast and afternoon refreshments, served in a cozy common room with a huge fireplace in the 1750 wing of the house. *Box 569, Cafferty and River Rds., Point Pleasant, PA 18950; tel. 215-297-8233. On Rte. 32, about 5 mi. northwest of Stockton.*

FOR MORE INFORMATION
Tourist Office:

■ **Bucks County Tourist Commission.** *152 Swamp Rd., Doylestown, PA 18901; tel. 215-345-4552, 800-836-2825; fax 215-345-4967. Open Mon.-Fri. 8:30-5 year-round, Sat. 10-4 Apr.-Oct.*

For Serious Walkers:

You can walk almost the entire 60-mile length of the Delaware Canal on the Pennsylvania side of the Delaware River (don't confuse the canal with the Delaware and Raritan Canal on the New Jersey side). For details and a map, contact Friends of the Delaware Canal (215-862-2021). The Delaware and Raritan Canal also can be walked for nearly 20 miles and is even better for mountain-biking. For a map, call the Delaware and Raritan Canal Commission (609-397-2000).

The Boys of Winter

EXPERIENCE 24: BOWMAN'S HILL

Tourists who make the trip to Washington Crossing State Park in Pennsylvania invariably visit the section adjacent to McConkey's Ferry Inn, where they can see the spot where General George Washington's troops clambered into Durham boats on a snowy Christmas night in 1776 to cross the Delaware River and make a successful, surprise attack on the British position in Trenton. It's a good place for a guided tour or to buy a souvenir, but if you want to really appreciate the boldness of Washington's deed and the heroism of the troops, drive north a few miles to the park's northern section at Bowman's Hill.

You can stroll in peace on pristine land camped on by the troops and visit the graves of some soldiers who made the ultimate sacrifice there. In addition, you can visit an old farmhouse where Washington and his staff hatched their plan and wander through a wild flower garden created in tribute to the men who

The Highlights: Scenic site of a Revolutionary War encampment, soldiers' graves, a historic house, a wild flower preserve.

Other Places Nearby: The towns of New Hope and Lambertville, historic parks, great restaurants.

▼

gave their lives for the cause of the Revolution.

Washington's attack on Trenton, New Jersey, had little long-term military significance. If one of its objectives was to prevent the British capture of Philadelphia, it ultimately failed. But no less a motive was the need for a victory. The first year of the Revolution was a rout in favor of the British, who had driven the patriots out of New York and back across the Delaware River. By December 1776, the Revolution was the laughingstock of European courts and had little support at home. Even many Americans who supported the Revolution had begun to give up hope, and the reluctance of farmers to sell food to a military without cash made life even harder for the 2,400 or so troops who camped on the western shores of the Delaware that month. Near the end of 1776, Thomas Paine wrote: "These are the times that try men's souls; the summer soldier and the sunshine patriot will, in this crisis, shrink from service of his country, but he that stands it now deserves the love and thanks of man and woman." Washington could not hope to find support in Europe or rally the spirits of the new nation unless he proved that the Americans could beat the British.

A mong those in Washington's inner circle who supported bold action was General William Alexander Stirling, who in December 1776 was quartered in the Thompson-Neely House you can visit along the walk. Stirling had surveyed the terrain from atop Bowman's Hill (where there is now a sightseeing tower and souvenir shop) and believed a surprise strike on Trenton could succeed.

While Washington's staff debated what to do, little was left of the army. Of nearly 8,000 soldiers who had helped in the futile defense of New York earlier that year, only about a third were with Washington at the Delaware. Many camped in the area where you'll walk near the river and up along Pidcock Creek. A mill whose site you will pass probably contributed to the men's meager rations. Contemporary descriptions of their

▼

condition paint a pitiful picture of men without shoes, clothes, or shelter, sleeping under rocks and in the brush to stay warm during a particularly cold December. Countless numbers died of disease and exposure. Washington had to worry constantly about the loyalty and morale of his troops, hoping that the "boys of summer" would last through the bleak winter. Despite the adverse conditions, his officers clung to their ideals, using in their letters words like "freedom" and "liberty" to justify their sacrifices.

As local historian Ann Hawkes Hutton tells it, a Captain James Moore lay dying in the pathetic makeshift hospital set up in the downstairs of the Thompson-Neely House in the days before the famous attack. He was a young man who had come from a comfortable family in New York. Moore certainly had plenty to lose by joining the Revolution, and he could easily have left during the dark hours when the patriots beat a hasty retreat across New Jersey. On the day before the attack, Washington is said to have visited the men in the hospital on his way upstairs to a planning session with Stirling and other officers. As he came alongside the gravely ill Captain Moore, Washington told him, "You are no summer soldier, son, no summer soldier."

On Christmas day, the men buried Moore next to the bodies of 49 unknown soldiers on a beautiful spot you can visit along the walk. That night, the ragged troops ventured out across the icy Delaware, walked 11 miles southeast to Trenton, and took the British and Hessian troops completely by surprise, routing them without the loss of a single man. Today, there's little doubt that this humble military victory ultimately helped change the war's equation in favor of the patriots.

As a tribute to the men who fought for American independence, a Depression-era work project created the Bowman's Hill State Wildflower Preserve, a 100-acre garden that both highlights local flora as well as habitats from other parts of the country. Here flower lovers can see hundreds of different species in

▼

bloom, depending on the season and rainfall, and enjoy a unique effort to preserve and study wild flowers of all kinds.

GETTING THERE
By car:

From Manhattan, take the bridge or the tunnel that's most convenient for you and go to I-78 westbound in New Jersey. Follow it to the exit for I-287 southbound, which you follow to exit 13, Rtes. 202/206. Follow the signs to Rte. 202 southbound and take it across the toll bridge into Pennsylvania. Take the first exit for New Hope, Rte. 32, and follow Rte. 32 southbound 4 mi. through the town of New Hope to the entrance for the Thompson-Neely House, which is part of the northern section of Pennsylvania's Washington Crossing State Park. Go left onto the park road and proceed a short distance to a gate. You do not park in the Thompson-Neely House lot for this walk, although you can if you intend to take a guided tour. Insert $1 in change (no pennies) into the automatic gate, then follow the road around to the right and park near the picnic shelter. (If you don't have change, tokens are available at the park headquarters, about 4 mi. to the south on Rte. 32.)

Walk Directions

TIME: 1 1/2 to 3 1/2 hours
LEVEL: Easy to difficult
DISTANCE: 2 1/2 to 7 miles
ACCESS: By car

The full walk, which is rated difficult only because of its length, takes you past the soldiers' graves down one of the most beautiful stretches of canal in the region, then brings you back up and through the Bowman's Hill Wildflower Preserve. You can signficantly shorten the walk by cutting out the canal extension. Follow the directions to Point 4; go right (instead of left to do the canal walk) and follow the directions from Point 4. Or, you

▼

can skip the wild flower preserve by doing the canal walk and then going right at the footbridge in Point 1. To take full advantage of the wild flower preserve, follow the walk directions to the visitors center and obtain a park map. It indicates the preserve's flowers and shrubs and allows you to use the numbered posts along the trails that identify the flowers. The itinerary below is only a suggestion; when you arrive, you might want to ask a park official which paths have the most flowers in bloom. Don't expect a flower garden like the ones you would see in an English gardening book; this park tries to display its flowers in the habitat you would find in the unmanaged wild. Pick up picnic foods in New Hope, Pennsylvania, or across the river in Lambertville, New Jersey. There are beautiful picnic spots along the canal and on the edge of the preserve, but you cannot picnic within the preserve.

TO BEGIN

With your back to the Delaware River, walk toward a pedestrian bridge that leads over the Delaware Canal.

1. Just before you cross the bridge, go left on the canal towpath. Proceed a short distance over a spillway that is dry except at times of very high water.

2. At a dirt path just beyond the spillway, bear left away from the towpath. When you reach a paved road, bear right and walk a short distance to the stone pillars marking the entrance to the tiny cemetery. Walk toward the Delaware River and the flagpole to see the graves.

3. At the graves, follow a small footpath down to the Delaware. *You'll get a much better idea here on this peaceful riverbank of what it looked like to the soldiers than you will at the main part of the park.* **Be careful: Poison ivy lines the trail down to the river.** When you're done enjoying this tran-

▼

quil spot, retrace your steps back to the stone pillars and cross a meadow straight back to the footpath.

4. At the towpath, go left. Follow the towpath as far as you want toward its intersection with Rte. 32 in about 2 1/2 miles. (You eventually must retrace your steps to Point 1.) *The canal and its towpath go through beautiful unspoiled countryside that's well away from the road. Beautiful views are disturbed only by a large quarry operation across the river to your left.* Just before Rte. 32, you reach an aqueduct that carries the canal over a small tributary of the Delaware. Retrace your steps to Point 1, where you go left over the canal on the pedestrian bridge. Follow the grassy path up to Rte. 32, past the front of the Thompson-Neely House.

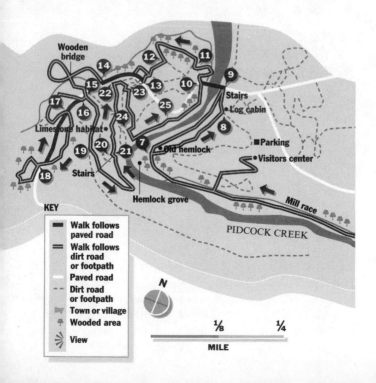

▼

5. Carefully cross Rte. 32. Proceed uphill in front of the Thompson-Neely gristmill following the outlines of the millrace on your left. When you reach the rest rooms, go left over a tiny wooden bridge. (Another option is to take a path that leads behind the old mill up to Point 6.) *The millrace is a trench that carried water directly downhill to the mill from an upstream pond to ensure a steady supply of water. Another mill was in operation near here before the Revolution, and soldiers camped here during December 1776.*

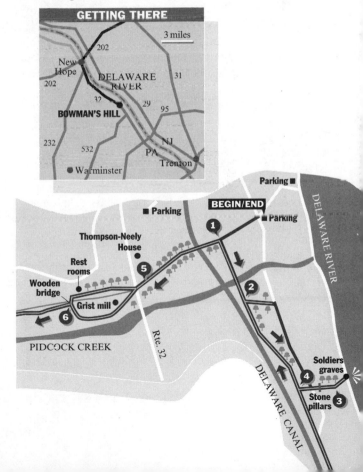

▼

6. After you cross the tiny bridge, go right uphill toward a metal gate. Proceed through the gate, and close it behind you. Continue uphill on the trail alongside the millrace to your right. In a short while you pass a small wooden bridge leading to a trail on your right. If you want to stop at the visitors center and pick up a map of the preserve, go right and walk uphill a short distance on the Parry Trail. Otherwise, continue uphill on the trail toward the dam, where the millrace begins. At the dam, continue straight, ignoring stairs uphill to your right, until you reach an intersection with the Azalea Trail indicated on a wooden post. *You're in a hemlock grove.*

7. Go right up a short hill to take the Azalea Trail's upper branch. As you go uphill, notice a huge old hemlock to your left that was there during the time of George Washington. *The white- and orange-flowered azealas on this trail bloom in June.*

8. When you reach a log cabin, go left downstairs to the lower branch of the Azelea trail. Go right a few feet toward a paved road.

9. Go left over a bridge and if you're passing through in June, admire the azalea blooms on the banks of the river to your left.

10. Immediately after crossing the bridge, take a tiny overgrown trail to your right called the Bluebell Trail and follow it around to your right and then to your left. *Look around carefully for the lavender-blue flowers of bluebells July through September.*

11. Go right at an intersection with the Audubon Trail, which leads along a fence into a tiny meadow whose berry-bearing plants attract birds year-round. Follow the trail as it loops around to the left through the meadow.

▼

12. At an intersection just a few feet into the woods, go right, continuing on the Audubon Trail past a shelter back toward the paved road. Take a tiny loop on the Sphagnum Bog Trail, which leads you through a very small bog and toward the paved road. *Notice the blue flowers of New York asters in October, the red flowers of the pitcher plant in early June, and the yellow flowers of swamp candles in July.*

13. Go right on the paved road and head uphill a short distance to the Harshberger Trail.

14. Go right on the Harshberger Trail, which leads over a small wooden bridge and loops around to your left. Continue straight at an intersection, and follow the trail around to your right back across the intersection. Proceed straight toward the road over another small wooden bridge. *You can see the orange flowers of the flame azalea in June, the white and pink flowers of pinxterbloom in April and May, and the pink-purple flowers of summer phlox from June through September.*

15. At the road, go right and proceed a very short distance.

16. Go right on the Medicinal Trail and follow it around to the left back toward the road. *Those interested in medicinal plants can look for twinleaf, goldenseal, prickly ash, and sarsaparilla here.*

17. Cross the paved road. Proceed uphill on the Poconos Laurel Trail, where you see lichen, moss, and mushrooms. *Beech, chestnut oak, and sweet birch trees grow in the forest.*

18. The trail comes out on the paved road. Cross it and do the final loop of the Poconos Laurel Trail. *On this part of the trail, you will see an old stand of mountain laurel that blooms white and pink in early summer.* Return to Point 18, where you

▼

go left and walk downhill to Point 15. Go right on the Ecology Trail past a shelter. Ignore the Evergreen Trail that's a short distance away on your left. Continue straight through an intersection with a trail that's on your right.

19. At a Y, bear left on the Lloyd Evergreen Trail, which you follow a short distance around a loop to the left.

20. Go right at the stairs heading downhill.

21. Go left on the trail that begins at the foot of the stairs. This is the Fern Trail. Follow it along a ridge toward the paved park road. *You're passing a limestone habitat enclosed in a fence, as well as many varieties of ferns.*

22. When you reach the road, go right, continuing on the Fern Trail. Ignore the Wayside Trail to your left and continue downhill.

23. At an intersection at the base of the hill, go left. Immediately turn right, and follow the sign to the Gentian Trail, which you follow around to the left side of a tiny pond. *The pond is home to painted and snapping turtles, birds, and water lilies that bloom much of the summer.*

24. Just beyond a bench and a sign, go left on the Gentian Trail. Follow it as it loops to the left. *Dozens of wild flowers can be found along this trail, which you can identify with the help of the map sold at the park headquarters.*

25. When you reach the road, bear right. Continue on the Azaleas-at-the-Bridge Trail, where you can enjoy the sight of blooming azaleas in early summer on your way back to the stone bridge. Go right across the bridge, and go right again at Point 9, down the lower portion of the Azalea Trail that runs

▼

along the riverbank. Follow it to Point 7, where you continue straight, retracing your steps to your car.

PLACES ALONG THE WALK

■ **Bowman's Hill State Wildflower Preserve.** In addition to several miles of trails, it features special programs and exhibits. *Rte. 32, Washington Crossing, PA 18977; tel. 215-862-2924. Grounds open daily 8-sunset. Headquarters building open Tue.-Sat. 9-5, Sun. 12-5. Gate is closed on Mon. but you can enter by following the walk directions.*

■ **Thompson-Neely House.** This beautiful 18th-century house was the site of critical meetings leading to General George Washington's decision to cross the Delaware in 1776. *Rte. 32, Washington Crossing, PA 18977; tel. 215-493-4076. Open Tue.-Sat. 9-5, Sun. 12-5. Admission.*

OTHER PLACES NEARBY

For additional attractions in the area, *see* Experience 23, Delaware Canals.

■ **Lambertville, NJ.** Those who have a high tolerance for throngs of tourists and enjoy cute shops may prefer frenetic New Hope, Pennsylvania. But, right across the bridge is Lambertville, a very pretty little town with excellent restaurants and a relatively undiscovered feel to it. A local guide and walking tour map are available from the Lambertville Chamber of Commerce (609-397-0055).

■ **Washington Crossing Historic Park.** The park's northern Thompson's Mill section includes Bowman's Hill Wildflower Preserve and Bowman's Hill Tower, from which you can get a sweeping view of the countryside. The tower was built in the 1930s, but the hill on which it stands was the lookout point for General George Washington's scouts. The park's southern McConkey's Ferry section includes a visitors center and numerous historical buildings. Special events include a re-enactment of the crossing. *Rtes. 32 and 532, Washington Crossing, PA 18977;*

▼

tel. 215-493-4076. Grounds open daily 8-sunset. Buildings open Tue.-Sat. 9-5, Sun. 12-5. There's an admission charge to the buildings and to some parking lots; the grounds are free. Bowman's Hill Tower is off Rte. 32, immediately south of the walk. The park's southern section is about 3 1/2 mi. south on Rte. 32 (you can also walk there via the canal towpath).

DINING

Many local restaurants have a "BYOB" policy, because liquor licenses are difficult to obtain. For additional restaurants nearby, *see* Experience 23, Delaware Canals.

■ **Anton's at the Swan** (expensive). Chef-owner Anton Dodel offers excellent modern American cuisine. The menu, which changes monthly, features items such as basil-crusted salmon with a ginger and beet sauce, or sauteed crab with pine nuts on saffron pasta. The dining room's darkish decor is brightened by the works of area artists. *Swan Hotel, 43 S. Main St., Lambertville, NJ 08530; tel. 609-397-1960. Open Wed.-Sun. for dinner. About 3 mi. northeast of Bowman's Hill.*

■ **The Ferry House** (expensive). One of the most popular restaurants in an area with many good ones, The Ferry House attracts regulars with its innovative, eclectic American menu, created by chef-owner Bobby Trigg. Try the roasted baby rack of lamb with mustard crust and roasted garlic au jus; a popular appetizer is roasted Portobello mushrooms with baby greens and goat cheese. Bring your own wine or beer. *21 Ferry St., Lambertville, NJ 08530; tel. 609-397-9222; fax 609-397-1429. Open daily for dinner (Mon.-Tue. prix-fixe dinner only) and Sun. for brunch. About 3 mi. north of Bowman's Hill.*

■ **Inn at Phillips Mill** (moderate). Housed in a 260-year-old stone barn, this inn offers excellent food and a romantic ambience. The interior has low-beamed ceilings and three fireplaces; a tiny courtyard for outdoor dining is very picturesque. The French country menu includes such delicacies as escargots, garlic-crusted swordfish with beurre blanc, and a variety of

▼

naughty desserts. Bring your own wine. No credit cards. *2590 N. River Rd., New Hope, PA 18938; tel. 215-862-9919. Open daily for dinner. Closed Jan. About 4 mi. north of Bowman's Hill.*

■ **Hotel du Village** (moderate). French-trained chef-owner Omar Arbani creates a country-style French cuisine that includes appetizers such as shrimp sauteed in garlic butter and entrees such as tournedos of beef with artichoke hearts and Bearnaise sauce. The dark Tudor-style decor and three working fireplaces give a pleasant old-world feel. *Phillips Mill Rd. and River Rd., New Hope, PA 18938; tel. 215-862-9911. Open Wed.-Sun. for dinner Mar.-Dec.; Thu.-Sat. Jan.-Feb. On Rte. 32, about 4 mi. north of Bowman's Hill.*

LODGING

Many charming and historic lodgings are near busy roads, so you may want to ask for a room in the back.

■ **Ash Mill Farm** (expensive). Your attentive hosts create a gracious, relaxed environment at this B&B, a plastered stone house on ten rural acres, with a cozy common room and a walk-in fireplace that were built in 1790. The three guest rooms and two suites all have private baths and air conditioning. They're comfortably furnished in a mix of antiques and reproductions, including pencil-post canopy beds. *5358 Old York Rd., Holicong, PA 18928; tel. 215-794-5373. On Rte. 202, about 8 mi. northwest of Bowman's Hill.*

■ **Barley Sheaf Farm** (expensive). When this was playwright George S. Kaufman's estate in the 1930s, guests included Lillian Hellman and the Marx Brothers. Now you can invite yourself to this B&B, and you'll receive warm, Swiss hospitality. Set on 30 acres, the 1740 stone farmhouse (with modern additions), a renovated barn, and a sweet little cottage contain a total of 12 rooms and suites, all with private bath. *5281 Old York Rd., Holicong, PA 18928; tel. 215-794-5104; fax 215-794-5332. On Rte. 202, about 8 mi. northwest of Bowman's Hill.*

■ **Chimney Hill Farm** (expensive). This hilltop estate on

▼

more than eight acres offers a quiet country escape. To maintain the tranquillity, there are no TVs or radios. Part of the 1927 house was built in 1820, including the cozy dining room. A spacious living room and a sun room invite guests to relax. All eight guest rooms have air conditioning and private baths (though some are in the hall). *207 Goat Hill Rd., Lambertville, NJ 08530; tel. 609-397-1516. About 3 1/2 mi. north of Bowman's Hill.*

■ **Whitehall Inn** (expensive). Don't be misled by the address; this B&B is in the country, far from traffic and tourist frenzy. Its 12 acres include a horse paddock, a swimming pool, and a tennis court. The 1794 house has six guest rooms, four with private baths; some have working fireplaces and canopy beds. *1370 Pineville Rd., New Hope, PA 18938; tel. 215-598-7945. About 6 mi. west of Bowman's Hill.*

■ **Inn at Phillips Mill** (moderate). If you're looking for a rustic, romantic hideaway, consider this historic inn. The main building, originally built in 1750 as a stone barn, holds one suite and four rooms, whose small size and simple but quaint furnishings are reflected in the price. All have double beds, air conditioning, and private baths. There's also an expensively priced private cottage, featuring a living room with a stone fireplace, a kitchenette, and a tiny bedroom tucked under the eaves. *2590 N. River Rd., New Hope, PA 18938; tel. 215-862-2984. Closed Jan. On Rte. 32, about 4 mi. north of Bowman's Hill.*

FOR MORE INFORMATION
Tourist Office:

■ **Bucks County Tourist Commission.** *152 Swamp Rd., Doylestown, PA 18901; tel. 215-345-4552, 800-836-2825; fax 215-345-4967. Open Mon.-Fri. 8:30-5 year-round, and Sat. 10-4 Apr.-Oct.*

For Serious Walkers:
Besides the walks described in this chapter, *see* Experience 23, Delaware Canals.

The Wonder of the Gap

EXPERIENCE 25:
DELAWARE WATER GAP

The Delaware Water Gap was born some 30 million years ago. It was not, as you might imagine while looking down on it on this walking tour, created by the Delaware River forcing its way through the already existing mountain wall. Instead, the Delaware River came first, flow-

The Highlights: Gorgeous views of the Delaware Water Gap, a walk along the Appalachian Trail.

Other Places Nearby: One of the country's oldest scenic byways, a restored 19th-century village, tumbling waterfalls, a small town with good restaurants, lodging, and live jazz.

ing gently across a wide plain sloping toward the Atlantic Ocean. Then, over eons, a slow upheaval caused the plain on either side of the river to lift and fold. As the new mountains rose up, the river ate a channel through them, exposing layer upon layer of steeply slanting gray sandstone walls.

Today, the Delaware Water Gap and the 40-mile-long valley extending northward from it form one of the most dramatic geological features anywhere in the New York metropolitan area. The 1,000-foot-deep gorge through which the Delaware River sweeps in a lazy "S" curve is a popular resort destination for

▼

artists, canoeists, walkers, hikers, and outdoor pleasure-seekers.

Steeped in history and prehistory, "the Gap" was home to Native Americans 10,000 years ago. When these first peoples wandered into this fertile river valley, it looked far different than it does today. The postglacial climate was cold, resembling that of northern Canada. By the beginning of the woodland period, a mere 3,000 years ago, earth's climate had warmed, and the landscape had changed dramatically, looking much as it does today. Up and down the river, the Lenape tribe lived in small villages, fishing, hunting in the old-growth forests, and cultivating crops.

The first Europeans to arrive were the Dutch in the early 1600s. They did little to disrupt the Lenape way of life at first, seeking mineral wealth rather than a permanent place to live. Then came Dutch settlers, who left a mark on the valley with their place and family names and their simple farmhouse architecture. The Van Campen Inn (on the New Jersey side of the Gap), built in 1746, is one of the oldest residences in the valley and a perfect example of the vernacular architectural style (combining Dutch details with a Georgian stone facade). Another Dutch contribution to the area is the Old Mine Road paralleling the Delaware's east shore from the Gap north. Still drivable, this beautiful byway is one of the oldest in the United States.

When the British took over the Dutch colony of New Amsterdam, they almost immediately sought to drive out the Delaware Valley's peaceful Lenape tribe. In doing so, they devised one of the most devious of all colonial land swindles. The Lenape, besieged by the flood of English farmers, begrudgingly agreed to sell a small piece of their ancestral lands: a squared-off territory equal to the distance a man could walk in a day-and-a-half (about 30 miles at most). But the English cut and blazed a trail along the route. They advertised in newspapers for fast runners and trained them. One "walker" ran 55 miles in the allotted time period, a total loss to the tribe of

▼

1,200 square miles. The enraged Lenape declared that the whites should have stopped to rest, smoke a pipe, or shoot a squirrel. But the tribe was forced to keep the bargain. The Lenape returned briefly to seek revenge during the Indian Wars, burning farms and killing settlers, but for them, the Delaware Valley was forever lost.

By the mid-1800s city dwellers, suffering from a shortage of fresh air and open space, took advantage of newly built rail-roads and came to the Gap on vacation. Great hotels sprang up everywhere along the river. One of the largest, the Kittatinny House, could host 500 guests and boasted four bowling alleys, a pool, and an illuminated electric fountain. Hard financial times after World War I killed the resorts.

In the 1960s, the peaceful life of the upper Delaware Valley was shattered when the U.S. Congress authorized a plan to construct the Tocks Island Dam. This planned 160-foot-tall earthen dam would have flooded 12,300 acres of land, destroyed 2,500 homes and 100 farms, and ruined large wilderness tracts famous for their populations of black bear and migrating eagles.

Property owners rose up in anger, but the Army Corps of Engineers moved in, condemning properties and driving out residents. Hippie squatters settled on vacated lands, setting up utopian communes, cultivating marijuana, and sabotaging Army Corps bulldozers. Angry evicted residents set fire to some historic buildings rather than let others use them. In the end, dawn raids by armed federal marshals were used to quell the unrest.

The fight to stop the dam went on. Such luminaries as Supreme Court Justice William O. Douglas rallied to the cause. In the end, a coalition of one-time residents, environmental groups, and squatting hippies defeated the "Tocks" dam, leaving behind what became the sprawling green oasis of the 70,000-acre Delaware Water Gap National Recreation Area. This outdoor playground is host to four million visitors each year who come to walk, canoe, bike, and swim. Eagles still can be

▼

seen gliding the updrafts above the Appalachian Trail in the Gap. Bear, bobcat, coyote, and Delaware River shad are again plentiful. In some ways, the surroundings of the Delaware Water Gap are as peaceful now as they were 100 years ago.

GETTING THERE

By car:

From New York City, take I-80 west through New Jersey to the Delaware Water Gap. Cross the Delaware River into Pennsylvania and get off at the first exit after the toll booth. Proceed into the town of Delaware Water Gap on Rte. 611 south. At the far edge of town, turn right onto Mountain Rd. Go a few hundred yards and fork left onto Lake St. At the end of this short street, enter the Appalachian Trail parking area.

Walk Directions

TIME: 2 1/2 or 3 1/2 hours
LEVEL: Moderate or difficult
DISTANCE: 2 1/2 or 4 miles
ACCESS: By car

This scenic walk on the Appalachian Trail, unlike nearly all others in this book, is not a loop. But it offers many beautiful sights and shouldn't be missed. There is a short and a long version of the walk. The short version goes to Winona Cliff, which looks out at the rocky "Indian Head" profile of Chief Tammany, the Lenape leader for whom the mountain on the New Jersey side of the Gap is named. The walk climbs 400 feet. If you climb an additional strenuous 500 feet to Lookout Rock near the top of Mount Minsi, there is another vista, looking across the Gap to Mount Tammany.

TO BEGIN

From the parking lot, face the National Park Service gate. Walk around the gate and straight ahead on the paved fire

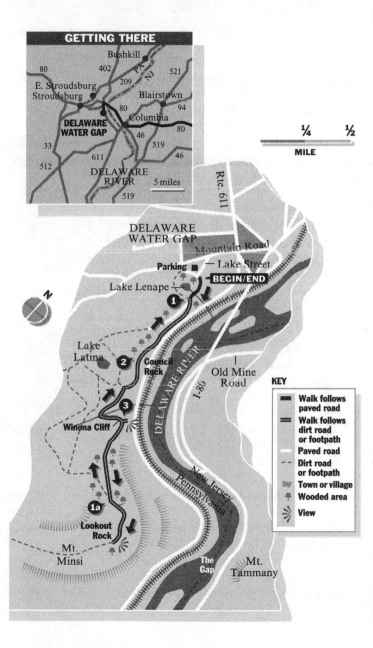

Bushkill

80   402

E. Stroudsburg
Stroudsburg

209   PA   521
        NJ

Blairstown

80

DELAWARE
WATER GAP

Columbia

94

80

46

33

611

512

DELAWARE
RIVER

519

46

519

¼   ½

MILE

5 miles

DELAWARE
WATER GAP

Rte. 611

Mountain Road

Parking   Lake Street

BEGIN/END

Lake Lenape

1

Lake
Latina

2

Council
Rock

Old Mine
Road

I-80

DELAWARE RIVER

3

Winona Cliff

N

1a

Lookout
Rock

Mt.
Minsi

New Jersey
Pennsylvania

The
Gap

Mt.
Tammany

KEY

▮ Walk follows
  paved road

▬ Walk follows
  dirt road
  or footpath

▭ Paved road

▪▪▪ Dirt road
  or footpath

▮ Town or village

🌲 Wooded area

≈ View

▼

road. *This road is part of the Appalachian Trail, a 2,100-mile footpath running from Maine to Georgia.* Notice the two-inch-by-six-inch white blazes on the trees. These white blazes mark the Appalachian Trail along its entire length, and you follow them throughout your walk.

In a very short distance, you come to lily-covered Lenape Lake (ignore the unmarked path that makes a loop around the lake). Continue following the white blazes and fire road over a small stream which drains out of the lake. Now you ascend slightly on the road through a grove of hemlock trees. *These stately trees, though apparently healthy, are all slowly dying due to the attack of Japanese insects accidentally introduced by man.* Ignore the many small unmarked side trails that lead away to the left to partial views of the Water Gap. Stay on the fire road. Note the 50-foot-tall rock face on your right.

1. When you reach this rock face, leave the fire road and continue on the Appalachian Trail by turning sharply left onto a wide hard-packed dirt path that goes into the woods. (You can always tell when the Appalachian Trail is making a turn because there will be two white Appalachian Trail blazes on a single tree, one blaze atop another.) You now descend gently on the packed-earth pathway through a hemlock grove, then level out and walk along a flat trail. Notice and **be wary of the steep drop-off to your left** that descends several hundred feet down through thick woods to the Delaware River.

2. Reach Council Rock, your first vista, about a half mile into the walk. *Though partly blocked by trees, you can clearly see the Delaware Water Gap with its profiles of Pennsylvania's Mount Minsi on the right and New Jersey's Mount Tammany on the left.* After enjoying the view, continue on the Appalachian Trail, descending to a small seasonal stream, then ascending gently through six-foot-tall rhododendron. Ascend through an even denser stand of hemlocks, rhododendron, and forest-floor

▼

ferns. Then ascend more gradually through a mixed deciduous forest of maple, chestnut oak, and hickory. *Wild geranium and delicate bluets bloom here in springtime.*

Level off and step on stones across a small cascading stream. Ignore the unmarked side trail leading uphill along the stream. *Notice that just below the Appalachian Trail, the stream dives steeply down toward the Delaware River.* Enter a small hollow and again step on stones across another little mountain stream, ignoring an unmarked trail running uphill along the stream. Level out through more hemlocks and interesting rock formations. *Look at the steep slope above and below the pathway and realize that Appalachian Trail volunteers actually carved this level trail into the hillside.*

3. At an intersection where the Appalachian Trail turns sharply right and steeply uphill, leave the trail by walking straight ahead on a level, well-used but unmarked packed-earth trail that extends 50 feet to Winona Cliff. *Take some time here and **be very careful when you walk out onto any of several rock outcrops.** The vista opens wide to the sky and gives you sweeping panoramas of the Delaware River and the Water Gap. You can see Mounts Minsi and Tammany, the "S" curve of the Delaware River, and Rte. 80.* Retrace your steps back to the parking lot and your car, unless you would like to follow the short, rugged extension described below.

To complete the steep, longer walk up Mount Minsi, retrace your steps from the Winona Cliff vista 50 feet to Point 3, where the Appalachian Trail turns steeply uphill. Following the white blazes, climb uphill on natural stone steps. Follow the Appalachian Trail as it climbs and twists left, right, and left away from the cliff, until you come to an open area with more views of the Gap.

Continue walking to the right and further away from the cliff, then climb steadily to a long flat sheet of open rock. Follow the trail into the forest. Climb steadily, occasionally leveling off.

▼

Enter a lush shaded tunnel of rhododendron, leading upward to a small rock face. After a steep continuous climb, level off briefly, then make another steep climb to a wide woods road.

1A. Follow the Appalachian Trail as it turns left briefly on the woods road. It then turns sharply right, leaving the woods road and re-entering the forest. Make one last steep climb before reaching Lookout Rock, which is located somewhat below the true summit of Mount Minsi. *From Lookout Rock you'll be looking straight across to the top of Mount Tammany, where folded layers of rock strata tip at a 45-degree angle.* Retrace your steps to the parking lot.

OTHER PLACES NEARBY

■ **Kittatinny Point Visitor Center.** This is a good first stop to orient yourself to the Delaware Water Gap National Recreation Area. A short walk from the visitors center along the bank of the Delaware River provides breathtaking views of the towering heights of Mounts Minsi and Tammany. Inside the center are nature exhibits, a slide show, and a bookshop with a fine collection of field guides to local flora and fauna, geology, and history. *I-80, New Jersey; tel. 908-496-4458. Open daily 9-5 May-Oct.; open Sat.-Sun. 9-4:30 Nov.-Apr. In the heart of the Water Gap, on the New Jersey side.*

■ **Old Mine Road.** Built sometime in the 17th century, this is one of America's oldest commercial roads. It hugs the New Jersey side of the Delaware River for much of its length and then heads northeast towards the Hudson River. Today, this scenic drive north of the Gap provides a marvelous diversity of natural landscape. A five-mile section is unpaved, much as it was in colonial times. *From the town of Delaware Water Gap, PA, take Rte. 611 north to I-80 east. Cross the Delaware River bridge and get off at the first NJ exit. Head north.*

■ **Town of Delaware Water Gap.** This small Pennsylvania town is a resort area, yet remains rural: A black bear and her cubs recently stopped traffic on Main Street. The

▼

town offers a cluster of crafts shops, a few good restaurants, jazz at the Deerhead Inn, plus the little Antoine Dutot Museum, a 19th-century schoolhouse displaying local historic and craft exhibits. An annual Celebration of the Arts, a jazz festival and crafts fair, is held the weekend after Labor Day (contact the Deerhead Inn at 717-424-2000). *Antoine Dutot Museum (717-421-5809) open Sat.-Sun. 1-5 May-Oct. Deerhead Inn (717-424-2000) presents live jazz Fri.-Sat. evenings. Both the Deerhead Inn and the Antoine Dutot Museum are on Main St.*

DINING

■ **Smuggler's Cove** (moderate). Some of the best fresh seafood in the area can be found here. Catch of the day may be Norwegian salmon or Alaskan halibut, and Alaskan king crab and Maryland soft-shell crab are delicious favorites. Cajun specialties, terrific pastas, Black Angus steaks, homemade soups, and wonderful salads fill out an extensive menu. The pub offers an inexpensive menu. *Rte. 611, Tannersville, PA 18372; tel. 717-629-2277. Open daily for lunch and dinner. About 14 mi. west of the town of Delaware Water Gap.*

■ **Saen Thai Cuisine** (moderate). You don't come to this little place for the ambience or the location—in a quasi-rustic strip mall— but for the good, authentic Thai food, delicately seasoned. Look for green or yellow curry with chicken, beef, or vegetables in coconut milk. *Box 167, Shawnee Square Shopping Center, Shawnee-on-Delaware, PA 18356; tel. 717-476-4911. Open Tue.-Sun. for lunch and dinner. On Buttermilk Falls Rd., about 4 mi. northeast of the town of Delaware Water Gap.*

■ **The Stroudsmoor Country Inn** (moderate). Providing sweeping views of the Pocono Plateau, the Stroudsmoor is most famous for its grand buffet served on Saturday night. It's a food orgy with 16 different salads (don't miss the seafood salad), seven outstanding entrees from filet mignon to lobster tails, plus extraordinary desserts. On weeknights, a five-course dinner with choice of entree is served. The elegant decor includes

▼

bentwood chairs and linen napkins. *Box 153, Stroudsmoor Rd., Stroudsburg, PA 18360; tel. 717-421-6431. Open Mon.-Sat. for lunch and dinner; Sun. for brunch and dinner. Off Rte. 191 south, about 4 mi. west of the town of Delaware Water Gap.*

■ **Trail's End Cafe** (inexpensive). Straight out of David Lynch's imagination, a six-foot-tall wooden raccoon welcomes you to this little cafe, a popular spot for backpackers. Enjoy specialty sandwiches and pizzas, or a pasta of the day. Breakfast may include homemade granola topped with fruit or Napoli eggs—scrambled eggs sauteed in olive oil, tossed with pepperoni, and served with home fries and Sicilian toast. The dinner menu features such entrees as roast duckling and tuna steak. *Main St., Delaware Water Gap, PA 18327; tel. 717-421-1928. Open Wed.-Sat. for breakfast and lunch, Fri. for dinner (bring your own alcoholic beverages), and Sun. for brunch.*

LODGING

■ **Eagle Rock Lodge** (expensive). Atop a hillside overlooking the Delaware, this is a quiet B&B where you can sit in the spacious yard or on the screened-in porch, listening to songbirds and watching the world pass by. The 19th-century farmhouse stands on more than ten acres and includes seven cozy bedrooms decorated with period furnishings. A hearty country breakfast on the porch is a good way to begin the day. *Box 265, River Rd., Shawnee-On-Delaware, PA 18356; tel. 717-421-2139. Open daily Jul. 4-Labor Day; weekends the rest of the year. About 4 mi. north of the town of Delaware Water Gap.*

■ **Shawnee Inn** (moderate). Founded in 1912, this inn on the Delaware is a full-service resort that, unlike most accommodations in this book, doesn't allow you to escape away from it all. But it has a beautiful river view and plenty to do: tennis, golf, canoeing, horseback riding, and two pools. The rooms are okay, clean and comfortable with modern furnishings. *Box 93, River Rd., Shawnee-on-Delaware, PA 18356; tel. 717-421-1500. About 4 mi. north of the town of Delaware Water Gap.*

▼

■ **The Shepard House** (moderate). This cozy country Victorian B&B is conveniently located on a quiet street near the town's restaurants and the Appalachian Trail. Carve out some time to enjoy the wrap-around veranda, with its flowering plants, rockers, and wicker gliders. Each of the six rooms (two with private bath) is furnished with antiques. Gourmet breakfasts are served. *Box 486, 108 Shepard Ave., Delaware Water Gap, PA 18327; tel. 717-424-9779. A few blocks from Main St.*

■ **The Stroudsmoor Country Inn** (moderate). This turn-of-the-century, 150-acre mountain retreat overlooks the Pocono mountain range. It includes a main inn with 15 distinctive and comfortable rooms, a superb restaurant, a piano lounge, and a small pub, plus 16 outlying cottages. Every room within the inn is furnished with antiques and has a private bath. There are shops and two swimming pools. *Box 153, Stroudsmoor Rd., Stroudsburg, PA 18360; tel. 717-421-6431. Off Rte. 191 south, about 4 mi. west of the town of Delaware Water Gap.*

FOR MORE INFORMATION
Tourist Offices:
■ **Delaware Water Gap National Recreation Area.** The most convenient information center for motorists is the Kittatinny Point Visitor Center (*see* Other Places Nearby).

■ **Poconos Mountains Vacation Bureau.** *1004 Main St., Stroudsburg, PA 18360; tel. 717-424-6050, 800-762-6667. Office open Mon.-Fri. 9-5. About 4 mi. west of the town of Delaware Water Gap. Satellite office located off I-80 at exit 53, on PA side of the Water Gap. Open Mon.-Thu. 9:30-5:30, Sat. 9:30-6:30, Sun. 9:30-4:30.*

For Serious Walkers:
The National Recreation Area is crisscrossed by hundreds of miles of trails ranging from easy to difficult. The Appalachian Trail climbs both sides of the Gap. The Kittatinny Point Visitor Center has a Selected Hiking Trails map. The best maps are published by the New York-New Jersey Trail Conference.

BIBLIOGRAPHY

■ **Anglin, Brian.** "Twin Peaks" and "Twin Peaks: The Sequel" in *Ulster* magazine (Woodstock and New Paltz, NY: Ulster Publishing Co., summer and autumn, 1993).

■ **Bryant, William Cullen.** *Orations and Addresses* (New York: Putnam, 1873).

■ **Burgess, Larry E.** *Mohonk: Its People and Spirit* (Fleischmanns, NY: Purple Mountain Press, 1980).

■ **Cawley, James & Margaret.** *Along the Delaware and Raritan Canal* (New York: A. S. Barnes & Co., 1970).

■ **Downing, Andrew Jackson.** *Landscape Gardening and Rural Architecture* (New York: Dover Publications, 1991; reprint of 1865 ed.).

■ **Dunwell, Frances F.** *The Hudson River Highlands* (New York: Columbia University Press, 1991).

■ **Dupont, Ronald J., Jr. and Wright, Kevin.** *High Point of the Blue Mountains* (Newton, NJ: Minisink Press, 1990).

■ **Dupont, Ronald J., Jr.** The History of Wawayanda State Park, unfinished manuscript.

■ **Dupuy, E. Ernest and Dupuy, Trevor N.** *An Outline History of the American Revolution* (New York: Harper & Row, 1975).

■ **Evers, Alf.** *The Catskills* (Garden City, NY: Doubleday, 1972).

■ **Grumet, Robert S.** *The Lenapes* (New York: Dover Publications, 1989).

■ **Hale, Edward Everett.** *The Early Art of Thomas Cole, Art in America* (Vol. IV, 1916).

■ **Hutchinson, Lucille and Theodore.** *The Centennial History of North Tarrytown* (Cambridge, MD: Western Publishing Co., 1974).

■ **Keller, Allan.** *Life Along the Hudson* (Tarrytown, NY: A Sleepy Hollow Book, 1976).

■ **Lanset, Andy.** *Camp Midvale: An Oral History* (radio documentary).

■ **Leighton, Ann.** *American Gardens of the Nineteenth Century* (Amherst, MA: U. of Mass. Press, 1987).

■ **Madeira, Crawford Clark Jr.** *The Delaware and Raritan Canal* (E. Orange, NJ: The Easterwood Press, 1941).

■ **Myles, William J.** *Harriman Trails: A Guide and History* (New York: New York-New Jersey Trail Conference, 1992).

■ **Ransom, Hames.** *Vanishing Ironworks of the Ramapos* (New Brunswick, NJ: Rutgers U. Press, 1966).

■ **Ruttenber, E. M.** *History of the Indian Tribes of Hudson's River* (Port Washington, NY: Kennikat Press, 1875).

■ **Scheer, George and Weigley, Russell.** *Morristown Official National Park Handbook* (New York: National Park Service Division of Publications, 1983).

■ **Stevens, William Oliver.** *Discovering Long Island* (New York: Dodd, Mead, & Co., 1939).

■ **Van Zandt, Roland.** *The Catskill Mountain House* (New Brunswick, NJ, 1966).

■ **Vaux, Calvert.** *Villas and Cottages* (New York: Dover Publications, 1970; reprint of 1864 ed.).

■ **Weaver, Muriel Porter.** *Where They Go By Water* (The Nature Conservancy, 1990).

■ *Wolfert's Roost* (Irvington, NY: Washington Irving Press, 1971).

■ **Zukowsky, John, and Stimson, Robbie Pierce.** *Hudson River Villas* (New York: Rizzoli International Publications, 1985).